Giono

MASTER OF FICTIONAL MODES

Giono

MASTER OF FICTIONAL MODES

By Norma L. Goodrich

Princeton University Press

Copyright © 1973 by Princeton University Press
ALL RIGHTS RESERVED.
LCC: 72-4041
ISBN: 0-691-06239-0
This book has been composed in Linotype Granjon
Printed in the United States of America
by Princeton University Press,
Princeton, New Jersey

This book is most affectionately dedicated to
Professor Jean-Albert Bédé
Columbia University

Table of Contents

Giono

MASTER OF FICTIONAL MODES

Introduction

"Thus, Ulysses was like a flowering almond tree in the midst of furrows, and covered the black earth with light perfumed petals."—Jean Giono.

The following chapters were written in an attempt to explain the fascination exerted by the fiction of Jean Giono. They present him as a major writer in our century, first as a master of French prose who reinforced tastes cultivated earlier by Marcel Proust and André Gide, and then more widely as an Americanophile renewing Melville and William Faulkner. No American studies a French novelist with such gratitude, it would seem, unless he has found him not only authenticating modern existence and personal ethic, but moreover handling as if by request our most plaguing problems: the disquieting relationships, in what appears to be another revolutionary century, within the family and among mothers and women generally; our dilemmas due to the collapses of religions and *raisons d'être*; our daily metamorphosis on earth despite eyes upon liberating space; our growing awareness of the cruelties of justice and governments; our dismay in the face of barbaric persuaders and savage wars upon persons and plants, urban disintegration, sudden mass pollutions of water and air—all heaped upon our natural anguish.

Occasionally Giono seized the direct address of the essayist in order courageously to attack his own government.[1] Then Socratically he led astray the young from military serv-

---

[1] *Lettre aux paysans sur la pauvreté et la paix* (Paris, 1938), notably.

ice before World War II and into the fastnesses of the Basses Alpes. His idiosyncratic views he expressed foolhardily in polemics, history, and prefaces[2] (as he consequently suffered retaliations under inhumane prison conditions). He also attempted poetry[3] and achieved considerable success in the mass media,[4] meanwhile stealing several marches upon other contemporary masters of prose fiction. In the following essays he will concern us mainly thus, as a master in prose fiction. Because of his scholarship, obvious intellectual independence, and study of such artists as Melville, Proust, Gide, Breton, Sartre, and Faulkner, he became a craftsman and technician par excellence of the novel, the tale, and story collection or cycle.

Self-educated, a lone visionary residing mainly in his native Manosque, thus isolating himself from Parisian notables by distance, climate, and way of life, Giono established himself for a wide, international reading public[5] as an unrepentant social critic, as champion of the poor, as theologian, mythographer, scholar, revolutionary, and humanist. We shall see him also, and in the tradition first proposed at considerable length by Pierre R. Robert, as a chief innovator in the field of the novel.[6]

[2] *Les Vraies richesses* (Paris, 1936), *Refus d'obéissance* (1937), *Voyage en Italie* (1953), *Le Désastre de Pavie* (1963), "Machiavelli" (1952), "Bernard Buffet" (1956), "Blaise de Monluc" (1964), etc.

[3] *Accompagnés de la flûte* (1924), *Fragments d'un déluge* (1948).

[4] Nine films are listed by Pierre de Boisdeffre in his *Giono* (Paris, 1963), bibliographical assistant, Jean Bottin, p. 277.

[5] Translations include fiction in German, Czech, Polish, English, Finnish, Portuguese, Swedish, Spanish, Italian, Dutch, and Hungarian.

[6] *Jean Giono et les techniques du roman* (Berkeley and Los Angeles, 1961). Robert concludes (p. 97): "En utilisant des sujets conventionnels, Giono a cependant rénové l'art du roman. Beaucoup plus qu'à aucun autre domaine, cet art appartient à l'esthétique. . . . L'autodidacte Giono se développe, et avec lui ses romans: formes nouvelles, personnages nouveaux, techniques nouvelles—. . ."

4

Giono shone unforgettably because of his charm, friendliness, modesty, genuine simplicity; his unmistakable nobility of bearing and speech; the joy of intellect that radiated from the man. When I met him during the sunny summer days of 1970, he sparkled with wit and the joys of talking about old books and of planning new ones. He was unusually pressed for time, he said, since momentarily he expected to die of a heart attack.

With very little acclaim for his virtuosity, but generally with confidence—perhaps with the modest assurance of polar explorers whom as a class of men he much admired—Jean Giono widened our understanding of the uses and the possibilities of prose fiction. He elevated the novel particularly, the very form thought by many to be moribund, to new artistic preeminence. Working experimentally in book after book, as we shall see, Giono demonstrated over forty odd years of daily practice how brilliantly the novel fulfills the conditions, and therefore meets the needs customarily satisfied by several hallowed literary modes.

A learned man, very well read, with a personal library of over 7,000 volumes, Giono often experimented by placing certain of his novels carefully within literary traditions. In such cases he proceeded by first arousing and then meeting in his readers a thirst for literary decorum, where components fit properly into what are recognizable modes. Various of his novels thus clearly recreate long-established sets, or literary structures. Such books read as if the author, having first categorized human experience, set forth its mysteries upon which he imposed order and form. Behind his approach, in other words, underlie not only the super-narrator's watchful decision made *a priori*, as Giono explained in the Preface to his *Chroniques romanesques* (1962),[7] concerning the basis for

[7] N.R.F. (Gallimard), pp. 7-8.

each conception but, even more important, his awareness of those certain issues—political, moral, religious, historical, aesthetic—best treated traditionally by each mode. Thus, adapting in some cases old formats to present use, Giono handled with striking originality various reconstitutions of a frightening, mysterious world. He hoped meanwhile, he added, that his *modus operandi* passed unperceived.

Adopting several different attitudes towards reality, then, and studying mankind from several different perspectives, Giono began by writing fiction according to the pastoral mode, which to the great comfort of his pre-war reader he initially preferred as an explanation of the world. Then he branched out into what we shall suggest is an apocalyptic mode, when in a spirit of prophecy he chose to treat history and theology. Much later he chose a surrealistic mode, when he undertook unearthly, fictional voyages through time and space; a symbolic mode, when he felt constrained to convey, or to suggest, by patterns, knowledge not made explicit in the text, and/or not comprehended fully by him either; an epic mode, when he proposed the ways of saints and barbaric heroes, lest their stories were thought irrelevant to modern life; a tragic mode, either according to Sophocles or to Shakespeare, when he realized that sacrificial offerings were still being made, even in the twentieth century; and twice an autobiographical and Proustian mode, when he resumed his puzzling about motherhood, creativity, and childhood, relying here, of course, upon the *Bildungsroman*,[8] or portrait of the artist.

[8] While no particular *Bildungsroman* seems the immediate source of inspiration for Giono, his *Jean le bleu* would bear a close comparison to Tolstoy's *Childhood* (1852), particularly for its frank admissions of sensitivity to people and to the world: beauty, cruelty, memory, shyness, women, vision, great-heartedness leading to genius,

While in the following chapters only twelve texts have been selected for detailed analysis, two per major fictional mode, all of Giono's novels will be brought in for corroborative evidence, comparison, or contrast. The only works more or less neglected are the early pastorals, published from 1928 through *Que ma joie demeure* of 1935, that famous novel which forms a swan song in the pastoral vein, but also, and far more importantly, represents a sickening on Giono's part at the sweet optimism of his youth. No depth of mature consciousness, no great awareness of craft, and no accession to bitter adulthood occur in Giono much before his first near-masterpiece, *Batailles dans la montagne* of 1937.

This book, in other words, presumes to fly, however feebly, in the face of common consensus, when it suggests that Jean Giono came of age as an artist only with *Un Roi sans divertissement*, ten years later, in 1947. Most critics, and all readers, doubtless, know best and still largely prefer the young Giono of the lovely pastorals, much as Victor Hugo always preferred the Molière who wrote before 1659. One need not quarrel with the world, however, by asserting categorically that the twelve novels or works selected here are therefore better works of art; it is only that they appear more interesting technically, or that they experiment more consciously. Furthermore, one cannot even assert that the novels chosen fit absolutely, pair by pair, or even singly, into the modes so

---

emotion leading to action. Specifically, both young *personae*, Tolstoy and Giono, react to the color blue.

Dostoevsky on the other hand, a novelist to whom Giono often referred in print, in his work translated as *Raw Youth* (1875), like Giono focusses upon women, motherhood, and social problems. Giono does not follow him into psychological complications, such as the double nature of Arkady's father Versilov. With both Russian novelists, however, Giono envisions this novelistic form as more fictional than autobiographical.

arbitrarily chosen; it is merely that one has enjoyed making a case for their several categorizations. Hopefully, such relegations and comparisons will heighten one's enjoyment of Giono's masterpieces. In any case, feeble though he was in the summer of 1970, Giono delightedly rummaged through his books, racked his brains, and aided and abetted my plan.

Two French critics, Jacques Pugnet[9] and Claudine Chonez,[10] noted some fifteen years ago how Giono's novels fell into differently characteristic forms. Both critics then clarified their observations by postulating the musical analogies invited by Giono in such titles as *Que ma joie demeure*,[11] and thus alluding to Giono's novels as composed musically according to "modes majeurs" and "tempo différent." Giono's own emphasis upon musical themes and structures within his novels, especially from Bach as in *Jean le bleu*, which we shall examine finally, places him with the Symbolists, certainly with Proust and Gide.[12] A philosopher such as Etienne Souriau might characterize the same novels as "artistic categories" representing varying artistic climates.[13]

When Jean Giono, a young and poor bank runner and clerk in Provence, published his first verses in 1924 and began writing in a French heavily accented with Provençalisms[14] his early pastorals, novels soaring lyrically with praise of countrymen and countryside alike, André Gide was the man of the hour. After Giono's sensational success in 1928 with his first such attempt to liberate modern man into a joyful paganism

---

[9] *Jean Giono* (Paris, 1955), p. 64.

[10] *Giono par lui-même* (Paris, 1956), p. 63.

[11] Bach's chorale "Jesu, joy of man's desiring."

[12] See *Jean Giono* of Pugnet, p. 128.

[13] *Clefs pour l'esthétique* (Paris, 1970), pp. 28, 48, *et passim*.

[14] See "Les Provençalismes et la question du régionalisme dans l'oeuvre de Jean Giono," by Alphonse Roche, *PMLA*, Vol. 63, No. 4 (December 1948), p. 1,322 ff.

—what Justin O'Brien called his "natures mortes"[15]—a curious Gide, whose *Symphonie pastorale* dated from 1919, condescended to call upon the young novelist. Arriving around 10:00 a.m. from the Marseilles train, Gide dispatched Giono's mother Pauline—she who would years hence become the girlish heroine Marquise Pauline de Théus in *Le Hussard sur le toit* (1951) notably, but also the mother of Orpheus, Eurydice (*sic*), in *Mort d'un personnage* (1949)—to the bank to fetch her son away from his flunkey's bowing and scraping so that he could entertain the great northerner. It is not Gide, curious but nonetheless disdaining Giono, who tells the story, but the latter in his "Hommage" at Gide's death in 1951.[16] Gide's entry for June 18, 1929, barely mentions a train journey from Marseilles to Manosque, but once there and again later, this self-appointed mentor read to his protégé and follower, correcting him about everything from art to botany, even when Giono happened not to be in error.

Diverging elsewhere widely from Gide, as in his reverence for Greek mythology, Giono still gratefully learned fictional theory from Gide and felt reinforced by that great man's interest and by his defiance of the traditional novel or *roman d'analyse*. Both the wealthy Gide and the penniless Giono sprang from mixed marriages, Catholic and Protestant. Both approached life and art as moralists, and both wrestled mightily with angels, studied William Blake, Shakespeare, and Christian theology, both men actually rewriting Scripture. Both novelists felt immeasurable propensities to pity and constant inclinations to suffer on behalf of the poor, the

[15] Professor O'Brien referred to Cézanne in particular. See his "Giono's *Harvest*," *The Nation* (June 3, 1939), reprinted in his *The French Literary Horizon* (Rutgers, 1967), pp. 257-58.

[16] See "Lundi," *Hommage à André Gide, 1869-1951* (Paris, 1951), p. 206 ff., and Gide's *Journal* (1923-1931), Vol. III, pp. 192, 296, 368.

oppressed, and those indicted for punishment in the courts. Giono's *Notes sur l'affaire Dominici* (1955), which lies beyond the scope of our present inquiry, constitutes his attempt to exonerate an old farmer, whose language diverged radically from that used by the court, of first-degree murders. Ponder as he could, Giono never succeeded in understanding any of this trial, neither the allegations nor the prosecution, neither the defense nor the justice alleged, and certainly therefore not the punishments proposed. Again, Giono perhaps followed Gide when he too insisted that every portrait by an artist amounts to a self-portrait. Both writers also weighed the merits of Marxism and were disillusioned by it, Giono during his brief pre-World War II association with André Breton. Always embarrassed by Parisians, and especially angry to have been intimidated by them, and glibly misrepresented, Giono doubtless also resented to some degree Gide's authority. Still championing Giono, however, Gide died unfortunately just after his young friend had finally published his first masterpieces.

The literary career of Giono as a novelist falls easily into three periods of very uneven production: (1) 1910-1935, (2) 1936-1946, and (3) 1947-1972. During the regionalistic phase 1,[17] Giono published nine novels and two collections of tales. Aside from eight pastorals, this group contains the two extraordinary works with which we will commence and conclude our present inquiry, so influential have they already become: the novel of World War I viewed apocalyptically in the wake of Tolstoy's *War and Peace*, Giono's *Le Grand troupeau* (1931), and, secondly, his first portrait of the artist, his attempt in *Jean le bleu* (1932) to remember his nascent creativity. Here he studies himself only as a child and young man apprenticed to a bank.

[17] See Charts 1, 2, and 3, and also the Bibliography.

PHASE I

1930-1935

MAJOR FICTION

Colline	1928
Un de Baumugnes	1929
Naissance de l'Odyssée	1930
Regain	1930
Le Grand troupeau	1931
Solitude de la pitié	1932*
Jean le bleu	1932
L'Eau vive	1933**
Le Serpent d'étoiles	1933
Le Chant du monde	1934
Que ma joie demeure	1935

* Collection of pastoral tales, which is even more than that, a short story cycle having unity and depth.

** Collection of tales of uneven quality, interspersed with prose pieces that appeared, it seems, from as early as 1910. They will be reprinted as *Rondeur des jours*. They seem to constitute Giono's apprenticeship.

During his tragic second period of World War II and two imprisonments, Giono published only one work of fiction, *Batailles dans la montagne* (1937). It was, because of an old taboo, badly received. In this long novel, as during these years, doubtless, one last time before a final rejection, Giono re-examined Protestantism, studying even the Christian epic, which had long been frowned upon in France but superbly practiced in England by John Milton. During the war years, in other words, Giono again followed Gide's lead into the liberating English language, gateway to such pioneers as Whitman,[18] Melville, and Faulkner and to English and American

[18] See W. T. Starr's "Jean Giono et Walt Whitman," *French Review*, No. 14 (December, 1940), pp. 118-29.

literature. The horrors of a second major war on home soil (Giono had been badly gassed in World War I) brought down upon his fictional characters a medieval scourge, in this case obliteration by flood or the personally administered wrath of a punishing God. Only the angel and saint was in the end privileged to intercede for man.

Three major political tracts also stem from this period, when Giono became a radical activist, as well as his tribute to Melville, some drama, and what is probably his first long expository celebration of his pastoral land, *Provence* (1939). Seven works of non-fiction from 1936-1947 made it appear that Jean Giono had, like some of his contemporaries in France, rejected the novel forever. What followed, however, only proves that one can hardly predict genius.

PHASE 2
1936-1946
MAJOR WORKS

Les Vraies richesses (polemic)	1936
(and supplement, *Triomphe de la vie,* 1941)	
Rondeur des jours	1936
(reprinted from *L'Eau vive,* of 1933, 1943)	
Le Bout de la route (theater)	1937
Refus d'obéissance (polemic)	1937
Batailles dans la montagne (fiction)	1937
Le Poids du ciel (essay on astronomy)	1938
Lettre aux paysans sur la pauvreté et la paix	1938
(polemic)	
Provence (essay)	1939
Pour saluer Melville (essay, according to Giono)	1939

From 1947, or from the end of World War II to his death in 1970, Giono staggers the imagination because of the sophistication, extent, and virtuosity of his mature productions: thirteen novels, all superior in quality, each worthy of many books of essays; four major works of non-fiction, ending in the last two years of his life with *Provence perdue* (1968), his most scathing accusation and renewed indictment of modern civilization for the pollution of Provence that resulted in part from the diversion of the Durance River; the second apocalypse text; plus four new tales that, although published separately, obviously form part of a new story cycle, and that appear posthumously in 1972 as *Les Récits de la demi-brigade*.

Phase 3

1947-1972

MAJOR FICTION

Un Roi sans divertissement	1947
Noé	
(*Fragments d'un paradis*, out of print,	1948)
Mort d'un personnage	1949
Les Ames fortes	1949
Les Grands chemins	1951
Le Hussard sur le toit	1951
Le Moulin de Pologne	1952
"L'Ecossais" (tale)	1955
Le Bonheur fou	1957
Angelo	1958
"La Nuit du 24 decembre 1826" (tale)	1962
"Une Histoire d'amour" (tale)	1962
"Le Grand théâtre"	1964
"Le Bal" (tale)	1965
Deux cavaliers de l'orage	1965
Ennemonde	1968

MAJOR FICTION (*continued*)

MAJOR NON-FICTION

This stormy third phase continues as we await not only Giono's posthumous fiction but the collecting of the unknown numbers of works that he so generously over the decades contributed to charity. The third phase commenced in 1947 with two astonishingly forceful novels that we shall examine in some depth: *Un Roi sans divertissement* and *Noé,* followed in 1948 by the still unavailable *Fragments d'un paradis*, in 1949 by *Mort d'un personnage* and *Les Ames fortes*, in 1951 by *Les Grands chemins* and *Le Hussard sur le toit*, in 1952 by *Le Moulin de Pologne,* and what may be an irreversible climax of resourcefulness in *Le Bonheur fou*,[19] where Giono probably moved into a last new domain. Nine of the following twelve chapters deal with phase 3, the major period of Giono's writing. These books almost instantly brought the

---

[19] Gaëtan Picon terms *"Le Bonheur fou"* a search for a new novelistic technique: *"Le Bonheur fou* est un roman expérimental où l'expérimentation recherche la survie du vieux charme romanesque. . . . D'une façon générale, nous écoutons trop bien Giono: nous ne l'interrogeons pas assez." See *Mercure de France*, No. 1129 (September 1957), p. 125.

In his *Panorama de la littérature française* (Paris, 1960) Picon added (p. 81): "Seul peut-être de tous les grands écrivains de sa génération, Giono est parvenu à donner à son oeuvre des prolongements imprévus. Et elle s'accompagne d'une audace technique et d'une maîtrise croissantes."

novelist the acclaim of critics and his only honors in the world's eyes, the Prix Monégasque from Prince Rainier III, followed in 1954 by the Prix Goncourt.

On March 7, 1953, the French critic André Rousseaux,[20] following congratulatory studies by Maurice Nadeau[21] and Marcel Arland,[22] described phase 3 for *Le Figaro Littéraire* as Giono's "seconde manière." There had been many changes of style from the lyrical novels of phase 1, for even Giono himself fell back upon the term "chronicle" to distinguish these ironical masterpieces, which sardonically castigate the reader and which are narrated by auxiliaries in often hateful and vulgar terms, via blocks of superimposed durations, from the simpler "natures mortes," or pastorals. Shielding himself from future punishments and from past charges of muddy lyricism and mawkish sentimentality, Giono thus found in adversity the stoical immunity and the methods by which better to "chronicle" the ongoing breakdowns of modern civilization: the warring centers of culture, the powerlessnesses of governments, the dissolution of the family, the world-wide economic collapses, the imminent crises in foodstuffs and power, an exhaustion of the resources of the earth, and the forthcoming departure of man from this planet earth upon a voyage of no return.

By 1938 only two major critical works had been devoted to Giono,[23] and Christian Michelfelder spoke more of Giono's pagan religious affiliations than of the early pastorals them-

[20] "Jean Giono, seconde manière" (March 7, 1953), p. 2 ff.

[21] "Un Nouveau Giono," *Mercure de France*, No. 317 (1953), p. 693 ff.

[22] "Le Chant du monde," *NNRF*, No. 9 (1953), p. 495 ff., and "A la hussarde," *NNRF*, No. 10 (1953), p. 687 ff.

[23] Katherine A. Clarke's *Lyrisme dans l'oeuvre de Giono*, unpublished thesis (Grenoble, 1938) and Christian Michelfelder's *Jean Giono et les religions de la terre* (Paris, 1938 and 1955).

15

selves—the designation "pastoral" is not his but ours. In 1955-1956 three book-length studies appeared by Villeneuve, Pugnet, and Chonez.[24] At this same time, when Giono's faithful champion Henri Peyre[25] characterized his return to fiction as "meteoric," seventeen new critics devoted articles to these third-phase novels.[26] In fact, six nations mentioned him in that year alone: France, England, Germany, Italy, Spain, and the United States. While Giono had in 1938 admitted to being a "fellow traveller," the *London Times Literary Supplement* exonerated him in 1954 as an "individual traveller."

In 1956 Chonez associated Giono with surrealism. In 1957 Stephen Ullmann, writing in Cambridge, England,[27] derived him from Rimbaud. Alphonse Roche in 1948 had already noted how his Provençalisms had by phase 3 been replaced by French, i.e., that Giono could no longer be dismissed as a mere regionalist. By 1959 Robert Poulet had placed Giono as

[24] Romée de Villeneuve's *Jean Giono, ce solitaire* (Avignon, 1955); Jacques Pugnet's *Jean Giono* (Paris and Brussels, 1955); Claudine Chonez's *Giono par lui-même* (Paris, 1956).

[25] The pages devoted to Giono in *The Contemporary French Novel* (New York, 1955) point to directions we shall explore: the epic qualities of Giono's fiction, relationships to Gide and Faulkner, Bach and Mozart, Greek tragedy and Ariosto, Huguenots and Protestantism. Professor Peyre noted (p. 143): "Giono is significant in French letters because he is, primarily, a great artist. This son of a Provençal shoemaker enriched the French novel of his age with an infusion of virility and of poetry. He broke with the tradition of the psychological novel of Stendhal, Proust, and Gide, as well as with the tradition of huge realistic scope that Roger Martin du Gard and Jules Romains had tried after Zola." See also pp. 124 ("meteoric") and pp. 125-54.

[26] Pugnet, Villeneuve, Arland, Chonez, Henry Miller (*The Books in My Life*, Norfolk, Conn., undated), plus Dominique Aury, René Bailly, Yves Bridault, Jean Dutourd, Jean-Claude Ibert, *TLS*, Peter de Mendelssohn, Christian Millau, F. Robichon, Pierre Seize, Marguerite Taos, Fernand Vial, etc.

[27] See *Style in the French Novel* for an essay on Giono's *Regain*, pp. 217-31.

a new leader of the avant-garde.[28] In 1965 Pierre de Boisdeffre found him nothing less than "métamorphosé" between
1938 and the post-war masterpieces of 1947: "Il était diffus,
lyrique et volontiers pathétique; il devint sec, ironique et
dur." Visiting Giono at home, examining him narrowly,
Boisdeffre thoughtfully concluded: "anarchiste impénitent"
(p. 102), "poète en prose" (p. 103), "solitaire" (p. 102).[29] Intent upon correcting Romée de Villeneuve in 1966, defending
Giono with all his learning and sense of justice, Maxwell A.
Smith,[30] dean of Giono scholars, roundly chastised the perse-
cutors, such as the *Comité National des Ecrivains, Les Lettres
Françaises*, and Tristan Tzara[31] for a personal vilification of
Giono on October 6, 1944. In 1967, W. D. Redfern raised
Giono to eminence among the latest realists, newer novelists
such as Beckett, Sarraute, Simon, and Robbe-Grillet.[32]

It seems certain that Giono will not lead into any retreat towards incommunicability and anguished incoherence, but
rather into a new phase for the novel. In Giono's hands it becomes anew, as in its greatest practitioners, a comforting
"refuge" (Giono's term for Melville's *Moby-Dick*), a guide
and new direction, and, once more, the means to individual
and collective revelation. In any case, Giono will not lie down
quietly with those novelists popular after 1950, for he scorned
them and their admirers upon occasion:

[28] "Giono à l'avant-garde," *Carrefour*, 16e année, No. 751 (Feb. 4,
1959), 13 (NYP).

[29] *Giono* (Paris, 1965).

[30] See among many publications his *Jean Giono* (New York, 1966).

[31] "Un Romancier de la lâcheté," *Les Lettres Françaises*, No. 24 (Oct.
7, 1944), NYP. Other attacks may be read: René Brochon's "De Giono
à Pétain," *Action* (Jan. 5, 1945) and René Bergeron's "Le Cas Giono,"
Les Lettres Françaises, No. 450 (Jan. 29 to Feb. 5, 1953).

For a defense, see also Herbert Read's work cited by Henry Miller in
defense of Giono: *Politics of the Unpolitical* (London, 1946).

[32] *The Private World of Jean Giono* (Durham, 1967).

"The fact is that in 1962 literature is in panic because of its past. Like all arts in terror, it hurtles headlong into rhetoric. When an author no longer dares to tell stories, or is no longer able to, he passes his time stringing words like beads. . . . Hence the distress, the nausea that those interested in groaning in cadence over the sadness of the human condition applaud; from this applause, and from the ephemeral success that ensues, arises the exaggerated self-esteem that impales a few mediocre performers on muted trumpets."[33]

Thus, even into phase 3, Giono remained, despite his seeming lack of involvement, a champion of happiness and a promoter of the joy of living.

SINCE WE are awaiting the publication of Giono's *Journal* and his complete works, it seemed best, in this book, to select an order of presentation that would deepen, as we advance, our knowledge both of the possibilities of prose fiction and of our own situation in the twentieth century. Born in the nineteenth century, Giono in his youth opened his eyes upon a conflict between harmony and disharmony, or the Vergilian and pastoral confrontation for *libertas* between *rusticitas* on the one hand and *urbanitas* on the other.[34] Like William Faulkner, Giono not only rejected the city and foresaw grass growing at the Paris subway exits, but he constructed from bits and geographical particulars what he acknowledged to be a mythical "High Country" peopled by hypothetical beings like those in Jefferson, at the hub of equally mythical Yoknapatawpha County in northwest Mississippi. As early as his novel *Naissance de l'Odyssée* of 1930—the novel so titled because it humorously offers a theory and practice for the creation of Homer's *Odyssey*—Giono had selected two of his chief

[33] Préface, *Chroniques romanesques* (Paris, 1962), p. 8.
[34] *Virgile par Giono* (Paris, 1960).

themes: the happiness of man released from society into the wide world as a free adventurer like Ulysses, and the privileged position of the artist, also like Ulysses, creating tales for the delight and knowledge of himself and anyone else. As an apocalypticist, Giono grappled later on at least two major occasions, 1931 and c. 1960, with the catastrophic end of modern civilization, and each man's personal abyss and absorption into the cosmos. As a surrealist rejecting reason and logic and summoning other ways of knowing, Giono imagined trips back into time in *Noé* and forward into space in *Fragments d'un paradis*. When he chose a symbolic mode, he summoned reader collaboration for *Les Grands chemins* as for *Le Hussard sur le toit*, soliciting theories and conclusions from the mazes of oblique referential patterns relating to twinships and brotherhoods, blacks and whites, warfare between nations and sexes. The epic novels call upon modern humanists to review the behavior of men and women, to decide upon what now in our days can be salvaged from what once were worshipful stances and actions, and to view the heroic women leaders of the future, after our present revolution. Always in the most noble mode, the tragic novels of Giono very movingly treat crimes and justice, triumphs, revenge, and ghastly sacrifices to olden gods, perhaps upon a frozen planet.

This book concludes with a discussion of the place where most novelists start, the autobiographical, perhaps the most difficult mode for fiction. Thence, in fact, every narrator moves on to imitate a crafty Ulysses coolly fabricating tales of vast ships and wrecks and whirlpools from mere wisps of reed dropped in the muddy pool of an irrigation ditch, swirled by gigantic waters past Scabiosa Shoals into the safe harbor of Ithaca at last. When Telemachus tells his true story, no matter how indignant he grows, he is not believed. But when Ulysses rises from his sober contemplation of that bit of wet reed which miraculously has navigated the fearful mud puddle, and when, advancing towards an incredulous Penelope, he recounts perilous peregrinations, he becomes again her own true love and a chief chronicler of ancient voyages. As an artist he alone spoke what all recognized instantly as the truth and as commonly experienced reality.

Looking about him, Ulysses, who is Giono's first portrait of the narrator, sees man's will faulty, his being corrupted, and the world he knows harassed by cruel gods and therefore fraught with perils. To him, as to Giono, two solutions provide deliverance from evil: the feeling of pity for the falling and the oppressed, and the aesthetic joys of creation. By liberating man from himself for a moment, art provides him not only the perspective but also the desire and the knowledge requisite for finishing his life. One may be a great depicter of men without loving them; to paint men well, the novelist must, in very fact, really despise them. Those villagers who lined up to sign the funeral book of the blacksmith Murataure in *L'Iris de Suze* (1969) truly resembled contemptible insects, being themselves devoid of pity. Thus, Giono loathes the twin companions in *Les Grands chemins* even as he describes them, much as Faulkner saw through such individuals in *A Fable*, a modern man, a ". . . foreigner who moved, breathed, not merely in an aura of bastardy and bachelordom but of homelessness too, like a half-wild pedigreeless pariah dog: fatherless, wifeless, sterile and perhaps even impotent too, misshapen, savage and foul: the world's portionless and intractable and inconsolable orphan, . . ."[35] In similar terms Giono also boldly castigates men and society, probably actually preferring women, appealing to them to outlaw wars, evolving in his understanding of them from the Arsules and

[35] *A Fable* (New York and Toronto, 1950), pp. 189-90.

20

Aurélies of his early fiction, pure beasts of burden and sorry but cherished victims, to the lofty Dr. Alithéa, the mathematical genius of *Ennemonde* (1970).

Maurice Nadeau pointed out in 1950 that Giono's overall view of society and the modern world had remained consistently from his earliest prose a tragic view: "As soon as he began to write, Giono wished to usher into our age . . . tragedy. Reread *Colline, Un de Baumugnes*, his presentation of Vergil. Does not this writing incorporate a complex, sometimes obscure plot, does it not require personages who are at the same time straightforward, mysterious, and enigmatic? Was not his goal, in the last analysis, to fill us with 'terror and pity' "?[36] Giono's accommodation of the modern world to the exigencies of both Greek classical and Shakespearean tragedies may be characteristic, in fact, of our best novelists. In discussing "The Novel as a Tragic Mode," Roger L. Cox concluded in 1969 that it "functions in relation to our age as tragic drama did in relation to the greatest periods of Greek and English history—by involving the members of its audience in moral life, by inviting them to put their own motives under examination, by suggesting that reality is not as their conventional education has led them to see it. Moreover, understanding and forgiveness are no less indigenous to tragic drama than to the novel."[37]

Thus, Giono claimed in his essay on Vergil that he always tried to pierce below what is generally considered "the truth" and "the real" to the underlying significance, or to be always "le maître du sens des choses." Otherwise, he added, he might

[36] "Un Nouveau Giono," *Mercure de France*, cccviii, No. 1040 (April 1, 1950), pp. 693-97, here, p. 697.

[37] See Chapter VI in *Between Earth and Heaven. Shakespeare, Dostoevsky, and the Meaning of Christian Tragedy* (New York, 1969) and p. 123.

have wanted to deify the first engineer whom he saw using nitroglycerine. Therefore he personally preferred not the positivistic scientists held up as heroes by Jules Verne, but the solitary essentialists like Robinson Crusoe, alone on the highest points of their islands.

When he wrote his *Notes on the Novel*, Ortega y Gasset observed that adventures no longer interested modern readers, at least not mature readers who had outgrown the "barbaric residue" of their childhoods. "It is not easy nowadays," he added, "to invent adventures capable of stirring the superior portion of our sensibility."[38] Yet to his reader, Giono offers sources of optimism after the adventures of his novels, for they consist generally of adventures in series: nature, or the beautiful world through which we travel (who could continue to feel anguish on a morning like this? asks Ulysses). Giono suggested that life itself can be lived every minute with the excitement and marvel of a great adventure, mysterious, unforeseeable, and unique for each human being. Thus, Giono's novels generally commence and close with departures. They commonly figure a circle and a road bisecting it, involve a tangential stranger and peripheral groups encountered by chance and rapidly spun out centrifugally. The latter heroes are unashamedly adventurers, handsome rogues like Pauline de Théus and Angélo Pardi,[39] dashing villains of the open road, lawmen on horseback, and coach travelers who spur on and vanish or burst like the iridescent bubbles they always were. All splendid people, truly the simple and splendid ones, live for the sake of living: "They understood that the deliberately ignominious members of the human race amounted to no more than a trifling minority, and that happily

[38] *Notes on the Novel* (Princeton, 1948); New York edition (1956), p. 60.
[39] Hero and heroine of *Angelo* and of *Le Hussard sur le toit*.

all over the world, the overwhelming majority of living, so-called inferior, beings continued to live for the sake of living."[40]

The great ironic novels of Jean Giono appeal, then, not only because he succeeded in clothing his vision in aesthetically admirable and identifiable forms, which allow the reader the pleasure of placing the works severally into familiar and rich literary traditions; they also afford shelter and comfort by reminding the modern reader, with whom the world is much too much, that beyond his routine and narrow horizons lies a vast, adventuresome universe of freedom and pure delight. They thrill some readers with their portraits of brave men and magnificent women, who trust the earth and their own bodies. Last of all, they delight eye and ear and bring joy to many hearts because, more than most authors, Giono possessed what Aristotle considered the surest mark of a born genius: the gift of abundant metaphor. There lies his waspish humor, and there also the reader's enjoyment.

Giono's Ulysses explained parabolically why even we moderns must have our new adventure stories. In the olden times, he said, when heroic poems were chanted and spinning songs sung, the toilers slumped at their tasks until they fell fast asleep. However, whenever tales of adventure were told, all hands worked busily away at tasks grown somehow less arduous, the yarns unfolding, no one dropping off to sleep, so that finally twice as much was accomplished happily in an evening, or an hour: "Thus, Ulysses was like a flowering almond tree in the midst of furrows, and covered the black earth with light and fragrant petals."[41]

[40] *Virgile*, p. 85.
[41] *Naissance de l'Odyssée*, p. 207.

I   The Apocalyptic Mode

Le Grand troupeau (1931)

When Jean Giono composed his historical novel of World War I, he revealed not only by the point of reference from which he hid himself in order to narrate but also because of the prophetic nature of his view that he considered himself chosen and ordained to have seen that war and to have spoken of it. According to *Revelation*, Saint John the Divine was also commanded to bear witness:

> "1. The Revelation of Jesus Christ, which God gave unto him, to shew unto his servants things which must shortly come to pass; and he sent and signified it by his angel unto his servant John:
> "2. Who bare record of the word of God, and of the testimony of Jesus Christ, and of all things that he saw."

Therefore the hidden narrator, Jean Giono, witnesses the departure for war, suffers in war, and returns because he has been enjoined like his namesake to record that event.

Far from being the first novelist to interpret war as a catastrophe predicted in *Apocalypse*, Giono here follows at least two of his favorite novelists: Melville and Tolstoy. In the former's *Israel Potter* (1855)[1] the naval battle is prompted by

---

[1] *Israel Potter: His Fifty Years of Exile (1855)*. Melville's Israel feels divinely appointed to undergo trials and witness catastrophes: "being of this race, felicity could never be his lot," says Melville (*Israel Potter*, Boston, 1926, introduction by C. A. Page, p. 284). The novel is sarcastically dedicated: "To His Highness, The Bunker-Hill Monument."

an evil agent or false Christ actually seen leering over the horizon's rim, and the bloody commander John Paul Jones represents another Satan insatiably evil. To Melville, the London where his hero Israel remains in bondage seems with its economic collapse, its fires, and its plagues as terrible a place as Babylon, Gomorrah, or Armageddon.[2]

Tolstoy's *War and Peace* (1865-1869),[3] like Melville's novel of Benjamin Franklin and the American Revolution, is to the same degree Christian, moral, and apocalyptic. On the opening page of his vast novel Tolstoy sets the tone by speaking of the Antichrist, while the idea of Apocalypse, as well as the continued allusions to catastrophe and the Napoleonic Beast, recur in both the fictional and historical passages. Although Tolstoy fails to identify a wicked city like Flaubert's Carthage, or Melville's "dirty Dis" or the coal-hued London near its River Styx, *War and Peace* does fulfill the prophecies of *Revelation*, where a reign of terror finally fades into a New Jerusalem and promised paradise of home and infants. Giono repeats this pattern, and his Natasha Rostov is called Madeleine.

Those historical novelists who could be separated because of their explicitly or implicitly apocalyptic theory of history certainly belong to the Judeo-Christian tradition or know at least one apocalypse text such as the book of *Daniel* in the Old Testament or the book of *Revelation* in the New Testa-

---

[2] Israel actually undergoes three Armageddons: (a) London, (b) adversity, and (c) the sea. See James E. Miller's *A Reader's Guide to Herman Melville* (New York, 1965), pp. 150 and 285. Harriet Beecher Stowe's *Uncle Tom's Cabin* of 1851 featured also, for Melville's benefit perhaps, an apocalyptic vision read and known by now around the world.

[3] See *Tolstoï en France (1886-1910* by Thaïs S. Lindstrom (Paris, 1952), for the influence of Tolstoy upon French thought. For earlier appraisals, see Eugène-Melchior de Vogüé's *Le Roman russe* (Paris, 1886) and, for its bibliography particularly, Vladimir Boutchek's *La Littérature russe* (Paris, 1947).

ment, no other texts besides these two having been admitted into the Christian canon.[4] Such novelists comprehend themselves, their characters, and their worlds as facing a cataclysm directed by some unimaginably wicked monster of evil, after whose reign will arrive the heralded world of a peaceful and a New Jerusalem.

The novelists who betray or openly propound such apocalyptic doctrines must not be confused with the apocalypticists themselves, such as Saint John the Divine, author at Patmos of *Revelation*. The latter prophesy or, placing themselves in the past, look forward to future events like the destruction of Babylon and/or the fall of Rome. They speak in the future prophetic tense, then, of plagues and earthquakes that *will* arrive because they have been revealed. Most modern novelists—and Jean Giono, who actually also wrote an apocalypse,[5] may perhaps be the sole modern exception—on the contrary, look back upon past history, which by apocalyptic vision they reconstruct, make to some degree clear, and explain in some measure.

Historical novelists of apocalypse tend generally, moreover, to envision history as divided into predetermined periods or ages. Since only God remains in control, such writers find supremely interesting the final and cataclysmic act within the world because it arrives by God's intervention. They see a long period of dominant evil, of abject fear and hideous suffering under such a totalitarianism as directly precludes the end of the world. At this moment events expand until they acquire a cosmic dimension or until they include universal significance on earth. At such a time in history no man dares

[4] See Chapters II and III of *The Relevance of Apocalyptic* (1944) by H. H. Rowley in the American edition (New York, 1964), where sixteen apocalypse texts are analyzed.

[5] "Le Grand théâtre" from *L'Apocalypse,* ed. Joseph Foret (Paris, 1964), pp. 269-306.

rise to oppose; surely no man succeeds, Tolstoy would have observed, in opposing the Satanic Antichrist, Nero or some other Caesar, Hitler or some other Napoleon. Certain novelists proceed thus far, and then bog down in the meres of despondency.

As in 1931 Roger Martin du Gard still meditated upon World War I,[6] he concluded that the future truly seemed to him laden with catastrophic events. That year Jean Giono published his apocalyptic novel *Le Grand troupeau*. Advancing beyond impending disaster, Giono sensed an inner and often forgotten affinity between philosophy and theology. Thus in the twentieth century, Judeo-Christian apocalypse furnished Giono an answer for the historical catastrophes of those days. Apocalyptic stipulates that what really "happens in history is salvation and disaster."[7] The disaster may be "empirically apprehensible," which does not mean that it constitutes, if the salvation is neglected, the only "element of historical reality."

Theology contributed, as Giono composed, its component to empirical knowledge, or its means of cognition by unfolding or by revelation, the novelist knowing because he has himself experienced and seen others swept along like sheep in a flock, but also knowing because it has been prophesied by a divine, who knew without any experience whatsoever other than his vision. The truly Christian writer thus awaits the catastrophic end of history, accepts the whole dreadful creation, rises to great activity as he aids the divinity inside mundane reality, and fixes his eyes upon the promised salvation, which allows him to hope even in the midst of terrors.

[6] See Norman Cohn's *The Pursuit of the Millennium* (New York, 1961), introduction and conclusion especially, for modern chiliasm.

[7] See *The End of Time. A Meditation on the Philosophy of History* by Josef Pieper, trans. Michael Bullock (London, undated), p. 22 ff.

"(Seen from the body of experience afforded by our own epoch, is it so unlikely that the Church, although ultimately concerned with a salvation that cannot be grounded on intra-mundane considerations, might remain the sole champion of the natural dignity of man?)"[8]

To a theologian in the Russian Orthodox tradition, E. Lampert in *The Apocalypse of History—Problems of Providence & Human Destiny* (London, 1948), the philosophy of apocalypse is properly and alone *the* philosophy of history; apocalypse is history defined, then, as "the disclosure and consummation of divine and human destiny" (p. 14). "It may be said that the problem of History in its apocalyptic and eschatological significance is the dominant issue in the contemporary world and the touch-stone of survival precisely because mankind has reached a stage in which nothing is sufficient to meet the challenge of History but the absolutely creative, complete, final, totally triumphant or totally disastrous, that is, the eschatological solution."

Such novelists whom we may also consider to have written masterpieces of modern apocalyptic fiction—Jean Giono in the 1930's, André Malraux in the 1940's, William Faulkner in *A Fable* of 1950, and William Styron in 1967—seem to compose their historical fiction in two modes. On the one hand, as we shall presently see, they accumulate and absorb historical evidence, create characters, study persons and situations, recreate actual revolts or wars, and formulate answers to questions. Thus, they deal with empirical evidence, facts, dates, personages, and philosophy, an activity that becomes diurnal and cataphatic. Coexistent with such accumulations of data occur the philosophical considerations, however, nearer to creation and to end, born perhaps in darkness, pos-

[8] *Ibid.*, p. 138.

sibly even revealed in night if ever unfolded at all luminously. Each author, then, lures his reader through the horrors of the predicted disasters, into the dark quietness of night, where by apophatic theology he draws him like Moses closer to God, both unknowable and undefinable, at least by affirmative and discursive statements.

ALTHOUGH Jean Giono was not the first veteran of World War I to associate his experiences at the front and in the trenches with the life and death of Christ, he may very well have written the first historical novel based throughout on apocalyptic in lieu of any other philosophy of history. Just before *Le Grand troupeau*[9] of 1931, which has been translated into German,[10] Polish, and Czech[11] and finally into English as *To the Slaughterhouse*,[12] but about which there has been otherwise virtual silence,[13] Ludwig Renn in his famous novel *War*

[9] Christian Michelfelder in *Jean Giono et les religions de la terre* (Paris, 1938), where he omits Christianity from the religions discernible in Giono's works, believes that there are 900 extra pages of *Le Grand troupeau* besides the 252 in the Gallimard edition (67e) of 1931. The novel appeared in the *Nouvelle Revue Française* of that year, and there are extra chapters in *Refus d'obéissance* (Gallimard, 1937). The poor English translation was very late, done only in 1969 by Norman Glass in London, and called *To the Slaughterhouse*, 215 pp.; see the review in the *LTLS* (5.6.69), p. 601. See also Michelfelder's book, pp. 79-84, for his "panique" or pagan theory of Jean Giono, and also W. D. Redfern's chapter "Apocalypse" from *The Private World of Jean Giono* (Duke University, 1967).

[10] Fischer Verlag customarily publishes Giono.

[11] Only these three translations are listed between 1931-1965 by Jean Bottin's Bibliographie.

[12] See *Giono* by Pierre de Boisdeffre (Paris, 1965), p. 270.

[13] Even with such consistent champions in America as Henri Peyre ("Jean Giono" in *French Novelists of Today*, pp. 123-53), Maxwell A. Smith (*Jean Giono*, New York, 1966), Katharine Allen Clarke (*French Review*, xxxv [April 1962], pp. 478-83), Pierre R. Robert (*Giono et les techniques du roman*, Berkeley, 1961), Hadlam Walker

(*Krieg*, and New York, 1929) had equated a soldier-hero with Christ.

Giono's allusions to apocalypse resemble Ludwig Renn's thoughts of Christ crucified, but, contrary to this German contemporary (*né* V. v. Golscenau), Giono openly attacked war, in the manner of Tolstoy—and Henri Peyre has several times associated Giono and Tolstoy.[14] There is, as far as war is concerned, neither ambiguity nor confusion in Giono's novel, which, of course, may have argued against it.

Maxwell A. Smith in his *Jean Giono* has, after André Gide, also spoken admiringly of this Giono novel with its memorable prologue (p. 63): "The most epic scene in the book, one of the most powerful and moving passages Giono has ever written, is the opening chapter which shows us the apparently endless procession of sheep and lambs coming down from the high plateaux and streaming painfully through the little Provençal town." As Smith argued,[15] the theme of the great flock returns to furnish, at the recovery of the God-like ram and the birth of a son, or blessed Lamb of God, a lyrical conclusion that affirms a Christian hope of a new and peaceful realm. According to apocalyptic tradition, Jean Giono emphasizes four major points in *Revelation*: (1) natural disaster (the descent of the great flock, or the departure of its shepherds to war), (2) a period of Great Tribulation (when the Beast of war reigned), (3) the Second Coming of Christ (the

---

("Myth in *Chant du monde*," *Symposium*, xv, 1961, pp. 139-46), and Henry Miller's enthusiasm as expressed in *The Books in My Life* (New York, 1950), for example, Giono has never become to the general public in America a novelist of great importance.

[14] See his "Jean Giono" from *French Novelists of Today* (New York, 1967), especially p. 152.

[15] He argues against the prior interpretation of Louis de Mondadon in "*Le Grand troupeau*," *Etudes* (July 5, 1932). See Smith's *Jean Giono*, pp. 63-65.

birth of the Lamb, or child), and (4) the ending with a Christian, "inverted," or hopeful solution to catastrophe.

Solidly but unobtrusively documented by the author's own experiences in World War I, the book proceeds from the mobilization of France in 1914 through the Battle of Mount Kemmel in 1918, or through the Battle of Passchendale, also called the third Battle of Ypres.[16] According to Giono's account, only two Frenchmen in his unit (140th Regiment?) survived. The ground was a heavy clay churned into mud by the long bombardment, and during the battle it rained heavily.

Giono begins his novel by describing the departure of men to war. That August night thick with the smell of wheat and the sweat of horses, the wagons drawn by work horses pulled up by the station and waited while the train loaded and then moved softly off into darkness, spitting sparks into the willows as it picked up speed. The horses moaned. Next morning the sheep, an ass and her foal, watched by old men, young women, and children, came down from the high pastures. A wounded ram lay down in the dusty road to die, swept aside by an irresistible current of dumb animals, no shepherd stopping them, no person healing. In houses where people could not eat for grief, a mother lay down to sleep in the place left vacant by the absent young husband.

In Chapter III the swift transition to a scene of three men lying beside a road jerks the reader abruptly into the actual world of war, where each man is totally expendable, for despite promises the ambulance will not return. Overhead a crow circles, waiting impatiently. As Smith has already observed, Giono alternates, via true Tolstoyan antinomies, home scenes with combat scenes: Julie and Madeleine at home

[16] See A. J. P. Taylor's *A History of the First World War* (New York, 1966).

fighting an evil force blindly bent on turning the cultivated fields back into wilderness, and a beast within themselves that longs to see them break the tenets of Christian morality and revert to lusting savagery. As the wounded soldier dies of gangrene, Joseph consoles him, with the tale of his happy home life with Julie. Ironically also, Madeleine skins a rabbit and wards off a hungry fly as she and Delphine talk desultorily of fly-covered corpses along the Marne.

On Olivier's last night in the village, the news arrives of the death of Félicie's husband, and old Jérôme fetches carefully home from school the stricken and orphaned son. Then follows in Chapter VII (Part II) the brilliantly composed wake for an absent body, which commences with ritual words and the ceremony of the salt on the table: " 'I share your loss.' 'I thank you kindly.' " The chapter ends tenderly as old pappy walks his only son to the station. The mourning women tacitly believe Olivier too young to survive such a war. And all around, "la nuit est comme si rien n'était," the cosmos remains indifferent to man.

Jean Giono's many such pictures of war remain unforgettable even today: a passing ambulance losing meat like a butcher's wagon, Olivier's friend Regotaz turning back into a primitive woodsman, Joseph warning the heedless captain not to lead his men over a footbridge in enemy crossfire, the dead moving in their piles as crows and rats feast on them, an epileptic boy passed by medical officers and drafted forthwith. Only a captain, Olivier, and one sleeping man survive Verdun, after which experience Olivier, who saw Regotaz die, keeps nervously repeating, "Me. Me."

At home the fifth angel has sounded his trump, and the Great Whore revels in cheap flesh. The butcher finds his obese daughter copulating with the adolescent apprentice. Julie blooms like a girl in Proust. Even the pullets ovulate

33

prematurely, while the washerwomen catch a boy in the wash water. After Julie and the butcher slide in blood as they slaughter a sow, Julie too wrestles with the apprentice, who has called her a sow. In her bed Madeleine wears, like the lady in the medieval romance of Coucy, Olivier's red wool sash under her nightgown. The waters turned gradually to wormwood, as *Revelation* foretold, by the time that Olivier returns home on leave.

In the wreck of a village called Santerre, soldiers go insane, try to borrow Olivier's love letter—an inestimably valuable treasure—become in their caves terrified at the mere ticking of a watch. One man even fabricates a slip-noose for a German, so that the prisoner will cruelly thrash about in slow and agonized strangulation, like a rabbit. Olivier again sees Regotaz, who brings him a gift, a pine cone in which one can hear lovely forest murmurs. He tells Olivier how much he would have liked to have brought him a little lizard just hatched from its egg, a little green lizard with water droplets on its tiny toenails, and with it some violets. Then too he would have brought a lovely new water snake which he saw swimming in the midst of a stream, like a water bird. As Regotaz talks, much as Giono's father will talk to him in our second apocalypse text, Olivier realizes that these sights were his own, that it is frozen winter all about. Finally he sees that Regotaz's face is merely a candle reflection on the shiny surface of a metal drum. Everywhere, men have suffered beyond their tolerance and are either slipping away into perpetual dreams or slyly returning to a crafty savagery.

In Chapter XIX, which is entitled "Le Grand troupeau," we return full circle to the commencement, or the structure of the book abruptly becomes apparent. Here near Ypres the French and British troops are deployed in northwestern Belgium for the defense of Dunkirk. The French army is the real

great flock, then, which descended from its peaceful pastures, and the Biblical title of Chapter I, "Elle mangera vos béliers, vos brebis et vos maisons," refers to war. Thus, Chapter I concerns flocks of sheep, but its title, referring to war, became clear only in the nineteenth chapter, which dealt with flocks of men. Between these two chapters Giono has arranged the intrigue chapter (house) by chapter (war) until this climax or flocklike war scene.

In the sour, green dawn, lakes and tides of soldiers slog through heavy mud, grit their teeth, weep, and bleed quietly until their first halt at a supply depot around noon. Their helmets are white with frost. It is spring now, and the English pour from Mt. Kemmel in full flight. In a series of short sentences Giono draws brief and vivid pictures of civilians in panic. The men are deep in the water of a pond; the very water also tries desperately to escape by flowing here and there as it is bombed and flailed. The casualties are so heavy that the chain of command passes downward in dizzy speed. Crawling from one dead body to another, Olivier finally finds two live friends, and with them watches the grey flock of Germans attacking. While a gentle rain falls, four planes with black crosses emerge from clouds: "They swoop down like swallows until they are skimming the earth with their bellies. They fire a few rounds of their machine guns, like beaks chattering." (p. 234)

The horrors have not ended yet, however, nor even properly begun at their worst, for as Olivier enters an abandoned farmyard, he comes upon a sow eating a corpse: "A naked newborn babe lies under the feet of the sow. She has torn off a shoulder, and has already eaten its chest. She stands there leaning over its tiny belly, which is still white; she bites into it; her mouth stuffed, she gulps in air in order to swallow the child's guts." (p. 238)

Olivier draws his farmer's knife from his pocket. The ensuing combat is characteristically recounted in two-, three-, and four-word sentences. After the beast's death, Olivier looks up at the sky, very much as do Tolstoy's Prince Andrei and Pierre Bezuhof: "Au-dessus, le ciel, un peu de bleu. . . . La paix! La paix!"

As his friend mounts a black horse, Olivier leaps on the white mare. From this height they now can see burning barns and houses, willow hedgerows flattened on the ground, and a lone airplane. Leaning, like Fabrice del Dongo at near-by Waterloo, on their horses' necks, the two French soldiers let themselves be carried away from the sea, where the German troops are converging.

In their headlong retreat Olivier and his friend meet troops moving up to combat. In the distance, German machine guns begin to crackle like oil in a frying pan. Gassed in May of 1918, the author was demobilized in October 1919. Thus, he knows no more at first-hand of World War I.

Chapter XX serves as an epilogue, entitled "Dieu bénisse l'agneau." In the closing nine pages Julie helps Madeleine deliver the latter's second son, a baby born well and strong, not deformed like her first child because of the abortion attempt. Olivier has miraculously returned in time to welcome his son, and the old shepherd of Chapter I has also returned for his ram. As the venerable shepherd blesses the newborn baby, the star of Bethlehem rises in the east:

> "The shepherd lifts the child high . . .
> The ram lows towards the horizon . . .
> Visibly . . . the night brightens:
> 'Saint John! Saint John!' Julie gasps . . . ."

Thus, the book ends with the name of the author of *Revelation*.

Jean Giono typically has constructed his only war novel about a series of symbols that, said D. H. Lawrence in his *Apocalypse*, appeal to "deep emotional centers."[17] By dwelling upon the rams that died in Chapter I, for example, he seems to be insisting upon symbols of power and might. The flock in its complimentary sense represents God's pastoral care for man, as in both Testaments. The Psalmist says (77:22): "Thou leddest thy people like a flock by the hand of Moses and Aaron." Pejoratively Giono scolds man for dumb conformity and mass acquiescence in his own slaughter.

The carnivorous birds, which the narrator saw feasting on soldiers' corpses, were also foretold in *Revelation* 19:17-18:

"And I saw an angel standing in the sun; and he cried with a loud voice, saying to all the fowls that fly in the midst of heaven, come and gather yourselves together unto the supper of the great God;

"That ye may eat the flesh of kings, and the flesh of captains, and the flesh of mighty men, and the flesh of horses, and of them that sit on them, and the flesh of all men, both free and bond, both small and great."

Both dragon and serpent, or lizard in Giono's case, are apocalyptic symbols of life. The jovial white horse ridden by Olivier as one of a pair, with his saturnine friend on the black horse, form two of the famous four horsemen of the Apocalypse, Olivier being the conqueror crowned, the survivor, and, as here, slayer of the beast.

Julie properly represents the apocalyptic Scarlet Whore of Babylon, or the woman turned beastly and lustful because of the war. The author's anger and scorn for a faithless wife whose husband is a soldier in wartime—and Jean Giono is otherwise a notorious champion and defender of woman,

---

[17] *Apocalypse* with an introduction by Richard Aldington (New York, 1966), p. 184.

where, as usual, he stands athwart the prevailing temper of his own times—causes her also to be qualified as a "sow." The author leaves her thereafter for Madeleine, who can be redeemed at least by the birth of a second son.

Giono is fascinated by Chapters VIII and IX of *Revelation*, particularly verses 10 through 1 of the latter chapter: the third angel blew his trumpet, and a star called Wormwood fell, turning one-third of the rivers and springs on earth very bitter. A fifth angel blew and another star fell from heaven to earth, "and to him was given the key to the bottomless pit." Albrecht Dürer preferred a similar subject in the fifteenth century, when he made his woodcut numbered 110: "And the stars of heaven fell unto the earth, even as a fig tree casteth her untimely figs, when she is shaken of a mighty wind" (*Revelation* 6:13). Dürer represents the lamb (woodcut numbered 118) as throned in the sun, spurting blood from his breast to fill an extended chalice.[18] To Giono the lamb of God, or newborn son associated with Saint John as author of *Apocalypse,* means the Christian's hope that at the advent of Jesus, as Boris Pasternak would so often say in his apocalyptic *Doctor Zhivago*, savagery was replaced by gentleness.

Both the second and fourth horses of *Revelation* are passed over in this novel, the second or red horseman because to him was given the power to take peace from the earth, cause killing among men, and wield his great sword. The rider of the pale, or green, or yellow horse—interpretations of this color differ—was named Death, with Hades following after him. In his later apocalypse text Giono will smilingly say that Saint John may in any case have been so dazzled by the sea at Patmos that he only imagined he saw a fourth or green horse. At the sight of such a horse, the tumults on earth

[18] *The Complete Woodcuts of Albrecht Dürer*, ed. Willi Kurth (New York, 1946), pp. 110 and 118.

would have been replaced by eternal silence. Therefore there never was a fourth horse.[19]

Thus in 1931 Giono renewed a tradition of interpreting history according to nocturnal apocalyptic theory,[20] as Melville had done almost a hundred years earlier. To both writers there are certain data susceptible of empirical verification, beyond which lie mysteries, which are mysteries, or other forms of knowledge.

In 1936, or five years after having published *Le Grand troupeau*, Giono presented as a Preface to his essays on true riches, *Les Vraies richesses* (1937), a short history of his own philosophical development. He had always felt, he said, that his own life's road had been marked out for him in advance. Man he early defined widely as nothing less than a "cosmic element." By rejecting Jesus' renunciation of the body, modern man can proceed from the collective terror in which he presently lives to a boundless hope, which surges in man precisely from a body alive and joyous. Such a man must not let any society based upon money destroy either him or his peace. Giono wrote for man, to give him joy, he said, and he fulfills D. H. Lawrence's dictum: "The human heart needs, needs, needs, splendour...."

"Le Grand théâtre" (1964)

Between the years 1958 and 1961 M. Joseph Foret assembled in France the manuscript pages of a book that took its title from its key text, the *Apocalypse* of Saint John. To other pages of this book seven painters, including the late Jean Cocteau, and seven writers, including Jean Giono, contributed

[19] *Apocalypse*, p. 31.
[20] In his *Jean Giono* (Paris, 1955) Jacques Pugnet pointed out the importance of night in Giono's fiction.

paintings and/or hand-calligraphed texts. The resulting book, weighing 460 pounds and valued at one million dollars (its jeweled cover was constructed by Salvador Dali), was exhibited in Los Angeles in the fall of 1964. At that time M. Foret also presented a film based upon the making of this book, with a sequence devoted to Jean Giono, showing him in Manosque copying his text into the volume. Giono's contribution, "Le Grand théâtre,"[1] has not to my knowledge as yet been entered in Giono bibliographies,[2] nor has it as yet received scholarly comment.

This text of Giono, dated June 2, 1961, falls neither into the category of literary criticism nor exactly into that of prose fiction. Although it purports ostensibly to be a "conversation" between the boy Jean Giono and his father, also named Jean Giono, its first section is largely the latter's monologue, with glosses only by the author. "Le Grand théâtre" is both theology and that branch of philosophy termed eschatology. It is divided first into a main section of nineteen pages narrated inside quotation marks by the author's father, third of that name, whose words are interspersed with three short paragraphs by the author explaining the circumstances: Jean III (the father) and Jean IV (the author, when he was ten years old) escape the August heat by taking refuge on a stable roof. It is night. The father begins by quoting Jesus' words on the Mount of Olives, as reported by Matthew, and these words lead into *Apocalypse,* or the biblical book called in Protestant Bibles *Revelation.* The second section of six pages, written more predominantly in authorial first person, although again

---

[1] *Apocalypse*, ed. Foret, Joseph (Paris, 1964), pp. 281-306.

[2] See Pierre de Boisdeffre's *Giono* (Paris, 1965), p. 251 ff.; Maxwell A. Smith's *Jean Giono* (New York, 1966), p. 183 ff.; and W. D. Redfern's *The Private World of Jean Giono* (Duke University Press, 1967), p. 197 ff.

relying upon the father's *oratio recta*, serves primarily to illustrate apocalypse in our century. Giono here, then, has not only rewritten the most famous of all apocalyptic texts,[3] but has furthermore modified and restated it. Rising from a starry night, thus higher to beginning and to ending, the words of this text constitute a modern apocalypse.

As we approach this complicated work—and when did Jean Giono regale us with simplicity?—it will be less crucial to list the author's recollections of his best-known predecessor than to discuss his variations and his additions to the text attributed to John of Patmos. They are modern additions, which stem largely from two specialized areas: mathematics and astronomy. Giono's artistic method, always distinctive and unpredictable, consists here of a sliding from well-known apocalyptic to his own illustration. It may also be of some interest to note in passing how Giono's approach here differs from that of D. H. Lawrence, for example, since he is a novelist to whom Jean Giono is often compared. We should note *a priori* how this Giono text, a subtle mystification, bears witness to Giono's consistency and to the fact that his prison experiences neither altered his convictions, nor silenced him, nor caused him to forswear political apocalyptic.[4]

The text commences, as we have seen, with a voice, later to be identified as the author's father, quoting Matthew (24:6, 7

[3] A very helpful and clear listing and discussion of 16 apocalypse texts, from *Daniel* in the *Old Testament* through *Revelation* in the *New Testament*, was made by H. H. Rowley in *The Relevance of Apocalyptic* (New York, 1944, etc., but see in particular the revised edition of 1963), pp. 29-149. For medieval apocalypse, see Norman Cohn's *The Pursuit of the Millennium* (New York, 1961), p. 13 ff.

[4] Because W. D. Redfern was unaware of "Le Grand théâtre," he confined Giono's "apocalyptic stage" roughly from 1935 to 1939, and treated in his Chapter VI only Giono's pre-war political and sociological views. In my opinion, Giono's most distinguished and most artistic apocalypse text is still *Le Grand troupeau* (Paris, 1931).

and 8): there will be wars, clashes of nations, earthquakes, famines—and this only a beginning of misfortunes—the sun will be darkened, the moon will no longer give light. During this preliminary list of catastrophes, the author has begun, very subtly, to substitute for *Matthew* the Book of *Revelation* (7:8, 5, 8, 12, 11; 8 and 9), and then *Job* (41 and 40), until he forsakes Biblical statement altogether to forecast at the last three original prophetic visions: hell will light up the world like a dawn, the sun will sink like a shipwrecked craft, and the cracking of the world's mechanism will be heard all the way to Sirius. Instead of continuing the earlier prognosis of Jesus, Giono blended His prophecies with those of John of Patmos, whom he assumes, incidentally, to be the same John son of Zebedee who wrote the Fourth Gospel.[5] He left it to the reader to recall that in *Matthew* (24:17) Jesus had gone on to say that there would be no time to leave the rooftops "pour prendre ce qui est dans la maison. . . ." This verse, however, gave Giono his second paragraph: "Nous étions . . . mon père et moi . . . sur une toiture, au-dessus de la ville. . . ." Inside their house, says the author in a first-person narrative passage

[5] Giono follows a traditional ascription here to Saint John the Evangelist (Saint John the Divine), brother of Saint James. The Book of *Revelation*, as H. H. Rowley points out (p. 138), is not pseudonymous, but claims to have been composed by a John who was at that time in exile in Patmos; this is not necessarily the Apostle John. In his *Apocalypse* (copyright 1931, but New York, 1966), D. H. Lawrence distinguishes most definitely, from tone, subject matter, attitude, and internal evidence, between John the Apostle and John of Patmos. He attributes *Revelation* to the latter, in other words.

For recent works by literary critics treating apocalypse, see "Days of Wrath and Laughter" from R. W. B. Lewis' *Trials of the World* (Yale University Press, 1965); Frank Kermode's *The Sense of an Ending. Studies in the Theory of Fiction* (Oxford University Press, 1967); and an earlier work on Kierkegaard, Dostoevsky, Nietzsche, and Kafka by William Hubben, *Four Prophets of Our Destiny* (New York, 1954).

where he has shifted to the imperfect tense, remained the mother of the family, whose nightly sleep represented a daily death with which she fought their old house, letting in from all directions wind, rain, and the filthy vermin that scampered from its decaying walls. On such nights Giono's father, a poor and work-worn cobbler, would awaken his son. Together the pair would scramble up on the stable roof, under the summer stars, or under Sirius, brightest star in the heavens and a true symbol for the stifling summer dog days in Manosque. Thus, by establishing the social level of his father, whose lore is about to unfold, Giono tacitly attributes to him what certain Biblical scholars consider a constant prophetic bent among anarchistic and autodidactic men,[6] an apocalyptic tendency that Giono derives for his father principally from Saint John's *Apocalypse*.

There will be illnesses, continues the father, alluding to the seven angels who from vials full of wrath cast plagues upon the earth and upon men (*Rev.* 16). During the course of his prediction, the father speaks of the famous four horsemen and of the first rider on the white horse, of the second death, of the beast and the abyss, of the seven seals, of the trumpets and the fifth angel, of Babylon as obviously representing the

[6] Giono strives, during Part 1 of the text, at least, to disassociate himself and his father from the sort of fanaticism that Norman Cohn and many others trace as a "revolutionary messianism" or as an irresponsible chiliasm, apocalyptic derivatives that apparently led to such modern ideologies as Communism and Nazism. Giono's present work, straining to remain purely theological, becomes largely Christian. The basic Christianity of Jean Giono is an issue that Maxwell A. Smith seems to have raised when he objected, and I believe quite rightly, to our blanket acceptance today of Christian Michelfelder's early *Jean Giono et les religions de la terre* (Paris, 1938). Professor Smith felt that there has been too great an insistence upon Giono's previous and exclusive inspiration from Greek mythology, for instance. See *Jean Giono*, p. 186, for example.

Roman Empire, of Armageddon and Gog, of the plague of locusts, and also indirectly, perhaps, of the Great Whore. Like *Revelation*, the father, or the author in his stead conjures deftly with numbers; like the authors of the Bible, he proffers what he terms "grandiose commonplaces," in what we may all agree is unlike Giono's own colorful and highly metaphorical style. Like John of Patmos, Giono's father looks as a matter of course towards cosmic cataclysms, universal catastrophes, all announcing the approaching end of the world. Giono's father does not, on the other hand, accede to the New Jerusalem (*Rev.* 21:9 ff.).

Once having anchored an unsuspecting reader to familiar imagery, Giono proceeds to reinterpret suavely and to refute calmly several major points of apocalyptic. Soon after having added his own prophecies, he rejects the future prophetic, declaring that the present tense must be rigorously employed since apocalypse is upon us all, here and now "à l'echelle planétaire même universelle, et elle ne fait pas le moindre bruit" (p. 282). The predictions are thus modified to corroborate the end of the world in the sense that the end of our personal worlds is close, is here, is now—ergo that apocalypse is present. The human history that here interests Giono "becomes not merely a series of happenings but the disclosure and consummation of . . . human destiny. . . ."[7] Even were the world to end, however, "the end-situation within history" need not be "construed as the ultimately valid end,"[8] since the father-prophet does not confuse apocalypse with death. There can be no green horse with Death and Hades accompanying him, asserts the father, for this would be mistaking the remedy for the evil. John of Patmos was dazzled by the

[7] See E. Lampert's *The Apocalypse of History* (London, 1948), p. 14.
[8] See Joseph Pieper's *The End of Time. A Meditation on the Philosophy of History*. Trans. Michael Bullock (London, undated), p. 80.

shimmer of sun on bright seas! There could be no green (or pale) horse in any *Apocalypse*, but three horsemen only; for death itself is the cure. Therefore so-called eternal suffering is not eternal at all, but only a state that comes to an end. Apocalypse itself refers to the state, "l'ensemble des évènements qui font désirer la Mort" (p. 284). If there had been a green or fourth horse, moreover, all terrors like the rumbling and hissing of volcanoes would have been replaced by choirs of angels, i.e., by everlasting silence.

Human nature being what it is, insists the author from his unquestioned authority, we would all crowd into the vast theatre of the universe to witness apocalypse, just as we scramble up volcanic craters to sniff sulphurous fumes (*Rev.* 9:17-18), to see rivers of blood (*Rev.* 16:4) and the uprooting of mountains (*Rev.* 8:8). We would run to watch the beast rise from the abyss (*Rev.* 13:1 and 11) when now we throng to see beasts and abysses, even separately. In short, as evidenced in many illustrations, which it doubtless amused Giono to detail, as it amuses the reader to recognize, we would thoroughly enjoy apocalypse. There is a dearth of pure joy in the universe, spoke Giono's father, and also Nietzsche's Zarathustra. We would therefore stay to the last curtain, for apocalypse as previously defined does not necessarily destroy our lives. In fact, while it may worry us in some world where we live, it does not preclude either hope or happiness, both being independent of it. And, in any case, there exist most assuredly other worlds.

Now recall the fifth angel, says the father: "And the fifth angel sounded, and I saw a star fall from heaven and unto the earth: and to him was given the key of the bottomless pit" (*Rev.* 9:1). And recall Apollyon, who appeared from the abyss, the god of numbers, which express that which does not exist and which illustrate how scholars construct a non-existent present from some long-disintegrated past. What happened? Nothing, except that a star fell, whose light took millions of years to reach us, or to reach John son of Zebedee, to whom it resembled a star. Therefore, there is no need to use the future tense for past apocalypse: "On ne peut pas nous menacer du futur; on ne peut nous menacer que du passé" (p. 300).

What is *Apocalypse*? To Giono's father, who loved the sweet shadows under the centaurs, the golden locusts with lion's teeth, and all such splendors, it is also literature in the line from Vergil to Ariosto's *Orlando furioso*. What else? With its patent allusions to Rome, it is political writing, its author pouncing upon and utilizing events like foundlings. But most of all, it constitutes a timely warning to beware of super-civilizations that would forbid to man the sovereign remedy for all holocausts: death itself, that final triumph, as Giono would characteristically believe.

In addition to these refutations of *Revelation,* Giono's modern apocalyptic contains two blocks of material (pp. 288-92, and pp. 296-99) relating to astronomy, cut by a third or central block (pp. 293-96) treating mathematical thinking. Number theory, we recall, is ruled by the angel Apollyon, recalled from the abyss by the fifth angel's trumpet. Numbers are the flesh of this fallen angel. As for numbers, argues the father, we possess only an infinitive form perfectly unsusceptible therefore of stating even past tenses, since numbers cannot be conjugated. Nothing, in fact, that we human beings invent can apply elsewhere than in the limited world of our invention, from which it follows that our mathematics cannot obtain in any other world. Other worlds may already be dead, or may require for their description a subjunctive mood or a pluperfect statement. This limitation of numbers is a pity because, were they more flexible, we might hope to understand the creation—although, to be sure, we may witness it daily without ever being the wiser, and with no hope, for example, of attending our own births. While the father-narrator dreams of the subjunctive of the number one, scholars depend upon figures, all relative like those proclaimed by John of Patmos, to express the present of a past—a present that exists only so far as our memory stretches.

In the first passage dealing with astronomy, which Giono studied for a period of some years, the text equates the aurora borealis, with its scarlet and purple hues, with the memory of a faithless wife, possibly the Biblical Whore of Babylon, whom the author thus appears again to condemn—fairly typically of Giono. He speaks of floating in space; of our world, which is "ténèbres et silence" (p. 290); of our planet, upon which we are all spectators; and of our universe, that which does not exist, faceless like all things that likewise do not exist. He points to Vega, whence light reaches us in twenty million years, a few years more or less making no difference, while to a human being seconds are so precious. When we name the constellations that we observe and turn in desperation to numbering them, we are really characterizing Saint John's vast abyss in all of which nothing has ever occurred, except for traces of explosions seen by astronomers that happened eons ago. Look, for example, at the stars seemingly clustered in the Milky Way. Could not this very universe already have passed through apocalypse, with us none the better informed of it? "Ce soir est peut-être la fin du monde" (p. 298), which similarly may already have ended so that we may, each one of us, inhabit an extinct universe. All that we see with our eyes is truly more false than poetry (p. 298). Science continues to calculate in a non-existent present, using, for instance, the speed of light, which is nothing compared to the speed with which a present moment plunges into the past: "Tout se précipite dans le passé, rien n'est immuable, rien ne demeure dans un présent qui lui-même ne demeure pas" (p. 299). In such considerations Giono introduces new material, which marks his apocalypse as being of the twentieth century, while by its use he repudiates science, as he did in *Le Hussard sur le toit*, preferring poetry or art, on whose grounds he himself is probably to be preferred.

His own terrain, where he commands our instant respect, however, is human nature, which he can reliably observe and from whose case he can posit conclusions later generalized to apply to all humanity, then to our planet, and finally to the universe. Very wisely the novelist finds apocalypse verifiable in one person whom he takes, then, for his illustration. The father, as he quoted Matthew and John, as he discoursed on mathematics and astronomy, worried about a member of the family, an aged uncle named Eugène. This old man (*ecce homo*), concerning whom Jean III states facts, without any attempt on Giono's part to elicit pity from the reader, depends every day more heavily upon the father, the mother, and the son of the family. The uncle's wife abandoned him years ago because their lives lacked magnificence or transfiguration; Uncle Eugène was only a dull-witted, ordinary man. A tanner by trade, Uncle Eugène had become a part-time gardener, as he waited to become a nothing-at-all with digestive and eliminatory functions.

The reader is introduced to him via the father's discursions upon apocalyptic, but the method used, or the author's technique in this parallel material which serves as a concrete illustration of apocalypse, contains the chief interest of the piece. In the very opening lines of "Le Grand théâtre" the dire calamities predicted included "l'éclipse de la lumière," the most bearable of all the afflictions listed. Shortly thereafter the reader is introduced to *Oncle* Eugène, who has been "retranché de la lumière," or who is becoming blind: he has already virtually lost the sight of his right eye and *they* will doubtless manage shortly to make him lose that of his left eye: "on arrivera sans doute à lui faire perdre l'oeil gauche" (p. 282). The second calamity fallen upon *Oncle* Eugéne is a growing deafness, or he has also been "retranché des bruits," so that in his case, although we may imagine that apocalypse occurs amidst great noise because it takes place on a planetary level, or even upon a universal scale, "elle ne fait pas," on the contrary, "le moindre bruit" (p. 282). As a gardener in his personal Gethsemane, *Oncle* Eugène is now in his extremity able to become interested, not in malodorous hides, but in perfumed flowers, in roses, cyclamens, lilacs, violets. This feeble and unintelligent septuagenarian is himself a world, a universe even, in whom apocalypse unfolds; he typifies the only verifiable illustration *within our grasp* of man succumbing to a series of awful calamities: "le seul à notre portée" (p. 283). There is much apocalypse in this old man's frail body.

Apocalypse is apprehended, not intellectually, but by our senses, although John of Patmos in exile by the sea, betrayed by his eyes, mistook some mirage for the green horse of death. Uncle Eugène in his earlier career as a tanner and abandoned husband also composed his knowledge of the world through his five senses; but now, when he has been reduced almost to nothing as part-time gardener, his universe, no longer comprehended sensually, has expanded until it enfolds an infinity of knowledge. Thus, the white horse (*Rev.* 6:2) represents the Word of God, vanquisher of all beasts and lords of the earth; the white horse is the "Word . . . made flesh" (*John* 1:14) saying to Uncle Eugène, "Come . . ." (*Matthew* 25:34). Although he is a world within this world, the old man, tended by his sister, her husband, and the son

49

Jean Giono, so unloved and uninvited to earthly pleasures, is summoned nonetheless by the words of Jesus to enter the great theatre of revelation, where his physical sufferings have been firmly and solemnly promised an end. At this point the text recapitulates (p. 287) three physical deprivations upon earth: blindness, deafness, and lack of invitation to any feast or spectacle. Jesus had replied that He did not know how long calamities would last, we learned in the first series of predictions (p. 281). As he grows more feeble, Uncle Eugène will know, perhaps, that his nephew has helped him hobble to a seat in the sunshine, but as for his sufferings, "il va vivre ainsi, qui sait combien?" (p. 288)

The abyss of ten thousand years is the past into which all present plunges, then, faster than the speed of light. In this abyss of space Uncle Eugène floats with thousands of years to go, perhaps, before touching bottom, on his way towards a new universe, of which there are thousands. When we contemplate the heavens, we also gaze into this abyss in the description of which all our numbers are inadequate. Uncle Eugène arrives at the end of a world, which has perhaps also ended.

"I have always remembered these 'conversations' on the roof of a stable," resumes the author's voice antithetically in Part II of the text. These "conversations," which occurred, says Giono, fifty years previously, or from 1901, again a relative figure, paralleled our entrance into the twentieth century. The boy and his father attended their first moving picture, where the latter was impressed by a cinematographic representation of a typhoon. The typhoon, rephrased in more apocalyptic terms, was rather a manifestation of Typhon, antagonist of Jupiter, who from his lair in the abyss continued to exhale the hot blasts of August. Together they traveled to see their first reluctantly heroic aviator mount the Flying Horse of Ariosto like a modern knight in armor of shining steel. Together still, they heard a first record played by their first gramophone, and again the father wondered how such machines were to be understood and if their significance to the modern world, or their relationship to apocalypse, would not be, in the final analysis, what they carried inside them of danger to man. The Babylon[9] in Saint John's *Apocalypse* may now be translated as Paris or as Moscow, the crumbling Roman Empire seen as a continuing disintegration, politics as having remained the same: "to govern me is to force me to look elsewhere while somebody else handles my own affairs," resumes the father (p. 304). The apocalyptic Armageddon is 1914, and Verdun, the heavenly combat of airplanes, gas warfare. That is war. As for peace, it depends upon a new group in power, successors of Louis-Philippe and the middle class: the super-civilized. Our greatest danger, concludes the father, will come from those among us who, needing reserves of savagery hitherto unknown, will, if they discover how to abolish death, insist that man's suffering remain eternal. It is not they but poets alone who can predict the future, for did not John of Patmos realize: ". . . les hommes chercheront la

---

[9] Giono seems in his text to be in no way indebted either to modern Biblical scholarship or to such a contemporary exegesis of Saint John's *Apocalypse* as that of Paul Claudel: *Paul Claudel interroge l'Apocalypse* (Paris, 1952). Although Claudel's essays explain the Biblical book from a theological and orthodox point of view, he also at various points emphasizes a modern political lesson: as, for example, that the wrath of God may be seen in the "rictus de haine" of great revolutionaries such as Luther, Voltaire, Mirabeau, Lenin, and Marat (p. 109). When he comes to Babylon in the Bible, however, Claudel admits that the text of *Apocalypse* gives him a "headache," for how rejoice at the prophetic character of the book when Rome, future site of the Church, is thus doomed to destruction? Pp. 159-60.

mort . . . et la mort s'enfuit d'eux . . ." (*Rev.* 9:6). Jean Giono ends this text abruptly: "Peu de temps après il [the father] mourut."

The Giono text is itself a work of art and an apocalypse, rather than a criticism thereof, as in the case of D. H. Lawrence. Giono proceeds throughout more subtly even where he may agree with Lawrence. While Lawrence had demonstrated by argument that apocalyptic thinking represents a popular or mass reaction, Giono allows his father, a man of the poor, to speak the text. While Lawrence brilliantly analyzes the symbolism of the text, Giono-the-apocalypticist points out a philosophical error inconsistent with his knowledge of man: that apocalypse excludes death. Where Lawrence feels a grudging admiration mixed with contempt and scorn for John's *Apocalypse*, and while he concentrates upon the mythological interpretations of the text, Giono goes behind the text to put himself in the author's place and thus, allying himself with John of Patmos, whose real identity or possible historical identity he does not care to discuss, he is able to modify him authorially. Thus, while Lawrence treats various aspects of *Revelation* in chapters, Giono reconstructs the whole, making it apply to our own times. Lawrence is interested in *Revelation* as a past fact; Giono is interested in it as a present, living entity, a power still in the world.

Jean Giono's apocalypse text, "Le Grand théâtre," is, like all his writings, anthropocentric. Man, he says, is here on earth like a spectator in a vast theatre, a privileged viewer before whom and to whom revelations occur. Stars that he sees are born and die, or may already be extinct. Man also will die, a fact of no tragic consequence, for there are other worlds. Apocalypse is man, transpires in man, where it has a verifiable beginning and an end. Man's old age, when the predicted series of disasters normally strike, permits revelation as he approaches death, which is above all a beginning and an end. The harder the catastrophes strike, the more is revealed. Man can live always, then, with joy since he alone is most divinely diverted. Although he may suffer, such diversions arising from such invitations to such magnificent spectacles show him that he is somewhere preferred. Man need necessarily have neither terror of Antichrists, nor awe of judgments, nor even any fear of the future, unless death is refused him. Apocalypse cannot destroy his hope and his joy in living, both having nothing to do with environment (p. 290). Nor can suffering destroy man. Dangers to man, rising from the four cardinal points, threaten him only because of his past, asserts Jean Giono, author diverted from diurnal fiction for the nonce to become an apophatic theologian as he recomposed a book of the Bible.

Noé (1947)

When, passing suddenly to the mature novelist, we open a discussion of Giono's chronicle *Noé*, we see spread before us a most brilliant innovation in fictional form by an author whose literary career, commencing at the end of World War I, had just witnessed the close of World War II. The title *Noé*,[1] along with its associations of flood and ark, derives in part from the recent German occupation of France and from Giono's own war experiences at Manosque and in Marseilles. After June of 1940 it appeared that France had sunk under an ocean of suffering; members of the *Résistance*, finally adopting names of animals to mask their identities, were appropriately designated by the German forces as "Noah's Ark."[2]

The ideas of Noah, ark, flood, and voyage produced three Giono works, all published closely together, in 1947 and 1948: *Noé, Fragments d'un déluge*, and *Fragments d'un paradis*. The first is a prose chronicle of 356 pages, dated July 12, 1947, at Manosque, prefaced by a page of free verse entitled "Déluge" and quoted from *Fragments d'un déluge*,[3] Giono's

[1] Page references will refer to *Chroniques. Noé* (Paris, 1940), Editions de la Table Ronde.

[2] Marie-Madeleine Fourcade's *L'Arche de Noé* (Paris, 1968), and in particular the Preface and Chapter 1 ("Le Déluge").

[3] Unable to discover a copy of this work (Villeneuve-Saint-Georges, 1948), I am fortunately able to replace it with a gift from Jean Giono, a copy of his late poetry, privately published in Manosque in 1969: "La Chute des anges," "Un Déluge," and "Le Coeur Cerf."

late book of poetry. The third work, subtitled "Poème," which recounts a "voyage merveilleux"[4] in prose, is, aside from restating what were the current thematic preoccupations[5] of this author, not directly relevant to this preliminary appreciation of *Noé*.

The constant concern with form, which so distinctly marks the post-war fiction of Jean Giono, appears nowhere so prominently as in this chronicle, where the modern novelist seems to be implementing suggestions of Flaubert: "As form skillfully takes shape, it strips itself of trammels, casting aside all liturgy, regulations, limitations; . . . thus, form no longer recognizes orthodoxy, and is as free as each creative will that fashioned it."[6] Catching his second wind as a novelist at the close of World War II, then, and publishing the difficult first chronicle *Un Roi sans divertissement* along with *Noé*, Giono concurs with Flaubert that "l'avenir de l'Art est dans ses voies." "Je ne suis gêné par aucune réalité," says the first-person narrator of *Noé* (p. 109), or the voice whom the reader respectfully recognizes as that of a Noah.

The mature novelist represented by his narrative voice, about to embark like the Biblical hero upon stormy waters with a cargo of living beings, must first rid itself of its old attachments, or manage, however rending the separation, to cast off Langlois, the *Roi sans divertissement*. Only if Langlois stays dead can the narrator prepare this new voyage, ar-

[4] M. Giono spoke to me of this work during my last conversation with him in Manosque, Aug. 17, 1970, at which time he lent me his own copy.

[5] The various symbolisms must be studied separately and as a whole, particularly the meanings and types of voyages, and also, for another instance, the various levels of significance for narcissus and mollusk.

[6] *Oeuvres complètes. Correspondance (1847-52)*, Deuxième Série, Vol. 2 (Paris, 1926), pp. 345-46. Flaubert is writing to Louise Colet from Croisset on Friday evening, Jan. 16, 1852.

range his sources, review his readings, and select a date, however undistinguishable autumn seasons are from each other, "au siècle du voyage dans la lune" (p. 326). Before beginning *Noé* proper, he must also consider an aesthetic by again comparing fiction to music, to painting, and to the theatre. At the end of his introduction (pp. 9-53), the narrator has settled upon a plan involving *histoires intercalées* entwined with *drames avoisinants* so that he may study both their affinities and leurs *enchaînements*. His will constitute also a voyage of fictional discovery and minute observations amid superimposed realities, like Pieter Bruegel's technique.

In the room where he is working (p. 12 ff.), amid multiple characters clamoring for admission to the ark, the maps of the New World, a painting of Mongol horses, a Saint George in wood, a panoramic view over the countryside, and the road through the window form one integrated tapestry the same size as the real world. "Car, le *monde* inventé n'a pas effacé le monde réel: il est superposé" (p. 25). Before Noah's eyes stretches an "immense théâtre," where on a "tréteau particulier" such a ghastly drama as that of Langlois unfolded before lighted ramps. Every book is an inventory cataloguing vehicles, means, years, *and* pale shades from Hades: "Ah! to write all these stories. . . !" (p. 42) Bruegel could show them all simultaneously, but writing constitutes a much less docile medium, with its "monde qui s'est superposé au monde dit réel" (p. 23).

The date of the story will be the winter of 1943, February of 1945, and September of 1946—or five hundred days all told (p. 32). Autumn will be chosen, and perhaps November, or rather "fin novembre" (p. 11). Sometimes a drama will occur on a day in 1920, or even in 1843 (p. 14). Linking these dates extends the "époque de la prise de conscience de la solitude humaine, de 1800 à 1900, (when) les hommes ont fait l'apprentissage des temps modernes" (p. 28). Embarking in perilous times, a modern venturer must cease hoping for any "solution de continuité" (p. 37), time also being so many superimpositions. Despite such manifold difficulties, the narrator has nevertheless resolved: "Je vais donc entreprendre moi-même;—mais quoi? un voyage dans le but catégorique de me séparer d'ici" (p. 12).

The sharing of a problem of aesthetics with the reader should result, as here, in the latter's calmer acceptance of technical irregularity, for Noé delightfully assaults the canons of form, being a novel most closely affiliated with a collection of short stories. As Giono was, even then, particularly aware, having already published such collections of short fiction as Solitude de la pitié (1932) and Rondeur des jours (1936), the main aesthetic problem of the storyteller consists in avoiding claustrophobia. Tales and/or stories are connected variously but generally suffocatingly: by a similarity in subject matter, by a similarity in form, in mood, in central or minor characters, in tone or setting. Giono's first collection, for instance, as its title indicates, derives from the sense of pity that he, as super-narrator, felt for the country people in the stories, a sense of charity that he doubtless wished to arouse in his readers.

Noé consists, on the contrary, of a throwing open of doors and of a descent from Manosque to Marseilles in four stages, followed by a two-level return to the mountain. Thus, Giono's book is a marvel of form, opening to the reader vistas of sheer delight. Interpolated stories at several plateaus illustrate not only the simultaneity of epochs but also the affiliations between peoples of varying periods, all writhing in the "filets des dieux" (p. 103), each bound for a personal Waterloo (p. 266). As far as Noah can see, men pass the entrance requirements for admission to the ark: all are animals, all moved by the same passions—particularly that of avarice, no matter what their class or status (p. 292). Descending into the Hades of a fabulous metropolis, Noah also tells the stories which punctuated his journey, reminding the reader: "We must not forget that . . . all around us . . . the entire population of these suburbs was gradually slipping away into the slavery of the late nineteenth century" (p. 222).

The novel proper commences (p. 53) on the heights overlooking the Valley of the Durance; it is November 9, when in Provence mills open to press olives. In the very cold winds of autumn the harvester has climbed the trunk of an olive tree, where he "prend sa leçon d'avarice" (p. 93), or where he makes Ulysses's sacrifice to summon the greedy dead. Ecstatic as he grips his tree trunk like the mast of a windtossed craft, the narrator raises against human avarice four objections from the world: earth, waters, light, and wind. Earlier "voyages" to Toulon (hell) have taught him that, down below, avarice has become hereditary.

Behind Jean Giono's home in Manosque rises the Mont d'Or, crowned with the ruined tower of what was once a *château* and is, still today, girdled with olive trees. Standing beside the trees one looks down the hill past the Giono residence, across circular Manosque on the crest of a smaller dome, and thence directly down the main highway towards Marseilles. Thus, geographical reality confirms the origins of our Noah's travels, and Giono always found undistinguishable the rolling blue hills of Provence and the sweeps of ocean.

On a second level downwards, or at a second commencement (p. 95 ff.), the narrator approaches Marseilles characterized by its "violente odeur de narcisse," which evoked the sea and by a strong smell of shellfish redolent of human temptations or passions: love, plunder, sex—"un thème général valable pour toutes les rues de la ville que pour le monde

59

entier" (p. 108). Marseilles itself appears finally as "cette ville où tous les dieux barbares sont en liberté" (p. 229). The Rue de Rome resembles mythical Brocéliande, with its forest of faces, its shadows, its vanity. A hunchbacked bootblack before his shop is Vishnu with his fourteen arms. He and black-clad bookkeepers, sad adulteresses of forty or fifty, and a big Greek woman ante-Phèdre have all fallen before the weapon of the gods: the mollusk smell of passions.

In adventurous sentences,[7] Noah describes the great hellish city, and is then reminded of a story concerning the struggle for supremacy of two modern barons, "Charlemagne de l'Ouvèze" vs. "Saint Jérôme de Buis-les-Baronnies." (The struggle consists of warfare and physical force on the former's part with siege, attrition, and attenuation on the part of the latter. Presented with the Gordian knot, for instance, "Charlemagne" would cut it, while "Saint Jerome," who easily spends twenty years setting up his checkerboard without ever declaring himself interested in a game, would manage to untie it. Charlemagne's *bien* is so ancient that it injures no one, his avarice so majestic that it extends to generosity, and so secure that it dares feel weakness for a daughter.) Instead of finishing this first long story, which came to mind in Marseilles at 5 p.m. in late October, the narrator, descending to a lower or third depth, recounts another entrance into hell in a September which was probably 1943 (p. 137 ff.)[8]

During this trip to Marseilles Jean Giono realized how deeply he loved his "métier" of writer (p. 139), which had

[7] Giono says whimsically on pp. 110-11: "(Je prends en ce moment un grand plaisir à l'aventure de la phrase. Elle va dans au moins cinquante petites capitales de barons de ce pays.)"

[8] Quite appropriately because of this block of material, designated here as Level III (pp. 137-c. 170), Maxwell A. Smith speaks of *Noé* as "autobiographical." For his definitive treatment of Giono's "First Imprisonment," see his *Jean Giono* (New York, 1966), pp. 105-08.

taught him to dissimulate, to dream, to create, and to keep faith, training that stood him in excellent stead during his own imprisonment in Marseilles. There, from the prow of Fort Saint-Nicholas, he stood, confident as Noah, overlooking the Mediterranean. Descending through abandoned estates ruined by the arrival of the railroads, the narrator-author entered the great harbor, city of dreams, gleaming golden as Moscow seen from heights, city of honeymoons, where as a child he had walked the Canebière with his beloved father (pp. 157-58).

Marseilles and its domains evoke in the narrator the legendary world[9] of Harun al-Rashid (p. 144) as recelebrated in such works as *New Arabian Nights*: "New Arabian nights. Harun al-Rashid lord of the fleets. He would arrive from the city each night, hastening towards his fairyland come true. . . . Every morning on the terrace his wife would have them set up the telescope on its tripod so she could track across the boundless main her lord and master's fleet" (p. 144).[10] Thus, as in such famous collections of tales, the

[9] Bennett Cerf expresses this idea very well in his abridgement of the Burton edition, *The Arabian Nights' Entertainments or The Book of a Thousand Nights and a Night* (New York, 1932): "Romance lurks behind every shuttered window; every veiled glance begets an intrigue; and in every servant's hand nestles a scented note granting a speedy rendezvous. . . . A world in which apes may rival men, and a butcher win the hand of a king's daughter. . . . It is the world of a legendary Damascus, a legendary Cairo, and a legendary Constantinople; the world in which a legendary Harun al-Rashid walks the streets of a legendary Bagdad" (p. x).

[10] In a letter to me, from Manosque, dated July 24, 1970, Giono stated that he had in his library two editions of *Mille et une nuits*, including the twelve-volume translation by Antoine Galland (Paris, 1704-1717), which he reread two or three years before "avec un plaisir toujours renouvelé.": "Mais je n'ai puisé ni aux *Arabian Nights* ni aux *Mille et une nuits*. J'ai seulement essayé (in *Noé*) d'expliquer ce que je sentais." He also had a copy in English of Robert Louis Steven-

narrator Noah, like the narrator Scheherazade, imprisoned and under sentence of death—i.e., mortal like us all—meanwhile delights his fellows with stories[11] of princes, ship-owners, cargos, fortunes, palaces, eunuchs, ruined financiers, riches, angels of death, beautiful captives, whores, and voyages, all magical.

While Giono has not, to be sure, drawn any of his stories directly from Stevenson's *New Arabian Nights*,[12] still the fantastic and the marvelous dominate both collections. In Stevenson, as in Giono, great fortunes are made by devilish men, sophisticates gamble in gorgeous mansions, dissolute adven-

---

son's *New Arabian Nights*: "Oui (,) j'ai dans ma bibliothèque les New Arabian Nights de Stevenson en anglais et j'ai lu ce livre il y a très longtemps; . . ."

[11] Thus, Giono in prison, and in his memory here in *Noé*, uses the same rationale explained by Ivo Andrić many years later during his Nobel Prize acceptance speech, reprinted in French by the editor Aleksandar Stefanović in *Nouvel essai yugoslave* (Založba Obzorja Maribor, 1965). On December 10, 1961, Andrić explained the story teller's necessity to create: "A l'instar du récit de la légendaire Schéhérazade, ce conte semble vouloir tromper les bourreaux, retarder l'inéluctabilité de la tragique catastrophe qui nous menace, et perpétuer l'illusion de la vie et de la durée."

During one of my conversations with Giono in August 1970, I asked him if he knew this Nobel Prize speech, and then if he knew Andrić at all. He categorically answered "Non" each time. At that time I forgot to inquire whether he remembered Jean Giraudoux's enormously successful *Siegfried et le Limousin* (Paris, 1922), in which the empire of Harun al-Rashid is compared to Germany (p. 206 ff.) because of its brutal treatment of women, its learning, caste system, poetry, contempt for death, high frequency of nervous diseases, enthusiasm for tales, love of round buildings, and inability to conceive of hidden vices. Could one imagine Edward VII, or the French Prime Minister, or the King of Italy putting his wife to death? Giraudoux asks smartly. As a matter of fact, Giraudoux's novel ends like *Noé*, with a train ride home and a paean of praise for France.

[12] *The Novels and Tales of Robert Louis Stevenson*, Vol. 1 (*New Arabian Nights*), New York, 1903.

turers commit crimes for gold and diamonds, ruined palaces of long-dead millionnaires conceal macabre remains, murdering *carbonari* prowl the streets, prodigal November falls upon a great metropolis (Paris or Marseilles), and, particularly, the dilapidated castle-like structures typical of Gothic fiction chill the reader's heart.[13] Decadence, corruption, vice, and the evil that underlies the external glamor of attire, fortune, carriages, gold, rich foods, and jewels, recall, as Giono puts it, the fragile beauty of a narcissus blossom and the smell of mollusks—passion and the sea.

The center of this oriental Hades is reached again by Noah in a fourth and final descent into Marseilles, where the core of the book contains essentially four stories plus transitional passages, which we might for convenience entitle: (1) La Thébaïde (p. 170 ff.); (2) Melchior's Estate (p. 199 ff.); (3) The Emperor Jules (p. 204 ff.); and (4) Tramway #54, or Noah's Ark (p. 225 ff.). Not only could these stories, especially the third about Jules Empereur, whose name, given in French fashion, becomes "Empereur Jules," stand alone as they would do in any collection of tales, but they are so cleverly intertwined even from the earliest pages of the novel that the reader has been constantly conditioned by the omniscient and omnipotent narrator to accept them as gospel. Thus, tramway 54 passes a retaining wall that still confines, like some wall of China, an unkempt forest, or a "bois funèbre" (p. 234 ff.). The eye sweeps along "une véritable voie royale,"

---

[13] Stevenson's "The Pavilion on the Links," with its Italian *carbonari*, has seemed perhaps the most interesting to other authors of tales, not only vaguely recalled by Giono, but more expressly so by Isak Dinesen in her "Deluge at Norderney," the first of her *Seven Gothic Tales* (New York, 1934). In Dinesen as in the *Arabian Nights* the illustrious narrator is a noblewoman, but, contrary to Giono's equation of flood and creation, Dinesen rejoiced at flood and the destruction of an evil world (where women are persecuted).

leading past a stagnant fountain still dripping water. Beyond a small pavilion, with its Mansard roof, stands a temple of Angkor, and in the distance above the trees rise the turrets of a castle, style 1900. Thus slumbers like an enchanted kingdom the still fabulous domain of the Emperor Jules.

In the first story, searching for a lodging for the night, the awed narrator walks softly down an avenue of red trunks, past the frogs and stone toads of a Romantic grotto, a Greek temple, and a gazebo, into a dilapidated mansion called La Thébaide. Feeling like some King of Bactria or candidate Knight of the Grail, he smokes a pipe in the chamber assigned him, largely to exorcise an infernal odor. Total darkness falls just as he traces the odor to a large stain on the mattress, while lemurs and harpies frolic in cobwebbed corridors. Euripides' Hecuba, her hair curlers silvery like the crown of Troy, enters through the dreaded door. She is followed by six other fairies, smiles the narrator, their members fastened by sundry attachments: necklaces, bracelets, belts. The grease spot on the bed came from poor Madame Donnadieu, they whisper, who waited two days for her nephew, without his ever arriving to pay his last respects. Had the house mother postponed burial any longer, she would have had to have the once-fat woman carried to her place of eternal repose in buckets.

Having hastily fled this old ladies' home, Noah sleeps in its park under the "dômes apaisants de la nuit, des feuillages et des oiseaux."[14] Musing, he considers the great lords of the ending nineteenth century, taking into account their city and its climate, the gods they knew, their physiognomies, and their flexibility before the cruelty and brutality of commercial

[14] This refrain (pp. 191-93) adds another narrative feature, a standard practice in the New Realism of 1950 and later, for which Giono had not as yet been hailed as partially responsible.

struggles.[15] As democracy took shape, they were its real masters, owning fleets as far away as Jamaica and Florida, themselves long-legged like grasshoppers in tuxedos. Alpaca-clad
like scarab beetles, they tirelessly rolled their sticky egg-
cases, collecting gold and women. Their eyes like those of
harem dancers, their mouths pursed like those of candy sell-
ers, their glances melancholy and triumphant like the poise
of a narcissus, they darted with the speed of spiders, hairy-
bodied like them also, apparently spreadeagled helplessly
upon their webs, but in reality swift to the kill: "Each Sunday, the landaus hauled their cargoes under the portico of the
Church of Saint Vincent de Paul, cockroaches, beetles, tum-
blebugs, spiders, crickets, mantises, and centipedes whose
mandibles, jaws, claws, and stingers balled and defended
stockpiles of rum, coffee, groundnuts, copra, pepper, and all
species of cantharides and opium raw and refined; but the
elytras, the shells, the spectral posturings hid sensitive souls"
(p. 195).[16] Recognizing "la grandeur de ces âmes sublimes"

[15] This passage (pp. 190-204) provides an example of transition and
modulation in key from one story to another.

[16] Giono's novel contains other catalogues attesting to his research
on and knowledge of Marseilles, a port that grew tremendously through
commerce, particularly after the building of the Suez Canal. While
in 1787 only 600 ships were registered there, by 1893 there were
15,681. As Marcel Pagnol, the other modern celebrant of Marseilles,
wrote in "Midi Capitale Marseille" (*Figaro Littéraire*, May 4, 1969,
p. 8 ff.), this city, essentially Greek in origin—and Giono's novel
frequently recalls Greek mythology—passed the million mark in that
year. Around 1889 when Giono writes about his shipping tycoons,
Marseilles was the sixth port in the world.

In reading this celebration of a great city, one recalls, doubtless
with Giono, the attribution "Le Roman urbain" by Albert Thibaudet
in *Le Liseur de romans* (Paris, 1924), as follows: "Entre la complexité,
le grouillement d'un grand roman et ceux d'une grande ville, il
semble qu'il y ait affinité. . . . Et il me semble bien que l'auteur de
cette nouveauté féconde, le créateur du roman urbain, ce soit Victor
Hugo. . . ." (p. 215)

(p. 197), Noah admires that force which refused to accept pot luck for themselves or for their lovers. Their women, for example, decorated with large specimens of their booty, were usually painted by the best of the Italian masters.

Melchior's wife Rachel was just such a woman, living in the protection of a vast fortune derived from the refining of oil, Marseilles's richest industry. In love with his wife "au beau visage de pieuvre" (p. 197), who was becoming so fat that her rings and bracelets had constantly to be sawed from her flesh and who spent all her days in smiles and miscarriages, Melchior dreamed of the day when he could transform arid Périer Hill into the pleasure dome of Kubla Khan. For her sake he realized, at age fifty, this massive engineering and architectural project, three horses being required to haul Rachel up the hill past thin trees well pruned. Like another bearded Hercules, her husband cherished Rachel's naked and majestic white person. There in the dream garden high above the city and the sea, Melchior finally fed Rachel with the food of the gods. Giono's point, that the tycoons of the last century were very sensitive men, seems persuasive, the reader capitulating before such sheer originality.

The story "of the Emperor" analyzes two generations with a professional psychologist's brief but telling assessment, particularly of Madame Maxime Empereur, who became, like all wealthy young ladies of those days in Marseilles, an orphan at an early age, learning at that time to play the stock market for her own profit. At the time of his marriage Maxime owned only two cargo ships, but before his death his shipping business had become an empire. A wife such as his falls in love only with her son, if at all, however.

The Emperor Jules grew up with everything his heart desired, riding his pony "Mustang" through a kingdom, but the gold mines he most desired were always across another fence: "Let us realize how significant these children's games were. What he did, in fact, was to set off across the father's kingdom, through his pine-clad hills, intermittently glimpsing as he passed between their trunks the gray city, and its suburbs whence the streets fanned out, in whose corridors sad shadows slumbered, pierced by the reddish cars of massive trolleys somersaulting along the rails; at such moments he would gently knee the horse he called Mustang, and he would descend down into the grassy valleys brimming with crimson blossoms, and on to peaceful farmyards, where he was welcomed as the master's son, a young prince before whom one set offerings of currant jelly and goat's cheese. And often he would remain there until nightfall, inventing gold mines all for himself."

In such a sentence, where the imaginative furnishing by the author demonstrates the fabulatory function at work, clothing the anecdote that the narrator heard from his motherly hostess Mémé with details supposedly as observed by Jules, and yet sharply contrasting the unrest of the future *nabob* with the idyllic and pastoral serenity of the farmers, the author suggests the passage of time by graduating Jules from pony to horse, but more effectively by the slow rhythm of the exceedingly long periodic sentence. Thus, a green childhood passed slowly while outside the heavy reddish busses rumbled through a gray city.

At age twenty Jules lived aboard his own ships, and became a pirate on the stock exchange. At the death of his parents he was a slender bachelor of thirty-five, and then he met Hortense: "Sous sa peau, les plus fabuleuses bêtes qui font le bonheur de l'homme sont à l'ombre" (p. 212). They fell madly in love: "Ils étaient éblouis l'un de l'autre. Il n'y avait plus

67

pour eux de monde réel." When, that December 1920, the fire at the opera killed her and caused the Emperor's legs to be amputated at the hips, his eyes became "d'une dureté impitoyable" (p. 215). Henceforth during business crises no one could even lick his boots. From his father's firm of ten cargo ships, Jules then constructed the *Maison Empereur* of one hundred fifty ships.

With his heathen savage from Tierra del Fuego to carry him mounted high on his shoulder, even at a gallop on horseback, to roll and gambol with him among the Michaelmas daisies of his lawns and to worship him utterly as a god incarnate, the Emperor Jules underwent a metamorphosis into a "tricephalic centaur" (pp. 222-23). Thus again, Giono's stories of real life reverse the morphology of the fairy tale,[17] for by ordering plants and trees from Patagonia, the enchanted garden is made as the story finishes, and it was not the prince who turned into a monster, but the reverse.

No reminder that *Noé* from its opening pages is a novel treating principally the aesthetics of the novel could be more suitably placed, it would seem, than in the fourth Marseilles story, which has been called "Tramway 54, or Noah's Ark." The transitional material (pp. 225-47), as we have already seen, shows us *the* "Résidence," or the Emperor's estate, in its present dilapidation, and concludes that since Marseilles was from time out of mind a Greek city familiar with Orestes, Cassandra, and Oedipus, it hardly quibbled at all at the centaur Jules and his slave.

For the next fifty pages Noah rides his tramway 54, reminding the reader that the last entrance to Marseilles has been effected from the north, through the Saint-Charles Sta-

---

[17] *Morphologie du conte* by Vladimir Ja. Propp, trans. Claude Ligny (Paris, 1970).

tion, along the Boulevard d'Athènes, crossing the Canebière, into the Cours Lieutaud, Place de Rome, and Place Castellane, to Boulevard Baille. The tramway will take Noah and his passengers through the area circumscribed roughly by the Rue Paradis, the Rond Point du Prado, and the Boulevard Périer, and Notre-Dame de la Garde—or, as Noah says, will make a circumnavigation of a world (pp. 277-78) amidst howling colors, ending at individual Waterloos (p. 266).[18]

Surely few writers understand human nature better than Jean Giono, who aged so harmoniously with his craft that a few glances from his keen blue eyes sufficed to categorize, evaluate, compare, find the literary precedent, and express succinctly and caustically the background, career, and important personal experiences of a heterogeneity of people. A little prostitute climbing into the tram is Romeo's Juliet (p. 250). Here is the lady hairdresser: "The girl, the hairdresser, sails under full canvas down the Rue de Rome like a frigate ship-rigged for action, a hundred cannon to port of her. She casts a long glance, lightly at first in condescension, but which quickly turns to deep envy (in such an unsophisticated way!), at a giant billboard representing a movie star with pencilled lashes fanned in an arc, and with a mouth like a pink elephant's vulva" (pp. 275-76). Those passengers who ride for a considerable length of time with the narrator are subjected to a fine analysis, including diagnosis and prognosis: the X-rayed Woman (1), Yellow and Red (2), Cow's Eyes (3), The Thinking Woman (4), the Neutral Housewife (5), Flowered Earrings (7), Raincoats 1 and 2 (8), and the Hairdresser (6), whose name, for so she is addressed by an acquaintance, must be "mon petit." A numbering of the charac-

---

[18] Persons familiar with Marseilles must enjoy the score or so of street names listed between pp. 266-78.

ters shows how cleverly the narrator alternates them, and how carefully he weaves in a new one once he is sure that the reader can pleasantly juggle the old ones.

The principal resources used during this climactic section of the novel derive from psychology—sarcasm and derisive laughter coming from the narrator on the outside, a hitherto untried approach by the moralist Giono. The X-rayed Woman, who keeps getting down to shop for noodles (severely rationed in France for two or so years after World War II); Yellow and Red, whose papers are not in order; Cow's Eyes and her pregnancy test; the Thinking Woman and her stealthily concealed sugar cubes (saccharine being served then in cafés); and the naked men concealed by plastic-coated raincoats are not only surrealistically comical but so true as to be unforgettable. The narrator especially enjoys watching the pretty girl in the navy blue suit, whom he has called Flowered Earrings: "She trots, she gallops, she taps along on her high heels, she whisks herself diagonally between other pedestrians, avoiding collisions she swings her hips now to the right and then snaps back exactly the correct distance to the left; she hops, she plummets her body along all speed ahead, grinning to herself all this while" (p. 282). This passage culminates in a three-page tirade beginning, "A cette heure de la matinée, coulent là-dedans les égoïsmes tout frais émoulus de leur sommeil, les jalousies réveillées depuis deux heures à peine . . ." (p. 292), and concluding: "And I can well imagine that perhaps from the Rue Thiers up on the hill, or from the Rue Camas or Longchamp, having just wiped the blood from his hands on someone's curtains by way of signature, there will appear before us the Lautréamont, the Sade, or the Saint-Just of these fine days" (p. 295). During this climax of one paragraph Noah castigates the evil found in the "marshes" of Marseilles, where "sumptuous alligators of all sexes," purulent and obsequious, drag their foul bellies over the thresholds of Grand-Swamp-Hotels. And yet he has allowed these animals passage in his ark.

THE RETURN journey in another Noah's ark, where the narrator unfortunately enjoys only lateral vision from the window of his *micheline*, leads to Septêmes and Aix, above which on the highest level heavenly Manosque is perched. Along the slopes extends the forest of past literature, which the narrator interrogates in his quest for freedom, the trees themselves being also "éléments mystérieux de la liberté . . ." (p. 305) necessary for the creator's "vision des choses existantes" (p. 308). Before passing through the tunnel under the mountain, Noah ceases to invent stories, for in the tenderness of autumn he receives from his own sky country lavishly: "It gives to me unsparingly, in fact. What it gives to me (and consequently what is given to me from other sources as well) ranks very high in the hierarchy of gifts. It can most assuredly not be termed wisdom, nothing is less scholarly! It is my ability to feel the rapture of the creative artist" (p. 313). There again, he finds himself *"engagé dans le commerce du monde"* (p. 314) since his vision has demonstrated throughout time and space "la continuité de pensée qui unit l'assassin et le chirurgien" (p. 324), or all mankind.

Ending at the first level in conversations with those shepherds and other mountaineers who have survived, Noah concludes that in general "tout ce qui est derrière les visages date du déluge" (p. 344). There in the dark blue, violet autumn of the alpine valley he has acquired, simply by rolling ripe olives in his cold fingers, a knowledge of human passion, which he has expressed metaphorically.

In his poem "Un Déluge," a monologue spoken by God to an angel, the deity explains why He is preparing for mankind a second flood. Before the first flood He had simply told Noah to build himself an ark, which historiographers subsequently misunderstood and falsely reported as a boat, not realizing that they were facing the wrath of God, against which nothing stands. When God told Noah to preserve life in an ark, He meant him to shelter it *within his heart*. Then God's anger, and His waves pursuing the mountains around the earth, might yet allow Noah safely to set foot upon some summit so that even if God no longer existed, he (Noah) would be the creator. As for Noah himself, he is every or any man, clean or cleansed, but, importantly, a man without pretensions.

Much pondered in the modern world, having inspired such divergent artists as Rimbaud, Sir Benjamin Britten, and Giono's master, William Faulkner, the Noah legend of a flood seems particularly applicable in our century. A tradition that there would be other floods appeared in the well-known Atlantis passage of Plato's *Timaeus*, where an Egyptian priest tells Solon: "There have been, and will be hereafter, many and divers destructions of mankind, the greatest by fire and water(;) . . . when the gods cleanse the earth with a flood of waters, the herdsmen and shepherds in the mountains are saved. . . . To begin with, your people remember only one deluge, though there were many earlier; . . ."[19]

Similarly, in the same year as *Noé*, February 1947, André Breton published his "Ode à Charles Fourier," where he speaks like Plato of trial creations, the second having been in Europe and the third in America, both surviving a second flood. Very similarly to Giono, Breton castigates mankind: "Poverty graft oppression bloodshed these are still the same ills you have stamped upon civilization with a red-hot iron."

[19] *Plato's Cosmology*. The *Timaeus* of Plato translated with a running commentary, F. M. Cornford (London, 1937).

Reparation must be made, cries Breton, and to the Jews first of all: "Leaving it beyond dispute that without distinction of confession the freedom to plunder, artfully termed commerce, could under no cirumstances be re-instituted."[20] In a poem called "Vigilance" Breton also shared Giono's vision of the creative artist as Noah entering the ark:

"When everything is over, invisible I enter the ark . . ."

.   .   .

"I can hear the laundry of living flesh tear like a huge leaf . . ."

.   .   .

"No longer do I touch the heart of things but hold the thread."[21]

Both Giono and Breton, in short, imagined themselves very much as Marcel Proust had done before them: "When I was a child, the fate of no person in the Holy Writ seemed so wretched to me as that of Noah, because of the flood that keeps him closed in the ark for forty days. Later I was often ill, and during long days I too had to remain inside the ark. Then I understood that never was Noah so well able to see the world as from the ark, despite the fact that it was shut tight and that over the earth darkness reigned."[22]

Whether or not as a very young man Giono was struck by these lines of Proust, to whom he referred in conversation with great admiration, he had as early as 1937 in his own

[20] "Ode à Charles Fourier," first published in Parisot's series *L'Age d'or.*

[21] Thirteen verses of this poem are quoted by Anna Balakian in her "Mort d'André Breton," *Bulletin de la Société des Professeurs français en Amérique* (1966), pp. 49-59, here pp. 58-59.

[22] Quoted by Pierre-Henri Simon in *Témoins de l'homme* (Paris, 1951) in his essay on Proust.

consciousness associated a mercantile civilization with an avenging flood: "Civilization, which is based upon money, is now about to engulf us all under its flood waters; in the hollows of its waves are tossed about the corpses of women and of children who have starved to death."[23]

Having survived the war with his hope unimpaired and his trust in man as radiant, Jean Giono set to work again writing chronicles distinguished not only by their psychological depth, their wit, their symbolic patterns, and by the prestigious wealth and extent of their vocabulary and literary affiliations, but also by their treatment of aesthetics and their innovations in fictional technique.

As we have seen, Noé remains a notable case in point, not only one of Giono's richest and most intricate books, but also a novel closely related to a collection of short stories—a splendid innovation in fictional form. In addition, due to its sheer originality, Noé is in my opinion the most readable, even after many readings, of "modern" or "new" novels.

In a remarkably prophetic passage in his pre-war Les Vraies richesses, Giono seems to have foreseen his successful negotiation of the stormy seas of war and to have thought of his future narrator Noah just as a character, "le père Conache qui a parlé tout doucement de l'arche de Noé.—Sauvé des eaux, dit-il."[24] Therefore again Jean Giono assumed the novelist's burden, obeying God's injunction: "And I said to Noah what I say to all men: let enter into thy heart every living thing of all flesh that is in the world to keep them alive with thee and I will establish my covenant with thee."[25]

[23] 1937 being the publication date of Les Vraies richesses, pp. 148-49.
[24] Ibid.
[25] Rather than follow the reading of these verses of Giono used as an epigraph for Noé, I have substituted the revision from the 1969 edition of his poetry, p. 41.

Fragments d'un paradis (1948)

In the garden of his home in Manosque, France, on the morning of August 15, 1970, the conversation between Jean Giono and myself turned at one point upon the fictional voyage, always an admirable form, like Rabelais's *Quart livre*. Giono spoke of his own unknown "voyage merveilleux," *Fragments d'un paradis (Les Anges), Poème*,[1] which he said he dictated without plan and without retouching on August 6-10, 1940. Scheduled to appear in 1948, but consigned to oblivion through no fault of the author, this unfinished novel-called-poem has still to make its way, just as a hundred years earlier did *Moby-Dick*, the fantastic voyage that Giono was at that moment translating.[2] Although produced in an attempt at psychic automatism, the Giono work falls into a distinguished literary tradition, that of a surreal journey out of this world. What resulted will be foreseen by André Breton in *Entretiens, 1913-1952* (Paris, 1952): a "dictée de la pensée" will afford access to ". . . a land where the flora and fauna are recognizable among all others where the structure, apparently the same for all, asks only to be revealed" (p. 82).

Just as in *Moby-Dick* Ishmael tells us that for him an ocean voyage replaces suicide, particularly for a meditative man paid to go into "la pleine liberté de la mer" (M.D. 121), where

[1] Xerox and microfilm copies have been placed in the Doheny Library, University of Southern California. Publisher G. Dechalotte. Watercolors by Pierre Fonteinas. Page numbers will refer to this edition, number 270.

[2] *Moby Dick* by Lucien Jacques, Joan Smith, and Jean Giono, Gallimard (Paris, 1950). An idea of the influence exerted upon French letters by this particular translation comes from Léon Roudiez: "Camus and *Moby-Dick*," *Symposium* (Spring 1961), pp. 30-40; "Strangers in Melville and Camus," *French Review* (January 1958), pp. 217-26. Page numbers prefaced by M.D. refer to this collaborative translation, 144th edition.

the "émerveillements" of "choses lointaines" (M.D. 30) console him with the thought that beyond death lie infinite stretches of water (M.D. 467), so Giono's Captain, whose Journal constitutes Chapter IV, explains: "what I am seeking is the unknown. . . . If we find nothing unknown (which can heal us), then our returning to port will indicate our death . . ." (M.D. 44). Thus, radio contact has been broken with the known world, and no fuel has been stored. The departure was, through the force of some circumstances unknown to the reader, hasty (39), but seventy tons of foodstuffs will supply the crew for a voyage of five years.

Driven by winds southward from Madeira, two three-masted barques plough into an immense solitude, where, dizzy at the void beneath them through which seem to fly "choses totalement inconnues, sans commune mesure avec l'homme" (16), the crew suffer from "l'angoisse du manque d'appui." Around and about them an hallucinating "odeur de vie"—whether that of animals, plants, or gods cannot be determined—assails their nostrils while floating iridescently before their dazzled eyes. The odor seems synesthetically to recall a narcissus, a jonquil, a jasmine as the men long for something yellow amid this green-blue sea, or blue-green rain sometimes lasting for weeks (Chapter VIII).

The wonders of the ocean reaches furnish a solar bird, "oiseau de flammes," a "dorade" that lights up an underwater landscape over the void of bottomless firmament (32), and a marvelous shark killed, hauled upon the deck, and butchered, with a heart that even two hours later still refused to die. We are here again reminded that even before his *Hussard sur le toit*[3] Jean Giono shared Ishmael's opinion: men die when they wish to die (M.D. 463). When the Basque cook Quéréjéta eats the yellow fish, he gradually grows rounder

[3] (Paris, 1951.)

and more coppery, mottled with sun spots. Really proving itself hourly more inventive than any imagination (112), giant rays soar to the surface while an immense black cloud lowers until its showers of "migrating birds . . . fall on the sea . . . to rest" (114-15). If there are no more such marvels, then cease beating, hearts, murmurs the Captain and asserts his staff.

In one of the most unearthly passages, surely, in modern fiction, Giono holds his reader enchanted before this "immense nuage d'oiseaux," this "étrange escadre" draping "leurs terrifiantes écharpes noires autour du flanc de l'île . . . un très beau jour de printemps austral" (114-15). In an eery silence the now white birds camp upon the dorsal spine of a gigantic squid-like monster. Had it called them from the currents of air to clean its tentacles? "What was actually taking place was a monstrous and wonderful game being played between the immense white squid and all that throng of birds as white as it" (120). As the sailors watch, they see the birds caught fast in a monstrous excretion oozing from the giant mollusk as, fixing its phosphorescent blue eyes upon the ship, it submerged. It began to rain, as Giono makes the transition from monsters and marvels to paradise somewhere near the seventh continent. Chapter VIII, entitled "Pluie" (129-160), ends the novel.

Whenever he spoke of these monsters from the deep, the quartermaster Baléchat raised his arms and with his hands imitated their flight from the depths of heaven as, like fallen angels, they plummeted into the bottomless pit. Similarly, in his dialogue with Officer Larreguy, an astronomer aged twenty-five, the Captain inquires (Chapter IV): "'Do you not believe, Sir, that an angel could take the form of that monstrous fish that emerged the other day before our eyes? Everyone thought it was a skate . . .'" (51). In Chapter V, in a ship's log written by Officers Larreguy and Jaurena, an entry notes the savage ferocity with which the Captain devoured his portion of shark meat, or his part of a most cruel enemy.

In Chapter VI, which recounts Noël Guinard's strange adventure, Giono returns, as in Chapters I-III, to an impersonal, anonymous narrator. The storekeeper's adventure consists of a solitary climb during a day and a night up the extinct volcano of Tristan da Cunha, up the basalt cliffs through absolute lifelessness, silence, and immobility until in darkness he succeeds in obliterating from his consciousness all notion of the revolvant world about him. Then from this perfect zero he finally even hears the crackling of the stars.[4] All night long, "le temps que le transbordement des étoiles se fit d'Ouest en Est" (89), storekeeper Guinard puts his world in order or rejects his past—the purpose of the whole journey, in fact.

Thus, and despite the author's attempt at psychic automatism, many resemblances occur in Giono between this repudiation of the civilized world and Melville's repudiations, notably those in *Moby-Dick*. Even the marvelous creatures bear some likeness to each other, those of Giono resembling Melville's "Baleine du Sud" (M.D. 189) or "muraille devant l'inconnu" (M.D. 173), his Squid (M.D. 279), angels or devils (M.D. 368), and fallen angels (M.D. 541), as well as his Last Judgment (M.D. 545 ff.). Both novels also move through narrative changes, Melville speaking not only through Ishmael but also through Ahab, Stubb, Starbuck, as well as by dramatizations.

Thus, in both Melville's *Moby-Dick* and Giono's *Fragments*

[4] Many similarities of thought and image recur years later (1961) in Giono's "Grand Théâtre," or Apocalypse, so closely reproduced, in fact, that the latter appears to issue from the same period as *Fragments d'un paradis*, *Noé*, and Giono's poetry, or from 1947-1948.

d'un paradis, various narrators face an invisible world forged in fear (M.D. 203). Both the White Whale and the sea represent powers, whether incarnate or inanimate, in any case "tout ce qui est démoniaque dans la vie et dans la pensée" (M.D. 192). Furthermore, according to Chapter LVIII of *Moby-Dick*, the sea lies around Tahiti like a body about an immortal soul: "Consider all this; and then turn to this green, gentle, and most docile earth; consider them both, the sea and the land; and do you not find a strange analogy to something in yourself? For as this appalling ocean surrounds the verdant land, so in the soul of man there lies one insular Tahiti, full of peace and joy, but encompassed by all the horrors of the half known life. God keep thee! Push not off from that isle, thou canst never return!" (M.D. 277). Consonant with Melville's warning, it happens that, so far as the reader can ever know, the voyagers of Giono will not return, or cannot. In a sense both crews have been tricked by their captains since the "merveilleux vieillard" (M.D. 458) Ahab took pains not to divulge, until far distant at sea from Nantucket Island, the real purpose of his cruise.

While Giono's nameless captain, a man aged fifty-four, states in his log that the *acknowledged purpose* of the voyage is the exploration of Graham Land and the South Shetlands, he has already admitted that the real search involves finding a *new life* for all aboard. The world they leave has been "bouleversé," and so have men everywhere. "Nous partons," he says, "pour ne pas être changés en bêtes" (38-41). Their bitterness and disillusionment will for the first lapse of time sustain them: "*C'est à la rancune et aux désirs amers que nous devons d'abord naviguer.*" However, the charges made against this ravaged world are henceforth developed continuously, the various narrators remembering the subject, until they indict this century, with its science and illusory "progress" because of which "incontestably" people everywhere are literally dying from "ennui," "détresse," and "pauvreté." Their impoverishment is less economic than spiritual perhaps, a poverty of soul in a civilization devoid of marvels, and thus destitute spiritually. The Captain explains: "Je ne suis pas un philosophe: *je m'ennuie, comme tout le monde*" (43). The mortal sadness or *ennui* fallen like lead upon modern man also stems from the contempt he feels for others, and the reciprocal contempt in which he in turn is held—ergo from the resultant ostracism and isolation. In the following dialogue between *Lui,* the astronomer Larreguy, and *Moi,* the Captain, the young man testifies: had he believed that the only point to life was the gratification of his senses, he would long before have packed his duffle bag and departed thence, forevermore, as Ishmael threatened to do. That November, as they cross the Tropic of Capricorn, or just as the southern spring arrives, many feel sick at heart: (1) Gorri sees visions of an island, (2) Jacques Benoît (the blessed) drowns at sea, (3) Quéréjéta devours the sun in the shape of the golden fish, and (4) Noël Guinard withdraws to sterile volcanic precipices.

In Chapter VII the Captain himself attacks forms of government in the contaminated world, systems "constitués par les infâmes assassins," only themselves personally remaining above and beyond the reaches of the law. Others spin frantically like tops, their lives wretched and solitary. "'Hasn't your going in circles within these endless and desolate corridors on this strange segment of the globe . . . , and especially your being willing to lose contact with the real world, led you to adopt this dry sarcasm with which you have perhaps veiled . . . your own vast aspirations towards outer space and light' " (109).

Modern governments will in two more generations have rendered their subjects so ultimately wretched that by then people of quality will have retreated entirely within their imaginations: " 'And we have already entered the era of ugliness towards which our troubles have led us, and already we have been forced to create, just like the Aztecs before us, our gods of government whom we feed with raw children just to make ourselves feel less numb. . . . However, since we lack imagination, . . . we have thus far been powerless to endow these monstrous leaders of ours with the magic and the colors of the plumed serpent, or with the scorching brass of the god Moloch' " (111).

Thus, concludes the Captain for the moment, he has embarked, not upon a voyage of scientific exploration, but, quite simply, in search of paradise: " 'I left home in order to voyage through the very places which must formerly have been a prodigal paradise. I want us here to become witnesses able to testify that we still have the right to that *delirious joy which can enrich the longest life and even make us cherish the imminence of death.*' "

The paradise towards which these modern refugees steer is according to venerable tradition the land of Antarctica, and their ship (for now we have only one ship, named the *Indien*, doubtless in honor of the *Pequod*, itself so named for an Indian tribe) follows the pioneering routes into the vast south. Whereas the *Pequod* sank in the Pacific Ocean, however, and therefore did not complete her circumnavigation of the globe, over a three- to four-year period, the *Indien* appears before our fragment ends to have traversed only approximately 15,000 miles: Europe, Madeira, Tropic of Capricorn, Tristan da Cunha, Tierra del Fuego, Cape Horn, and past the Antarctic Circle towards the glaciers of the Palmer Peninsula. Curiously, the routes of both sailing ships cross near the Cape Verde Islands. The *Pequod*, departing Cape Cod at Christmas time, steered for the Azores, St. Helena, the Cape of Good Hope, and Crozet Island before veering northwards towards warmer climes at the Sunda Strait, thence up the China Sea to Formosa, and finally southward to the Equator, where all finally meet the Moby Dick they seek. Where the *Pequod*, after losing a man at sea, ends with a crew of thirty, the *Indien* seems never to have had more than twenty-two men aboard. Both captains are doctors, however, the *Indien's* Captain is more properly a bacteriologist. On board are also a meteorologist, a geologist, and a zoologist.

They set out, clarifies Giono, as in other voyages of 1920 (a remark that the reader can relate to Sir Ernest Shakleton's final voyage to South Georgia, 1920-1922,[5] which ended in his death; or to J. L. Cope's explorations, 1920-1922, in the South Shetland Islands;[6] also, perhaps, to the French Antarctic expedition actually in progress as Jean Giono wrote and/or prepared to publish *Fragments d'un paradis*. Reports from the *Commandant Charcot* began to appear in France, in fact, from about January 15, 1948.[7] Such plans perhaps reminded Giono of his long-standing affection, as for the French Arctic explorer Dumont d'Urville, for a famous French hero of the Antarctic: Dr. Jean-Baptiste Charcot, who was drowned at sea.

Captain Charcot, a Doctor of Medicine from the University

---

[5] There are three accounts of this expedition, one being as in Giono's novel, a diary: F. Wild's *Shakleton's Last Voyage: The Story of the Quest* (New York and London, 1923).

[6] See Thomas Wyatt Bagshawe's *Two Men in the Antarctic. An Expedition of Graham Land, 1920-1922* (New York, 1939).

[7] André F. Liotard's expedition (1948-1949) appears as reported in *La Nature*, Nos. 3,152 and 3,153, and as *Expéditions polaires françaises*, Centre de Documentation Universitaire, 1948.

of Paris, like Giono's Captain a bacteriologist at the Institut Pasteur, traveled to Antarctica for the first time in 1904-1905, also in a three-masted barque (*Le Français*) of low tonnage (250 tons) with a crew of twenty, en route also via Tierra del Fuego to explore the same land and *inlandsis* to which Giono's Captain alludes. In fact, Charcot's steward, named Robert Paumelle, seems to have become in the Giono novel the steward Paumolle. Like Giono's Captain, and often in similar terms, Charcot speaks eloquently of Antarctica: "Where lies the charm of countries in reality so desolate and fearful? Is it pleasure in the unknown . . . ? I have felt for a long time now that in the midst of this desolation and death I had a more vivid sense of delight in my own life. But now I feel that these regions make a kind of religious impression on one."[8]

Both Giono and Charcot before him feel the fascination of what Pomponius Mela had termed "terra australis incognita," or the sixteenth-century Sieur de Gonneville's Third World and Garden of Eden. This is the traditional Paradise towards which the *Indien* is bound, the "South France" or a part of this Eden that the French Chevalier Yves de Kerguélen discovered in 1772. It is not only paradise, says its modern historian, André Migot, but "a terrifying universe, quite outside human range," where in "supernatural silence" one feels on the "brink of a mysterious revelation."[9] As we shall shortly see is true in Giono, an explorer in Antarctica feels possessed of some cosmic kingdom: "And this self is no longer the narrow independent ego, but . . . an element of the cosmos, . . . uni-

[8] As quoted by Marthe Oulié in *Charcot of the Antarctic*, trans. (New York, 1939). See Charcot's own accounts: *Autour du pôle sud* (Paris, undated), and *Le "Français" au pôle sud* (Paris, 1906). Charcot's second voyage (1908-1909-1910) was on a new ship, also a three-masted barque named the *Pourquoi pas?* but of 800 tons.

[9] *Thin Edge of the World*, trans., illustrated by K. C. Jordan (Boston and Toronto, 1956), pp. 160-65.

83

versal river of life, one of the countless forms in which the absolute appears."[10] Charles Darwin had also noted in his *Journal of a Voyage round the World* that from the Strait of Magellan "the distant channels between the mountains appeared from their gloominess to lead beyond the confines of this world."[11]

The narrator of Chapter VIII, "Pluie," fears, in fact, lest his men fall through a hole in the world, to drift forever after through the abyss. In the brilliant opening pages to this final section of the novel, the ship starts and stiffens under the squalls like a balky horse, while the rain—and the extended metaphor here will eventually hover as drum beats—forms an opaque transparency through which the wind fitfully rips a passage across the sandy beaches of mid-ocean. Phrasing alliteratively whenever he thinks of the planet earth,[12] Giono accumulates magnificent sonorities about rain: "All night the rain comes down in wide sheets that we hear fume along the deck of the ship. Every now and then there are periods of dead calm, during which the breakers on either side of the bay howl as they crash against the cliffs, then from the far

[10] *Ibid.*, p. 69.

[11] Quoted by J. S. Jenkins in his *Recent Exploring Expeditions to the Pacific, and the South Sea under the American, English, and French Governments* (London and Edinburgh, 1853), p. 52. Melville includes Darwin in his epigraphs to *Moby-Dick*. In such a passage, Giono seems very close to the exiled Victor Hugo.

[12] Stephen Ullman's pioneer study of vocabulary and imagery in *Regain* remains a unique source for Giono's style: *Style in the French Novel* (Cambridge University Press, 1957). W. D. Redfern devotes a paragraph to *Fragments d'un paradis*, but he refers to it in terms of poetry: "idyll and counter-idyll." See *The Private World of Jean Giono* (Duke University Press, 1967). He also terms it, however, "the strange allegory" (p. 146). While Pierre de Boisdeffre does not mention this book at all, he does consider Giono essentially a writer of poetic prose, saying that he remains "notre grand poète en prose" of Provence, however (*Giono*, Paris, 1965), p. 242.

distance the next sheet of rainwater commences to patter as it sweeps down upon us. Collapsing across the ship, it tramples everything underfoot. . ." (129). Within four or so pages the reader can no longer cease phrasing these long, extremely rhythmic cadences into poetry, even into alexandrines, particularly when assisted, as here, by the author's poetic punctuation: "Throughout the nights beat ceaselessly the drums of rain on the deck. At first we could not hear but total darkness, levelling shadows, stayed the trembling spray and pacified the waves. They sounded two tones, tenor first, then bass. . . Heavy with rain, the sails flapped helplessly." Once the *Indien* is becalmed for a few pages, the author turns his attention to this crew, also about to vanish without a trace.

Among the interesting perceptions conveyed to the reader by means of significant impressions, the few traits that make Gorri le Rouge distinguishable from ordinary seamen involve his family rather than himself. In this passage (145), to explain Gorri's presence, Giono shows his reader two photographs, one of this sailor's wedding and another commemorating his daughter's first communion. In the first picture Gorri's "bony, black" wife resembles a fly in a pan of milk; the second photograph denotes the passage of time by only one wry difference: Gorri's aged mother is absent. Thus, to the reader Giono's conclusion becomes comical only at first sight: "Gorri ne parle jamais de sa famille. Gorri ne parle jamais de femme, de fille ou de parent" (146). Gorri has embarked in order to live like the solitary bachelor he is, dreaming of still more distant suns.

With loving care Giono dwells upon the steward's lovely tattoos or living paintings, which from wrist to shoulder represent first a snake coiled up to the elbow, then a heart pierced with an arrow and comically inscribed "Césarie," and higher yet a forest inhabited by four or five birds, three of which are chimerical. Proudly Paumolle's body flaunts this pulsating dream seen unclearly through graceful fronds of weeping willows: "On the left side of the body, the artist has recaptured his dream of birds and, from wrist to shoulder, Paumolle's arm is covered with phantasmagorical birds, part bird and partly flying tree" (135). Around the steward's neck extends a series of points with the instructions: "Tear along the dotted line." Immensely meticulous as he prepares to meet the sovereign Creator, Paumolle spends considerable time daily laundering his jerseys, which he prefers sleeveless so that they do not hide the moving pictures. Chaste nudes and huntresses are his pin-ups. With such seemingly tangential concerns, lulling the reader into false security, even when he explains why Baléchat worries naturally, interrogating not only silence but also daylight, night, noise, and everything, refusing even to accept nature as natural, Giono moves easily from officer to sailor, deriving each one's candidacy from his physical constitution and obvious thirsts.

When the roll seems complete, the spell is abruptly broken. The ship, and now the reader's heart leaps, has for a long period—days or even weeks, perhaps even for months—been enshrouded in heavy fog. More dangerously still, the men suddenly feel sure that they are not safe, not over deep water, not necessarily stationary either, but perhaps, even certainly, being swept towards jagged reefs by strong ocean currents: "Despite the fact that the deck itself was actually deep in shadow, still perceptibly it oscillated so that before our eyes, thus, the force that was bearing the ship irreversibly adrift, became manifest" (152). At dawn a haggard Archigard glimpses the reef upon which the becalmed *Indien* is being driven, less than two cable lengths away. A third reef directly off the bow turns out to be a whale.

The heavy fog into which the *Indien* drives recalls what Richard Evelyn Byrd described in 1935 along the Devil's Graveyard, overcome by the violence of far southern seas as by "a mood of Nature. For days a sleet-oozing, dripping, oppressive fog, so thick that the bow at times was lost from the view of the bridge, lay over the sea. . . . Fog alone is oppressive enough at sea. . . . A deep, brooding fog which, in Conrad's phrase, was one great circular ambush."[13] Furthermore, Giono's Captain had earlier felt personally, as he pursued his strange voyage, very much as did Admiral Byrd writing in 1938: "And in the hullabaloo the thinking man is driven to ponder where he is being blown and to long desperately for some quiet place where he can reason undisturbed and take inventory."[14] Like Admiral Byrd and Captain Charcot, Giono's skipper is returning another time to this Antarctica which summons his spirit. After the expeditions of Dr. Vivian Fuchs and Sir Edmund Hillary, Noel Barber further corroborates:

"Alone and apart, defiant and inexorable, Antarctica beckons to the mystic . . . [;] for the visionary it is a white heaven, and it is no fortuitous accident that makes the same men return time and again to its pitiless wastes, . . . many of them to die. . . .

"It has nothing of life, but it is clean, and perhaps because of this it is the last corner of our world where all adventure is clothed in the magic of the spirit. Because it is lifeless it is still of the ice age, so that man who travels to the bottom of the world is also travelling back in time."[15]

[13] *Discovery. The Story of the Second Byrd Antarctic Expedition* (New York, 1935), 40. Giono is referring to weather in February, while Byrd is recalling December 14-18.
[14] *Alone* (New York), 4.
[15] *The White Desert* (London, 1958), pp. 9-10.

Confusing and, indeed, fusing Ishmael together with his twin Queequeg (M.D. 317 ff.), for both are tattooed wanderers (M.D. 436), both sleep together, love each other, and worship together mystically, Giono permits his gloriously tattooed Paumolle to assume the narrative burden during the last pages of the book. Swinging like Queequeg upon the yardarms, the steward ardently longs to experience a foretaste of death—to drop down to a whale's back even and speed through icy, numbing waves. His is the long monologue (157-60) on the uncertainty of knowledge and every man's thirst for liberty. Thus ends this perhaps unfinished novel.

The powerless craft, becalmed and drifting, becomes a metaphor for every man, equally befogged, equally helpless and uncertain. No man knows where invisible currents draw him, any more than he knows what lies before him, even were he able to see, and all vision has been denied the *Indien*'s dreaming crew. In such gray daylight nothing at all occurs any more. No man knows, or longer expects to know, where he will be tomorrow. In these final pages Giono admits openly what other writers of marvelous travels may have sensed: all such displacements involve epistemology, or their ultimate purpose and originating force both derive from the desire for knowledge.

Giono's inquiry has moved into the unknown, for where better plumb the depths and interrogate the unseen than in that white, frigid silence where God may be?

What all men want in life, articulates Paumolle, is a breath of air for their sails, and then the slapping sounds as they fill with wind. It may as well continue to rain, but men want to be able to set a course and hold it. Only then will the endless spaces of ocean not trouble them. So long as men can steer, they are as alive surely as rain and waves: "There is the rudder; and there is this truth, equally as important as the vast endless stretches of ocean and the endless outpouring of the rain: that we act, that we get to the heart of things, and that we preserve our feeling of being free" (158). As long as a man can steer, he moves, and this motion immediately affords him the pleasures of freedom, even when he moves through a totally empty sky or across a bleak, forbidding sea over which only the sun voyages from the West to the East (158).

Thus, may we not maintain before apocalypse that for a man's contentment, as for his happiness, only motion along a route counts? " 'Nothing can cause the heart to stumble while the feet make time' " (159). Was it not given to man to steer towards something when he was born, between his birth and his death? Whatever the route he travels may be, is it not the route alone that counts? In spite of everything, a man feels his existence in this world only so long as the road runs before him, only so long as he travels, saying "left" and "right," recognizing "wrong" and "right" roads. Little does it matter that rain falls, that the sea extends in apparently limitless immensity, that cataracts of water rise from below or thunder from above. Let the sky turn to furnaces of fire, mountains crumble even though granite, or let the abyss open in black whirlpools beneath the feet of man, " 'So long as the hand holds the wheel, there is in the worst catastrophe a right, a left, a good and a bad road to take; so long as we are making time, we continue imperturbably, whether along the good road or on the bad, to take the most important step that a man can take, since forward motion is essentially what we were created for' " (159).

Having thus established man's purpose in life, his way of life, and his reason for living, having thus explained his equation of liberty and life, Giono has brought the reader also to the threshold. Counting slowly in terrifying silence, he measures out 105 more words, which pass through death's white, Antarctic curtain into the paradise that lies beyond for every voyager: the ship of life no longer responds to the helmsman's hand. The wheel spins crazily, rolling effortlessly right and then left. One no longer moves. The traveling has ended. The voyage has concluded. Motionlessness has set in permanently. A drifting hull, the once living ship has reverted to lifeless matter. Neither alive nor dead, all on and within it have become inanimate. To witness this unresponsive shell represents man's greatest moment of terror. After what becomes for the reader an even more frightening ellipse, Giono concludes thus: "C'est pourquoi tous les hommes du navire s'empressent de se découvrir une âme" (160). Only external proof can assure the reader that Jean Giono broke at this point from his self-hypnosis.

EVEN had Giono not mentioned by name in his novel André Breton's Emanuel Swedenborg (1688-1772),[16] the reader might have tracked him back to such texts as the *Arcana Coelestia* and *Heaven and Hell* by that Swedish scientist who left his earlier studies for theology rather late in life, at age fifty-nine (Jean Giono is here also, like his Captain, in his fifties at the time of composition). The novelist views man much as did the theologian, ". . . held by the Lord between heaven and hell, and thus in equilibrium, that he may be in freedom for the sake of reformation"[17]—or in order to create for himself an immortal soul before the terrors accompanying death:

"Therefore to be able to will good or evil, and to think what

---

[16] The Captain finds in such most icy regions "un Swedenborg et un Blake" to prompt him tirelessly with thoughts of angels (Chapter VII, p. 109). See Breton's *Entretiens. 1913-1952* (Paris, 1952), p. 284.

[17] See Swedenborg's *Heaven and Its Wonders and Hell from Things Heard and Seen*, trans. from the Latin of the first edition of 1758 in London (Philadelphia, 1907), and here an excerpt entitled "Freedom" from the *Arcana Coelestia*, pp. 447 ff.

is true or what is false, and to choose one in preference to the other, is the freedom of which we are now treating. This freedom is given to every man by the Lord, nor is it ever taken away[,] ... given to man with life[,] ... and this to the intent that he may be reformed and saved; for without freedom there is no reformation and salvation."[18]

Freely, then, have the men aboard the *Indien,* many already decorated and bedecked in glory to meet their Maker, chosen to become disembodied souls in paradise.

Content to visualize the last passage from life to death as the loss of vision and then of motion, Giono follows Swedenborg rather closely here. During the first months of the voyage the various narrators saw with the light from the natural, physical world; after their passage, as represented materially by enveloping fog, they perceived by means of another, accommodated vision inside a spiritual world, or with the very eyes of spirits and angels: "Such being the similarity between the spiritual world and the natural world, man after death scarcely knows otherwise than that he is in the world where he was born, and from which he has departed; for which reason also they call death only a translation from one world to another similar one."[19]

Coupled with Emanuel Swedenborg in the Captain's mind as he narrates the storekeeper's ascent of the volcano, is another mystic and apocalypticist, William Blake (1757-1827), who occasionally apostrophized Swedenborg.[20] Blake's *Vala,* or *The Four Zoas* (1797), are unfinished mystical poems, for example, which Giono's *Fragments* resemble in several respects, such as the idea common to both poets of an archetypal man, captain or Albion. The English poems, termed

---

[18] *Ibid.,* p. 443.   [19] *Ibid.,* pp. 430-31.
[20] *The Poetical Works of William Blake,* ed. John Sampson (London, 1925), p. 395, for instance.

"conceptual allegory,"[21] were written after a "slumber" beside the ocean, and dictated automatically or, as in Giono's case, without considered "premeditation" or reflective "revision." In Giono's *Poème*, as in the English poet, the apocalyptic vision issuing thus spontaneously includes beasts and "rulers of darkness in this world," and it excoriates real life, such as modern systems of government. Besides following Blake, or seconding his attacks on poverty and war, Giono makes the terrors of the abyss clearly visualized, before the "restoration to Eden." In Blake's case, as in Giono's, this crisis, which plunges the poet into the shrouds of mysticism, has occurred in full maturity, turning each poet's thoughts to religion— angels, paradise, and the fall therefrom. Giono's heartbroken Captain seemed already present in Blake's Man:

> "His eyes behold the Angelic spheres night
>   & day;
> The stars consum'd like a lamp blown out,
>   & in their stead behold
> The Expanding Eyes of Man behold the depths
>   of wondrous worlds!"[22]

Although in his *Fragments d'un paradis* Giono has not mentioned another marvelous voyage to which he was indebted, he has often elsewhere, as in his conversations, returned admiringly to Edgar Allan Poe's *Narrative of A. Gordon Pym* (1838), which French specialists of Melville consider a possible ancestor of *Moby-Dick*.[23] Poe's narrative

---

[21] See *Blake's Apocalypse* by Harold Bloom (New York, 1965), pp. 203 ff.

[22] As cited by Bloom, p. 307.

[23] Aside from the books *Melville par lui-même* (Bourges, 1958) of Jean-Jacques Mayoux and his *Melville*, trans. by John Ashbery (New York, 1960), there has been in France a sustained interest in Melville, as we have already seen (Note 2). In addition to three translations

also ceases without real ending somewhere in the Antarctic Circle and Ocean, in some white southland past Tristan d'Acunha and near the same South Shetland Islands. The sailor lost overboard, the gray vapor, drifting ship, and crew dreaming in immense whitenesses also appear to constitute virtually a morphology for this type of fictional voyage. In accordance with early notions of geography, the temperature becomes warmer and warmer in Poe's account as paradise draws recoverably close, but Giono makes little or no reference to either extreme of temperature, certainly not to great cold. Poe's shrouded and perhaps divine figure at the very close of his narration comes close to suggesting the idea of God and those immortal souls in quest of which Giono also ceases: "The heart ever desires to beat faster. Our passions are aroused by horizons (whence may loom the 'white being' appearing on the final pages of the *Narrative of A. Gordon Pym*)."[24]

What after Giono's fragments of paradise makes his ad-

---

of *Moby-Dick* into French since 1929 (Marguerite Gay's *Le Cachalot blanc* being perhaps the first), Jean Simon had written *Herman Melville, marin, métaphysicien et poète* (Paris, 1939); and Pierre Frédérix, *Herman Melville* (Paris, 1950). Mayoux refers to Poe's influence rather commonly, as in his discussion of *Omoo* (43), or in his treatment of style (5-6), as well as to Melville and Blake (70-72).

Recent French articles on Melville include: Robert André's "Melville et Shakespeare," *Critique*, xx (1964), pp. 705-15; Jean Greiner's "L'Utopie du mal," *Nouvelle Revue Française*, xiv (October 1966), pp. 678-88; André Le Vot's "Shakespeare et Melville: Le Thème impérial dans *Moby-Dick*," *Etudes Anglaises*, xvi (1964), pp. 549-63; and Léon-Pierre Quint's "Herman Melville," *Preuves*, xvii (May 1967), pp. 47-51. Mayoux contributed three articles: "La Langue et le Style de Melville," *Etudes Anglaises*, xiii (1960), pp. 337-45; "La *Saison en enfer* de Melville," *Lettres Nouvelles*, vi (1958), pp. 172-85. See also the "Checklist of Melville Criticism, 1958-1968," *Studies in the Novel*, i, No. 4 (Winter 1969), North Texas State University, pp. 507-35.

[24] *Provençe*. Les Albums des Guides Bleus (Paris, 1954), p. 8.

mirer pause for moments of thanksgiving is the realization that during the anguished years of the 1940's this great French novelist left behind by the Surrealists still managed to embark upon an ocean, although he consistently disliked the sea all his life, and that he himself willingly moved blindly through fog "into the face of death, the great adventure, the great undoing, the strange extension of the consciousness,"[25] *whence he returned*. Jean Giono returned fortified by what had begun as a tragic personal and artistic experience, but which he modified, after pondering surrealist aesthetics and the experiences of Swedenborg, Blake, Poe, and Herman Melville, into a *new life*. When he returned, he miraculously found himself able easily and bravely to deliver his great post-war masterpieces in a variety of fictional modes.

[25] In these words D. H. Lawrence speaks of Richard Henry Dana's marvelous voyage. See *Studies in Classic American Literature* (New York, 1964), pp. 112-24, and for Melville desire "to get out of *our* world," especially pp. 134-35.

The Symbolic Mode

Les Grands chemins (1951)

When Pierre-Henri Simon noted in *Témoins de l'homme*
(Paris, 1951, p. 190) that we are now witnessing in fiction a
century without women characters, he stated a fact undoubtedly true for a great many modern novels created by authors
generally considered foremost. However, the novel based
upon a love story involving a desirable heroine follows only
one novelistic tradition. As early as the sixteenth century authors had demonstrated that fiction can rise to great heights
when the problem of love is reduced to a minimum, with
women as coveted objects incidentally introduced, relegated
to shadowy presence in the periphery, or entirely absent. In
the twentieth century many writers of fiction besides Giono,
as we shall see from the following examples, have, particularly by studying a pair of bachelors, scrutinized problems
that concern men: money, occupations, friendship, responsibility to another, and the nature of man himself.

It may very well have been Balzac, perhaps following the
idea central to *Le Tiers livre*, who inaugurated in French fiction the general subject of celibacy, when for *Scènes de la vie
de province* he chose that theme for three works entitled *Les
Célibataires*: *Pierrette* (1839), *Le Curé de Tours* (1832), and
La Rabouilleuse (1842). His condemnation of bachelordom
is unequivocal, for he pits "ces deux célibataires," the brother
and sister Rogron and Sylvie from the first story, with their
evil hearts and their love of money, bourgeois comforts, and

political power, against an innocent child. In this Cinderella-type story, Balzac explains, as he studies "les immondices du coeur humain," that because of their isolation, celibates replace natural affections by factitious ones: love for dogs, cats, canaries, etc. In the third story the original bachelor is the imbecilic Rouget with his shrimp-netting mistress versus outsiders to the family circle at Issoudun. Balzac afflicts Rouget with physical and moral timidity.

In *Le Curé de Tours* Balzac grapples more closely with the problem. Here with unforgettable artistry he tells of the pitiful Abbé Birotteau, aged 60, "très mouton de sa nature," "grassouillet," his face reflecting good humor devoid of ideas. His adversary is Abbé Troubert, aged 50, whose orangeish eyes betray his "haute et profonde ambition." Naturally, Birotteau is defeated and despoiled by Troubert, seconded by the vicious spinster ("célibataire") Mademoiselle Gamard. Completely opposite, then, Birotteau yielded perforce to "ce grand sec" whose vaulted shoulders resembled yellow arches. The pitiful hero is disarmingly frank and expansive, easily diverted, "sans fiel ni malice," a plump man who rolled when he walked, juxtaposed to a gaunt man illustrating in his person "les forces des gens solitaires." These clerics are, if we omit Panurge and Pantagruel, perhaps the first carefully distinguished and well-known pair of bachelors in French fiction.

The characters of bachelors, portrayed in a manner very opposite to that of Balzac, interested Charles Dickens in 1837 when he gave us the four charming Pickwickians, two of whom remain celibate to the end. Smollett had already, and with equal tenderness, painted a comic bachelor in the neurasthenic Matthew Bramble. More to our pattern here, however, is Flaubert's last work in which he also chose as central characters, not two enemies, as in Balzac, but two friends, the widower Bouvard and the bachelor Pécuchet. Although both

47-year-old men are copyists, both weary of the city and long-ing for the country, both addicted to the same crazes, both snorers in the moonlight furnished with the same political views and desires, and equally fond of each other, Bouvard is methodically differentiated from his partner. The former appears amiable, is taller, wears linen garments and a hat on the back of his head, has half-closed bluish eyes, curly blond hair, and a childish face. Pécuchet appears grave, is shorter, *wears a brown redingote too large for him* and a cap with a pointed visor, has flat, black hair, and—always disconcerting in a little man—possesses a deep, cavernous voice. Even though they soon come to resemble each other, to borrow, in fact, each other's distinctive traits until "l'union . . . était absolue et profonde," Bouvard's confidence, giddiness, and generosity oppose Pécuchet's discretion, parsimony, and medi-tativeness. Flaubert still has not finished establishing the giv-ens: on their last day at the office, Bouvard offered punch to his fellow employees, while Pécuchet slammed the door as he departed. Bouvard was sad to leave his apartment, while Pécuchet, glad to be going, maliciously carved his name on the fireplace. On the way to Chavignolles, one took the coach (and by this time we can easily guess which one), while the other rode on the baggage cart. That first night in their new domain, Bouvard slept on his back, but the less secure Pécu-chet slept on his side.[1]

The situation of famous bachelors in French fiction at the turn of our century stood something as follows: it had been

---

[1] Similarly, in Maupassant's story *Deux amis* (from *Mademoiselle Fifi*) M. Morisot ("horloger," "pantouflard") is differentiated to some extent from M. Sauvage ("mercier," "petit homme replet et jovial"). Both are, however, "pêcheurs fanatiques" or "enragés," "hommes doux et bornés," with "des goûts semblables et des sensations identi-ques." When M. Morisot's eyes filled with tears just before he was shot, we learn that he was the taller of the two.

brilliantly proved that prose fiction can sustain a story where there is little or no love interest. Inheriting that tradition, Balzac contributed the following additions: (1) the problem of two bachelors is challenging to a novelist, (2) the pair must be carefully differentiated to orient the reader, (3) it seems psychologically sound to set one against the other (since bachelors are by the pressures of society and because of their own frustrations evil and unnatural), and (4) it is an excellent idea to enlist pity in the reader as he sees the weaker destroyed by the stronger. A recollection of *Bouvard et Pécuchet* finds Flaubert conditionally agreeing with Balzac's propositions 1 and 2, but disagreeing flatly with 3. As far as pity is concerned, Flaubert seems to have thought, bachelors in their union have no need of it; if they are comic, they are also and at the same time, tragic, but in their relationship to culture.

In 1932 the young novelist Giono, with several best-sellers already to his credit, published a collection of twenty short stories entitled for the first story, *Solitude de la pitié*. Thus Jean Giono opened what appears to me, at least, to have developed over the years into a dialogue between himself and his contemporary, the American novelist John Steinbeck. The keynote of this collection of hunting sketches is stated in the title: pity for one's fellow man.

The title story, barely fifteen pages in length, tells with much subtlety how two penniless men travel by coach to a neighboring city in search of work, appeal to the local priest, who, after having set them to the perilous job of repairing his well, cheats them of their due so that they recover for their pains only the minimal coin required for their fare. One man is big, wears a hat (Bouvard), and provides for the other, whom he helps and protects. The thin man "floated" in a gray cloak much too large for him (Pécuchet). He was apparently

98

dying, either of disease or of starvation, for his neck, "décharné comme une tresse de fer," rose with its prominent Adam's apple from the threadbare "houppelande." His "regard de mouton" (Birotteau) pierced people from blue eyes "immobiles comme de l'eau morte." As he stands shivering in the cold night air, on muddy feet, he sees through others "l'âme triste du monde." These unnamed bachelors do not feel united, as in Flaubert: "Je suis seul," says the big man, who fends for the other, decides for him, works for him even at the risk of life and limb, covers him from the cold with his own clothing, encourages him with a myth of eventual subsistence, and pledges to remain by his side. The little man is, like the author, clairvoyant. His gaze leaves a ring of pus around its impact point; others are rotten. The pair travel alone together, victimized by persons who should have shown them, if not charity, at least honesty in their dealings. In this story the thin man, "le maigre," attracts to his person the narrative focus. When the big man climbs twenty meters down into the dark well, for example, the narrator stops in the courtyard, describing sights and sounds seen by "the other." This particular story, along with Giono's *La Femme du boulanger*, has appeared regularly, thanks to the discernment of Henri Peyre,[2] in college textbooks since 1935.

A characterization of bachelors that is both comic and tragic, and because of its impersonality similar to the *credo* of Flaubert, is Henry de Montherlant's *Les Célibataires* (1934). Of the three bachelors here, the most important are the uncle and nephew, Elie de Coëtquidan and Léon de Coantré, aged 64 and 53 respectively. These "deux magots" wear (Giono's) "houppelandes." The virginal Baron de Coëtquidan, an imbecile with a good memory, steals food

---

[2] *Contes modernes*, ed. Henri Peyre and Yale University (New York, Evanston, and London).

from the kitchen, turns up the heat surreptitiously, does not care at all if his nephew is left penniless, and is, in short, as "mauvais" as Balzac's bachelors. He pushes and trips children, insults people by letter, renounces importance of any kind because he declines the inconvenience of a daily hour-long bus trip, and suffers from timidity aggravated by two sentiments caused by his shabby clothing and his impotence.

In this masterful novel the uncle abandons the nephew after four years of living together. Léon, the helpless one of the pair, a poor man who has neither situation, ambition, nor any love of money, although once excellent in music, in Latin poetry, and in painting, might have become an inventor, but he preferred manual labor. In his early years he had been supported by his mother, who feared that he might attempt suicide a second time. Once pushed out into the world, this aged fledgling soon dies of neglect, of humiliation, and perhaps also of malnutrition. The third bachelor, Baron Octave de Coëtquidan, on guard over his manias and prejudices, succeeds in remaining comfortably isolated from grim reality. He plays at being modern, pretends to read English, adopts American habits (including a rocking chair), and is bested by Elie. As far as bachelors in general are concerned, says Montherlant, "le monde est cette balle au bout d'un élastique: ils ont beau l'envoyer loin d'eux, il leur revient avec prestesse." It is a world in which no one is his nephew's keeper: "ce qu'il y a de tragique chez les anxieux, c'est qu'ils ont toujours raison de l'être." *Les Célibataires* of Montherlant, tragi-comic like *Bouvard et Pécuchet*, ignores the affirmation in Giono, however.

When these superb works of fiction are thus recalled together, they seem vigorously to pursue their colloquy, with the voices of their authors each asserting his own point of view, insisting upon his own variation upon the theme: Dickens and Flaubert versus Balzac, Balzac and Montherlant versus Giono. The debate resumed dramatically in 1937 in the United States, and by November of that year in France, on Giono's insistent question: Am I my brother's keeper? when John Steinbeck published *Of Mice and Men*, translated in 1939 as *Des Souris et des hommes*. Thus two individualistic and powerful novelists, so similar in age, background, native locale (California and Provence), interests, and particularly so similar in their sense of compassion for the unfortunate and the suffering underprivileged, meet in a similar bachelor fiction.[3]

[3] *Of Mice and Men* has been known in France since the November 1937 review in the *Mercure de France*. It was translated by Maurice E. Coindreau (1939, 1946, 1948), who in his introduction refers to Jean Giono. "In 1940 only the literati had known Steinbeck. In 1944 his name was a symbol of resistance and known by the average man in the street. And Gide's praise of *In Dubious Battle* (see Gide's entry in his *Journal* for Sept. 27, 1940) and comparison of Steinbeck's stories to Chekhov's had not hurt his initial reputation," wrote Thelma M. Smith and Ward L. Miner in *Transatlantic Migrations* (Duke University, 1955, p. 164). "The greatest literary development in France between 1929 and 1939," wrote Jean-Paul Sartre in "American Novelists in French Eyes" (*Atlantic Monthly*, August, 1946, pp. 114-18) "was the discovery of Faulkner, Dos Passos, Hemingway, Caldwell, Steinbeck." Jean Simon in *Le Roman américain au XXe siècle* (Paris, 1950, p. 169) called *Of Mice and Men* "une pure oeuvre d'art." Pierre Brodin had already pointed out in *Les Ecrivains américains de l'entre deux guerres* (Paris, 1946, pp. 247 ff.) that this work "est le livre de Steinbeck le plus connu des Français."

Steinbeck and Giono were again associated by Maxwell Geismar in *Writers in Crisis: the American Novel betweeen Two Wars* (Boston, 1942, p. 239 ff.): "Steinbeck's *To a God Unknown* retrogresses to the fallacious, primitive thinking of such writers as D. H. Lawrence, Jean Giono, and Sherwood Anderson." They were associated again in 1948 by the French critic Claude-Edmonde Magny in her essay, "Steinbeck, or the Limits of the Impersonal Novel" (reprinted by Tedlock Jr., E. W. and C. V. Wicker in *Steinbeck and His Critics*, Albuquerque, 1957, pp. 216-27). Joseph Warren Beach in the same collection (pp. 80-91) associated Steinbeck with Maupassant, and generally with "the

Just as in *Solitude de la pitié* we have two bachelors, one of whom protects the other, originally the memorable pair of George and Lennie in Steinbeck's masterful novel and play. As in Giono, it is the weaker one, Lennie, who appears intended as the real hero.[4] In every instance Steinbeck narrates his tale, divided into six chapters taking place (1) beside the Salinas River, (2) and (3) inside the bunkhouse, (4) inside Crooks' room, (5) inside the barn, and (6) beside the Salinas River, from a vantage point that allows him to see and to focus upon Lennie. The narrator does not, for example, follow George into town, any more than Giono followed his

---

great tradition in European writing." Jean Giono quotes John Steinbeck in the epigraph to a play, *Le Voyage en callèche* (Monaco, 1946).

Walter Allen in *The Modern Novel in Britain and the United States* (New York, 1964), on the other hand, places Steinbeck rather in an American tradition, saying that *Of Mice and Men* "is another example of what might be called the eternal American 'buddy novel' with its inescapable suggestion of latent homosexuality" (p. 163).

[4] R. Ganapathy in "Steinbeck's *Of Mice and Men*: A Study in Lyricism through Primitivism" (*Literary Criterion*, v, University of Mysore, 1962, pp. 101-04) feels that Lennie is the hero when he says: "Our sympathies are already with Lennie, however bad and primitive he might be, and his death comes as a shock to us. . . . The Modern Indian . . . is perhaps more fortunately situated to receive Steinbeck than the Americans themselves." See also Harry Slochower's *No Voice Is Wholly Lost* (New York, 1945), p. 299; and Margaret C. Roane's "John Steinbeck as a Spokesman for the Mentally Retarded" (*Wisconsin Studies in Contemporary Literature*, v [1964], pp. 127-32).

Charles C. Wolcutt in *American Literary Naturalism, A Divided Stream* (University of Minnesota, 1956) finds Lennie and George "spirit and power inchoate, mixed in chaos rather than fused in form" (p. 262). See also Warren French's *John Steinbeck* (New York, 1961); Stanley E. Hyman's "Some Notes on John Steinbeck" (*The Antioch Review*, June 1942); Josephs W. Beach's *American Fiction, 1920-1940* (New York, 1941), pp. 307-47; Joseph Fontenrose's *John Steinbeck: An Introduction and Interpretation* (New York, 1963); and such bibliographies as that of Walter Rahn (München, 1962) and Hildegard Schumann (Halle, 1958).

strong character. Only Lennie's sick mind is explored, as in Chapter VI through the vision of Aunt Clara and the giant rabbit. The narrator's pity and preference, in fact, seem lavished precisely upon those whom Curley's wife calls "the weak ones": Lennie, Candy, Crooks, and herself.

The babyish Lennie constantly pleads to leave the ranch because it is "mean" there. He worries, like "le maigre" in Giono, for fear that George will abandon him—not only because of Crooks' warning, but also that of the rabbit. Curley's wife, similar to Aurélie in Giono's story and celebrated film, *La Femme du boulanger*, when once the meanness, the discontent, and the ache are "gone from her face," is finally, and to the narrator also, "pretty" in death. The prolonged episode of Candy's dog, perhaps repeated as Salamano's dog by Albert Camus in *L'Etranger*, serves two purposes: to create sympathy for Candy, and to underline the true character of Slim. In the end, the strong ones of the story abandon the weak ones, two of whom are killed and two of whom plunge, in postures of self-defense, into hopelessness. Like the old dog, and like "l'autre" or "le maigre" in *Solitude de la pitié*, Curley's wife remains forever nameless.

As *Of Mice and Men* ends, we are left to continue the fiction ourselves with another pair of bachelors, George and Slim. Steinbeck's technique in the case of Slim subtly counterbalances deeds and words. The narrator *tells* us first that Slim is majestic, royal, masterful, capable (and "capable of killing . . ."), grave, profound, authoritative, hatchet-faced, with delicate hands like "those of a temple dancer." Since Slim is so wise, his first reaction—that George and Lennie travel together because of fear—must be weighed. When the narrator turns from telling to showing, we learn how Slim drowned the puppies. To George, Slim is "God-like," and George therefore speaks to him "on the tone of confession."

Neither George nor Lennie is intelligent, but Slim, who is very intelligent, says: "Take a real smart guy and he ain't hardly ever a nice fella." The real condemnations of Slim date from his approval of and insistence upon the death of Candy's old dog—he even reminds Carlson to "take a shovel." Slim feels "horror" for Lennie after seeing how strong he is; and the next time we meet Slim, he is condemning Lennie to death. He approves the murder, invites George to set out with him afterward, and departs with him. It is perhaps because of Slim that George fails to protect Lennie, "changes" towards Lennie, and repudiates Candy.

Both Giono and Steinbeck in these works set a time for the elapsing of their fictions; in the earlier work the repairing of the well occurs ironically during the music lesson given by the priest to a privileged youngster. The *curé*, although he enjoys books and music, although he is intelligent, is devoid of compassion. The narrator-author prejudicates his fictional world from the blind, dark courtyard. Steinbeck's novel begins at the Salinas River, a good place to behold visions, as Lennie does there. The narrator also, in a sense, sees visions there because *Of Mice and Men* comes "from out of" his head, or takes place in the author's mind between the inbound and the outbound flights of herons as a "water snake slipped along the pool, its head held up like a little periscope." Thus, we grasp in Steinbeck the logic of the change in tense after the first two paragraphs—from the author's present to the narrative past of fiction, which, once fabricated, is wafted upwards and out just after the heron "labored up into the air and pounded down river" (see pp. 9 and 173).[5] Giono's implied conclusion—that education and intelligence have not bred pity among the favored—is also

[5] See the Random House edition (New York) with an introduction by Joseph Henry Jackson.

implied by Steinbeck. Giono's original contention, *I am* my brother's keeper, is negated by Steinbeck. The dialogue between the two novelists, however, does not end there.

In 1951 Giono returned to bachelor fiction in a symbolic mode with his *Grands chemins*. This work is so different from what admirers of Giono expected from him in the post-war years, so allusive and so puzzling, that it has thus far passed without critical attention. *Les Grands chemins* is, first of all, a psychological novel, from an author supposedly not concerned with psychology. Secondly, it is Giono's only American novel to date, and thus a topical novel reflecting in its vocabulary American intervention during and following World War II[6] and this from the author who had been supremely content in his pre-war fiction to write glowing pastorals much more remote than *Sweet Thursday*. Thirdly, it is a novel virtually unrecognizable as having been composed by Giono. The language flows neither from Giono's old, lyrical voice nor with his usual rich imagery. The story is harshly told by a nameless bachelor, who, as one of a pair, resembles Steinbeck's George. Giono's narrator is, however, an accused hedonist, an opportunist, a manipulator of people and of situations, a total cynic, who while wanting to dominate the other bachelor (*l'artiste*) searches for affection; and

[6] Examples of contemporary allusions in this book (Gallimard, *Livre de Poche*) are as follows: "Indochine," "Vincent Auriol," "la Russie" (pp. 112, 142), "ravie de voter" (p. 149), "torpilleur" (p. 234), "planète Mars" (p. 161).
Specifically American vocabulary is as follows: "un gilette" (p. 236), "New York" (pp. 149, 150), "la chute de Niagara" (p. 233), "imperméable amércain" (pp. 219, 238, 251, 252), "gentleman" (p. 178), "baby-foot" (p. 147), "musique de nègre" (pp. 137, 150), "hammerless" (p. 242), "cigarette américaine" (pp. 35, 106), "bombe atomique" (p. 218), "poker" (pp. 64, 107), "tracteur américain" (pp. 40, 45), "armée américaine" (p. 87), "des salopettes américaines, des canadiennes de 'surplus' " (p. 49), "un Nègre" (p. 20).

he is a murderer. Beneath this surface lie several symbolic patterns.

With a new and uncompromising lucidity that makes the reader very uncomfortable, and with admirable fearlessness, Jean Giono thus ventures upon a Freudian terrain of homosexuality to probe beyond the George-Lennie relationship, as it can be imagined by the reader of *Of Mice and Men*. This Giono novel, as in Steinbeck's earlier work, deals with a pair of bachelors, one strong and one weak, where the stronger protects the weaker, and finally, rather than lose him, and in order to lose him, shoots him in the face. The murder takes place, with equally ironic protestations of love and tenderness, in a secluded glen or hollow.[7] The potential murderer is given a gun by another character, M. Albert, who here performs the function of Slim; and the murderer is disculpated, congratulated, approved by a grateful society, and therefore dismissed. The murder is, as in Steinbeck, preceded by the excited organization of a posse, or "battue," which the murderer outdistances. The other bachelor is also summarily executed, also, presumably, because he had strangled a woman. As in Steinbeck, *Les Grands chemins* deals with modern men seen as migrant workers and/or homeless wanderers, with relationships between

[7] See Peter Lisca's Chapter 8 (p. 135, in particular) from *The Wide World of John Steinbeck* (Rutgers University, 1958): "Sometimes . . . this retreat has explicit overtones of a return to the womb and rebirth." Giono has capitalized upon this same significance by having his narrator cling amorously to women in kitchens, to warm cooking ranges, to food and drink, etc. See also E. C. Richard's "The Challenge of John Steinbeck" (*North American Review*, CCXL, 1937, p. 412). "The world of John Steinbeck's novels is a beautiful warm valley with disaster hanging over it," observes Harry T. Moore in *The Novels of John Steinbeck: A First Critical Study* (Chicago, 1939), p. 11 *et passim*.

men,[8] and with their card games. The women in the book are regarded with contempt by the narrator, or seen merely as willing objects of sexual gratification; in either case their roles are incidental.

The virile blond narrator in *Les Grands chemins,* aged under forty-five, remarks that he has previously assisted a Paris psychiatrist to study prostitution. During the course of his relationship with the girlish, salivating "artiste" or card-sharp whom he befriends, he works at various temporary jobs. Why does he cling to the weaker man? Because of an "amitié" that he fails to comprehend, and also because "tout le monde a son type maigre" (p. 161). He sues the *artiste* for his company because the latter, by having cheated him at cards, has in a sense mastered him: "Si quelqu'un vous trompe et vous dupe, il est . . . votre maître . . . Il ne vous reste qu'à l'aimer ou à le

---

[8] Warren French (*op.cit.,* p. 3) derives Steinbeck's theology from "that of nineteenth-century American transcendentalists such as Emerson, Thoreau and Whitman who unite in asking 'How dare you place any thing before a man?'" This opinion might hold for Giono also, translator of *Moby-Dick* (Paris, 1941) and enthusiastic author of *Pour saluer Melville* (Paris, 1943). Claude E. Jones in "Proletarian Writings and John Steinbeck" (*Sewanee Review,* Vol. 48, 1950, p. 452 ff.) also points out the theme of "man's love for man." Joseph H. Jackson in his Introduction to *The Short Novels of John Steinbeck* (New York, 1953, p. ix) says that *Of Mice and Men* is "a statement of Steinbeck's drive to help one sort of man to understand another sort. . . ." R. W. B. Lewis in "John Steinbeck: The Fitful Daemon" (from *The Young Rebel in American Literature,* ed. Carl Bode, New York, 1959) speaks of a "contemporary motif" also apparent in Malraux, Silone, Camus, and Greene, which is in Steinbeck "awareness, of the fateful division between man and man; and of that division as a central feature of the mutilated life it is the novelist's business to give a direct impression."

Steinbeck himself says (*Figaro Littéraire,* July 17-23, 1967, p. 20, trans.) "que l'écrivain se sent poussé, au point d'en avoir mal, à transmettre au lecteur quelque chose qu'il ressent comme important."

tuer" (p. 159). The *artiste* wants no ties while the narrator, uncertain as to the "*mobiles*" behind his actions, seeks nonetheless "un peu d'amitié," "la gentillesse," "un peu d'attention," "je ne sais pas ce que j'aimerais," "quelque chose de valable, en bien ou en mal," "un évènement quelconque," "une certitude" (pp. 189-91).

The bachelors may be friends, in the sense of traveling companions, one of whom twice rescues the other, but they are also "ennemis intimes et d'autant plus inséparables." As long as the dark, curly-haired *artiste* depends upon the narrator, the latter keeps him attached. When that dependence is overcome, or when the *artiste* proves by strangling a woman that his injured hands have healed so that he can rely again upon legerdemain at cards, his doom is sealed. Giono has made the meaning of this murder doubly significant by prefacing in an epigraph Claudius' request to Hamlet not to go to Wittenberg (i.e., if he leaves, he will be murdered).

In *Les Grands chemins* Giono explores the relationship between two bachelors even further than Steinbeck in *Of Mice and Men*, inasmuch as the narrator attempts to discover what he means by friendship, why he plots to keep the *artiste* continually in a leading position, and also why his feelings towards the other are so ambivalent. The Giono novel is told in the first person by a narcissistic narrator whom the reader, struggling against the habits of a lifetime, must constantly remember not to admire. In fact, the reader can identify even less with Giono's narrator than with Bardamu, haunted by his mysteriously recurring Robinson, in Céline's notoriously first-person novel of 1932, *Voyage au bout de la nuit*. Giono seems to be saying that while there is some brotherly affection in a man that impels him tenderly to be his friend's keeper, there is, he finally concurs with Steinbeck, also another feeling, equally powerful but subterranean, the hatred that made Cain kill his brother.

As the reader fits the pieces together, it was the victim (Victor André, ultimately discovered to have been born at Algiers of unknown parentage) who gambled with his own life. The less contemptible *artiste*, who always sleeps with open knife in hand, had acquired in prison the taste for playing without safety net, "sans plafond." His "victory" lay, then, in forcing society to put an end to what he was: "C'est même une preuve qu'on ne pouvait pas mettre fin autrement à ce qu'il est" (p. 225).[9] The narrator killed him in the daylight because "les jours d'amour sont meilleurs que les nuits d'amour" (p. 254).

Thus, Giono ends the book, or the perplexing and uninterrupted flood of words[10] that have attempted for 255 pages to

[9] Having become familiar with Giono's train of thought, we know it is *l'artiste* whom he secretly admires. Claudine Chonez points out also that "le héros préféré de Giono adore, comme on dit, jouer avec le feu . . ." (*Giono par lui-même*, Editions du Seuil, 1959, p. 91). Thus, *l'artiste* would join other heroes whom she lists: Bobi, le Roi, Monsieur Joseph, Monsieur Numance. Had Giono himself narrated the story, he would doubtless have betrayed a certain admiration for *l'artiste*, who resembles to some degree the type of uncompromising man whom he considers heroic; since Giono could not justifiably admire a cardsharp, however, he veiled his admiration behind the auxiliary narrator's ugly voice.

[10] While there are neither chapter nor part divisions in this novel, it should still be understood that the author, or super-narrator, has exercised his controlling function in structuring the book into five sections, as follows:

1. Introduction (through the meeting with *l'artiste*, or for about 37 pages) in the autumn;

2. Places upon "les grands chemins": (a) The fair (to page 74); (b) The mill (to page 160), or winter hibernation; (c) The village of Sainte Jeanne (to page 192); (d) The village near the castle of M. Albert (to the end of the book, or page 255), or the March storm.

ensnare the reader until, forgetting himself, he too condones murder as a solution. By such a narrative device Giono demonstrates the uses of the symbolic mode, and the power and energy of modern fiction, which encourages the reader's reaction before such trickery, and incites fear and anger, exactly as the author desires. The reader does not, in fact, lay the book aside either without theorizing that Jean Giono succeeded in this experimental fiction in supplying a concrete example of a modern crisis. We follow his demonstration to its end, where, abandoned by the author, we are tempted to conclude by ourselves that the narrator's victory illustrated an illusory and, surely, a temporary triumph of day over night, of the "blond beast" over the dark artist, or of the Apollonian over the Dionysian hero, or of Germany over France.

By writing *Les Grands chemins* Giono seems again to have recognized America and American fiction, and to have acknowledged Steinbeck's artistry in *Of Mice and Men*; but he seems also to have considered that this American novel required an emendation lest the reader conclude that George is the hero, and that murder is the best way to handle Lennie's case.

Cain's punishment—that of wanderer and fugitive—would be no deterrent to George or to Giono's narrator, both only reconfirmed in their right to violence. Furthermore, Giono again attested to the fact that bachelors continue to be a proper subject for fiction, inspiring variations in symbolic patterns, supplying the novelist with a pretext for querying the very nature of man, with his need for responsibility and friendship and his propensity to errantry and violence. In addition, Giono used symbols for the purpose of inducing in the reader a heightened awareness of his world, of his culture, and of his values. With Steinbeck, Giono wondered whether or not our education has developed in us a sense of compassion, whether we are not all, as his narrator suggests for himself, Stanleys drawn towards Livingstons.

The symbolism in effect forces the reader to visualize concretely the modern condition, man as a vagrant upon a highway, escaping no less homeless than Faulkner's man described in *A Fable* from the city, the family, science, and traditional morality. The novel further forces the reader to shudder before all approaching winters, whitenesses, which always indicate for Giono, as we shall see not only in *Le Hussard sur le toit* but also in *Un Roi sans divertissement,* an empty and hostile cosmos. In years to come, Giono will decide that his twin hoboes, seen here as Cain and Abel, are perhaps even better grasped in their sinister implications as the primitive Greek gods, Castor and Pollux. For the moment, he throws out for the reader's reluctant acceptance, but only inasmuch as the latter will accept, the undercurrents of political reality, France and Germany. The reader remains fascinated by such possibilities, particularly because they remain latent, and spellbound by this vision of life as a highway trod by murderous bachelors, free and alien adventurers.

Le Hussard sur le toit (1951)

In 1951, twenty years into his career as a novelist, Giono came to the attention of literary critics at home and abroad with a major novel. His *Hussard sur le toit* deals with a celebrated novelistic subject, the bubonic plague, set by Giono as a background to the adventures of a central character, the aristocratic Angélo Pardi. Although the novel belongs to a cycle[1]

[1] In an article, "Giono's Cycle of the Hussard Novels," *French Review*, xxxv (1962), pp. 287-94, Maxwell A. Smith established, according to the information then available, the cycle as follows: (1) *L'Ecossais. La Fin des héros* (Manosque, 1955); (2) *Angelo* (N. R. F., 1953);

upon which the author was at his death reportedly still working, it requires a deliberate and careful study as a separate
work of fiction standing complete in itself, particularly since,
as probably Giono's greatest work, it presents problems common to the most distinguished of our modern novels.

Appearing when it did, four years after the widely ac-
claimed plague chronicle of Albert Camus, *La Peste* of 1947,
with its epigraph relating it to Daniel Defoe's *Journal of the
Plague Year* (1722), Giono's novel at once attracted a great
deal of scholarly comment. Critics first of all naturally related
the three novels. While establishing the fact that *La Peste* and
Le Hussard sur le toit are, despite their mutual subject matter, largely dissimilar, the critics wavered in their assessments
of the more troublesome, because much more complex, Giono
work. The major problem shared by the critics of this novel
was precisely whether the book could be best treated in terms
of another familiar literary genre, the epic perhaps, or the
medieval allegory. It would seem now that the romance, the
roman courtois from the Middle Ages, better interprets this
Giono novel, which is further complicated by the presence of
symbolic patterns.

Before examining *Le Hussard sur le toit* as a highly successful innovation in novelistic technique, the renovation not
of the epic nor of the allegory but of the *roman courtois*, and
before isolating its prototype or studying its symbolic patterns, we should proceed systematically and recall for this
novel the general lines of previous criticism and then the history of the book itself.

---

(3) *Le Hussard sur le toit* (Paris, 1951); (4) *Le Bonheur fou* (Paris,
1957); (5) *Pauline* (1962) [still unpublished]; (6) *Mort d'un personnage* (Paris, 1949). The next novel, released after *Angelo* appeared
in book form in 1958, however, was *Deux cavaliers de l'orage* (Paris,
1965).

Writing about this novel in October 1953, Marcel Arland agreed that it is a "roman," and further specified that it is a romance, or what French critics refer to as an "épopée": "L'épopée du choléra," "épopée lyrique."[2] His view was endorsed by the Giono specialist Claudine Chonez, who in 1959 repeated the term, calling the novel an "épopée de la jeunesse,"[3] and repeated by Maxwell A. Smith when he termed the novel "an epic."[4] When in 1965 the distinguished critic Pierre de Boisdeffre in his *Giono* set out to discuss *Le Hussard sur le toit*, he treated it rather in terms of Camus's *La Peste,* concluding that in the earlier work the plague was "une maladie symbolique," that Oran was "l'estrade symbolique," and that although Camus's chronicle was an "allégorie camusienne," there was "rien de tel chez Giono," or in *Le Hussard sur le toit.*[5] Smith stated again in his *Giono. Selections* of 1965 that *Le Hussard* is "not presented allegorically as in *La Peste* of Camus."[6] These samplings representing the majority opinion connect this novel, then, with the epic, or speak of *Le Hussard sur le toit* either as if it were of epic stature, or as if it were an epic recreated in modern prose fiction. Because of the subject matter of the work, critics contrasted Giono's plague novel with Camus's chronicle of the plague; the comparison yields the dissimilarity that the earlier work is alle-

[2] See "A la hussarde," *La Nouvelle N. R. F.,* No. 1,040 (1953), pp. 687-96.

[3] "Et qui peut nier que *Le Hussard,* à travers la mort et l'horreur, ne soit une épopée de la jeunesse, de la gaîté?" *Giono par lui-même* (Bourges, 1959), p. 107.

[4] In his article in the *French Review,* Professor Smith also likened the hero Angélo Pardi to Galahad and to Lancelot (p. 290).

[5] See pp. 81-82 of *Giono* (Paris, 1965).

[6] *Giono. Selections* (Boston, 1965) is a reading text edited by Professor Smith. The final selection, from the last 35 pages of Chapter VI of *Le Hussard sur le toit,* is admirably chosen for these are undoubtedly the finest pages of the novel. See introduction to this passage, pp. 147-48.

gorical and the later work without allegorical or symbolic meaning.

Tentatively dissenting views were expressed, however, from England and from France in 1965. When in June of that year Claude Michel Cluny wrote in the *Nouvelle Revue Française* that Angélo Pardi traversed the epidemic of cholera, "le choléra, ou la guerre—la guerre, ce choléra organisé," he implied that in the Giono novel cholera was a symbol.[7] Contributing from England to the *French Review* in October, Odile de Pomerai was more explicit: "Whatever Giono's avowed intentions may have been in *Le Hussard sur le toit*, it is certainly possible to look on it as an allegory of mankind faced with an overwhelming crisis. In *Deux cavaliers de l'orage*, the symbol is even plainer."[8]

While there is no absolute unanimity concerning the definition of *Le Hussard sur le toit,* many critics, struck by its medievalism, agree that its descriptions of the plague are macabre, or that the plague is described in terms similar to those used in reference to the *danse macabre*. As we have seen, critics have employed other literary terms frequently applied to medieval letters, epic and *épopée*, with insistence. They have not only called the hero Angélo Pardi a "chevalier servant,"[9] but have also equated him with medieval heroes whose names came to mind: Perceval, Galahad, and Lancelot.[10] What Pierre de Boisdeffre mentioned from the *Hussard* were, for instance, "des squelettes" which "paraissent échapper aux *Danses macabres* du Moyen Age."[11] In any case, we

[7] See page 1,061 from "Un Scandaleux bonheur," *Nouvelle Revue Française* (June 13, 1965), pp. 1,058-62.

[8] See "An Unknown Giono: *Deux cavaliers de l'orage,*" XXXIX, No. 1 (October 1965), pp. 78-84.

[9] Arland, *op.cit.* (above, note 2), p. 694.

[10] Smith (note 4) and Arland (note 9).

[11] Boisdeffre (note 5), p. 81. See also Gustave Cohen's Chapter VII

have not only the findings of scholars showing that *Le Hussard* is not based upon Camus's *La Peste*, but also certain words of Giono to the effect that he had not by 1965 read Camus.[12]

Words of caution for the critic of Giono had been spoken, as we have already seen, in September of 1957 by Gaëtan Picon: "D'une façon générale nous écoutons trop bien Giono: nous ne l'interrogeons pas assez. Il a plus de ruses et de masques qu'on ne croit—ou qu'Angelo Pardi ne nous le ferait croire."[13] Picon developed his theory that Giono's subsequent novel, *Le Bonheur fou* (1957), was an experiment in fictional technique, and it has already been demonstrated that such is also the case for *Le Moulin de Pologne* of 1952.[14] About *Le Hussard* Picon said: "*Le Hussard*, au moins avait un sujet: il y avait 200, 300 pages sur le choléra, sur la chaleur, sur l'air étouffant et malsain."

By a new interrogation of Giono's text, we shall see that although the author may originally have thought of writing what the nineteenth century termed a prose epic, and although he may originally have envisaged his hero Angélo as a medieval hero of a *chanson de geste* or of a *roman d'aventure*, he modified his intentions so that what he finally composed more nearly resembles a modern *roman courtois*.[15]

---

from *La Grande clarté du moyen âge* (New York, 1943) for a discussion of the *Danse Macabre* ("Danse Machabée").

[12] In answer to what appear to have been harassing questions, Giono told his interviewer Gilbert Gannes (*Nouvelles Littéraires*, April 1, 1965, pp. 1, 11) that he had glanced at Camus's writings but had not read them.

[13] See "*Le Bonheur fou*" from *Mercure de France*, No. 1,129 (September 1957), pp. 122-26.

[14] See "The Tragic Mode," Chapter V.

[15] I have preferred what I consider to be the narrower subdivision, *roman courtois*, to the generic term *roman d'aventure* (see Gaston

This novel under study should be classed equally with *Le Bonheur fou* and *Le Moulin de Pologne* as an innovation in fictional technique. In addition, and just as Picon clearly saw, there is not one focus of insistence in this work, but a symbol and its obverse: the plague, and the air or sky. It is these very

---

Paris's Chapter v from *La Littérature française au moyen âge* [Paris, 1889]) because it more narrowly defines the genre to which Giono seems to be adhering. In other words, a *roman d'aventure* of the thirteenth century, for instance, may not contain elements of *amour courtois* (Paris, pp. 199, 203); an example would be *Le Chevalier au cygne*. The converse is also true, however, as in the case of a *roman courtois* such as *Le Lai de l'ombre*, which might be defined by a word borrowed from Ilse Nolting-Hauff (*Die Stellung der Liebeskasuistik im höfischen Roman*, Heidelberg, 1959, p. 15) as a *Romankasuistik*, where there is no actual adventure but a *tenson* concerning seduction. A *roman courtois* in the Middle Ages is also a *roman de chevalerie* since, as Maurice Valency demonstrated, there are knights, ladies, and then love, in that order (*In Praise of Love*, New York, 1961). During that period a *chevalier* was by definition supposed to be and assumed to be *courtois*. However, the term *chevalier* in any sense other than horseman and *chevalier servant* does not apply to a nineteenth-century hero like Angélo. As Gustave Cohen pointed out (*L'Art du moyen âge et la civilisation française*, Louis Réau and Gustave Cohen [Paris, 1951] and see also Bibliography, p. 441), the "roman courtois . . . est le genre qui se crée aux alentours de 1150 et qui va dominer tyranniquement notre littérature dans la seconde moitié du XIIe et au XIIIe siècle, exprimant les tendances fondamentales et l'idéal d'une société non plus fondée sur la guerre, mais sur l'amour, où la force de l'homme s'incline volontairement devant la faiblesse de la femme" (351). *Le Hussard sur le toit* illustrates, in other words of Gustave Cohen, "le vieux pacte conclu . . . entre amour et bravoure" (*La Vie littéraire en France au moyen âge*, Paris, 1949, p. 396). See also Cohen's *La Grande clarté du moyen âge* (New York) 1943, Chapter III.

In his analysis of the Latin romance *Rodlieb* (*Romania*, XLIV, pp. 373-406), which he termed the first "roman courtois," Maurice Wilmotte found the following features typical of this genre, and they are also prominent in *Le Hussard*: (1) the subject matter, a wandering "chevalier" whose mother is at home; (2) detailed descriptions of ornaments (Angélo's clothing, for example), and "détails de la table" (Angélo preparing Pauline's meals); (3) "la peinture du décor" (the

two used in contra-distinction that form the stunning symbolic pattern.[16]

Le Hussard sur le toit has an interesting pre-history which it now seems appropriate to recapitulate so that the symbolic pattern may be seen in developmental sequence. While walking along a Marseilles street in 1934, Jean Giono caught a first glimpse of a fictional hero, Angélo Pardi, whose person and

---

attic in Chapter VI is the most striking example); (4) an interest in "le pittoresque de la vie quotidienne" (in Chapter I the incident of the woman serving coffee to Angélo is an early instance, and Giono is apparently fond of this recurring scene, from *Les Grands chemins* also of 1951); (5) "l'anecdote vulgaire coupant la monotonie des éternels combats" or adventures; and (6) "le détail descriptif" (in this case, the white sky and the cholera).

The character traits of Angélo (nobility, courage, generosity, devotion, tenderness, and spiritual affection for a noble married lady whose respect he has sought and won) are all listed by W. T. H. Jackson in his fifth chapter, "The Romance," from *The Literature of the Middle Ages* (Columbia University Press, 1960), pp. 80-159. As Professor Jackson also points out, the colors symbolizing heaven and hell in *Parzifal* are white and black (these colors are established in the opening lines of Wolfram von Eschenbach's romance), which perhaps explains why critics have compared Angélo to this hero.

Others have been troubled by what I term the *amour courtois* in the *Hussard*. Professor Smith has this to say in the *French Review* (above, Note 1): "Several critics have been astonished by the absolute chastity of these two creatures, by the total absence of amorous passion throughout their long cavalcade together. In answer to my query, Giono explained this to me through the psychological state created in both characters by the presence of so many corpses, adding that his study of population statistics at the time of the cholera epidemic in 1838 showed a striking decrease in natality" (290). In her analysis of *Le Bonheur fou*, Gennie Lucioni (*Esprit*, September, 1957, pp. 292-97) considered and then rejected the possibility that this later novel might be a "roman de chevalerie" patterned upon "le poème pseudo-chevaleresque de l'Arioste" (294).

[16] I am much indebted for this phrase, and for my method, to William M. Manly's article, "Journey to Consciousness: The Symbolic Pattern of Camus's *L'Etranger*," *PMLA*, LXXIX, pp. 321-28.

whose adventures during a severe epidemic of cholera never lost their fascination for him. In the six days following this initial inspiration, Giono dashed off a first draft of 243 pages, called *Angelo*. Instead of releasing *Angelo*, however, he put it aside for nineteen years, finding it unsuitable that his newly conceived hero should make his first public appearance involved merely or "tout bêtement avec des femmes" (P.A., 9).[17] This period of germination indicates two things: (1) how important Angélo was to Giono, or how fondly Giono hoped to present to the modern world a hero whom readers could fix as a lodestar; and (2) how difficult it is for a modern novelist to fit his material into the most meaningful form. For the next eight years, from 1934 to 1942, Giono worked on this very important *Hussard sur le toit*, which he did not release, however, until 1951. In 1953 he finally published *Angelo*, which appeared in book form with a preface of four pages in 1958. A comparison of *Angelo* and of *Le Hussard sur le toit* furnishes valuable insights into the genesis of the latter work, which is probably Giono's masterpiece.

While in the "première rédaction" (P.A., 7) Giono admittedly also saw Angélo in a trial situation somewhat similar to that of Stendhal's "Lucien Leuwen à Nancy (notamment chasseur vert)" (P.A., 9), he also related him initially to assorted heroes of epic and of romance, to Saint George (A., 101, 103), to Orlando, and to the horse Boiardo from *Orlando furioso* (A., 234), to Perceval in the episode where the knight contemplates the drops of blood on white snow (A., 234), to Don Quixote (A., 153), to the Cid Campeador (A., 149), and to

---

[17] The following abbreviations followed by page numbers signify: A = *Angelo*; P.A. = Preface to *Angelo*; P.S.M. = *Pour saluer Melville*; M.D. = *Moby Dick* (Giono's translation). Melville's novel is *Moby-Dick*. Where no letters (or an H) appear before numbers, then the page reference is to *Le Hussard sur le toit* (132nd edition, Gallimard).

Roland (A., 180). Most prominent among such allusions are those to the poet Ariosto (A., 56-57, 113, 179, 219), in particular to Canto XIX of *Orlando furioso*, which tells how Angelica meets Medor and heals him of his wounds. Among all such possible literary affiliations that came to mind as Giono dreamed and wrote of his new hero, of the Angelo who was to become the Angélo of *Le Hussard sur le toit*, only those to *Orlando furioso* are prominently retained in *Le Hussard*.[18]

It would seem that Giono once considered the feasibility of a novel based upon an epic. Such a novel was written by one of Giono's favorite authors, Gogol's *Taras Bulba* (1835, 1842).[19] He may also have considered a novel of epic stature;

---

[18] An early allusion established the fact that Angélo knows Ariosto sufficiently well to recognize a canto illustrated on a "paravent" which "portait les guerriers empanachés et les seins jaillissants des cuirasses d'un chant de l'Arioste" (173). During a later adventure Angélo frightens himself because instead of reality he had seen through the smoke and flame of a dark night a "chant de l'Arioste" (190). It is made quite clear, as Angélo talks to himself and recognizes that he is powerless to control his own "âme folle" (365), that Ariosto represents to him a way of life: "Il me faut l'Arioste. Là, oui, je suis à mon aise." It is a way of life, concurs the author humorously, that is applicable now: "Il (Angélo) imaginait fort bien qu'avec un peu de daube arrivant à point on pouvait dans la réalité domestiquer tous les héros et héroïnes de l'Arioste" (365).

[19] Gogol's composition of *Taras Bulba* coincided with his term as assistant professor of medieval history at the University of St. Petersburg. The work resembles a medieval epic, especially in Chapter ix, where there are even strong textual resemblances to *Roland*, to *Prince Igor*, and in the death of Andrei to the *Shah Nameh*. The work deals with a hero and heroes; its historical setting is inaccurate, as in the three epics just mentioned; patriotism, religion, and the state are everywhere exalted; the work glorifies war and the ruthless, physical exploits of the brave; the women are unhappy and play secondary and/or nefarious roles; and there is a childhood and even an old age of the hero, complete to the passing on of the sword. Leon Stilman calls *Taras Bulba* "the Ukrainian epic." See *The Diary of a Madman and Other Stories* by Nikolai Gogol, ed. and Afterword by Leon

such a novel again had already been written by one of his most cherished authors, Melville, in *Moby-Dick* (1851).[20] Giono, therefore, searching for a new fictional prototype, finally fixed upon the form of the "roman courtois" as written by Ariosto;[21] for *Le Hussard* cannot be better qualified than by this term from *Angelo* (132). The heroine of *Le Hussard* is a married lady, Pauline de Théus, whom Angélo attends as "chevalier servant."

Among the reasons that Giono may have had for selecting

Stilman (New York, 1961). For Giono's predilection for Gogol, see *Giono par lui-même*, p. 62.

[20] Various authorities on Melville, Richard Chase, Alfred Kazin, James E. Miller Jr., and Henry A. Murray, for example, have used the term "epic," either as a noun or as an adjective, in their treatments of *Moby-Dick*. Similar criticism has been applied to a French contemporary of Melville. In his recent study, *L'Inspiration épique dans les romans de Victor Hugo* (Paris, 1962), Raoul Simaika speaks of Hugo's later novels as possessing epic elements ("le grandiose, le pathétique, et l'horrible," p. 122), and of Hugo's "vision épique" (25), "grossissement épique" (27), and "respiration épique" (31), which make him an "auteur épique" (31). According to Simaika, Gilliatt is an epic character (119-20) because of his victorious struggle against the sea. For a study that categorizes fiction generally as epic, lyric, or dramatic, see Irène Simon's *Formes du roman anglais de Dickens à Joyce* (Université de Liège, 1949).

[21] When M. V. Philipon de la Madelaine made his prose translation of *Orlando furioso* (Paris, 1844), he stated in his Introduction that it was not a "poème épique" (xvii) but that it was "une épopée" or "un roman épique" (xx). Benedetto Croce in his essay "Ludovico Ariosto" from *Ariosto, Shakespeare and Corneille* (trans. Douglas Ainslee, New York, 1920) firmly established the irony in *Orlando Furioso* and argued that Ariosto is not an epic poet: "he could not be epic, because he had no national sentiment, no feeling for class or religion, and the marvelous in him is all fancy . . ." (106). Rev. E. W. Edwards in *The Orlando Furioso & its Predecessor* (Cambridge University Press, 1924) said that since it dealt with "knights and ladies moved to gallant deeds by love and courtesy, . . ." it is "a romance and not an epic" (125).

Orlando Furioso as a model is, first of all, the fact that it is Italian like the hero Angélo. Secondly, there are personal considerations that bind the author to Italy and to Ariosto. Giono's paternal grandfather, with the father of Emile Zola, emigrated from Italy to France in 1832; he served as medical attendant during an epidemic of cholera in Algiers. Giono's mother, who died in 1946 and whom he had already celebrated in *Mort d'un personnage* (1949), was named Pauline. Then too Giono has told us that he was fond of quoting Ariosto in the original from a volume that was a family heirloom.[22] Aside from the fact that Ariosto played an important part in his life, Giono chose this romance for all the reasons that have made it perennially popular, not only because it is a model worthy of emulation but also because it derives a hero from an epic, as Giono did in the case of Angélo. Another bond is the poetry, for Giono was not only an essayist, dramatist, and historian, but also a poet who wrote remarkably lyrical prose. As a matter of supposition, Angélo seems to be a masculine counterpart of Ariosto's heroine Angelica, who feels no love until she has healed Medor.

Then too, there is the same pervasive irony in both Ariosto and Giono; the latter does not always treat young Angélo seriously (he is twenty-five years old [146], or twenty-six years old [350]), as, for example, when he amuses the reader by implying a literal meaning to an idiomatic expression, repeating that Angélo inclines towards "jouer la fille de l'air" (48, 62, 101, 304), or when he sees the vain, strutting Angélo as Puss-in-Boots (59), as a crow (226), a lion (214, 216), or even when he describes him sparingly as "maigre aux yeux de feu" (331), with "beaux cheveux bruns" (364). On occasion,

[22] This information comes from *L'Apocalypse* (ed. Joseph Foret, Paris, 1961), to which Giono contributed *Le Grand théâtre*, pp. 269-306, as we saw in Chapter 1.

Giono tolerated Angélo with what amounted to an amused and fatherly detachment. The author's irony in regard to the plague, however—what have been called the "macabre" elements of the novel—is both stinging and violent.

In *Orlando Furioso* we see Giono's liberated woman's format of a lady and strange gentleman traveling through woods and forests, fantasies like Angélo's escapade on the roofs, beautiful place descriptions, touching love scenes followed by dramas tense with anxious suspense, and praise of idyllic comradeship between men and women. Ariosto would have approved Giono's modern woman, Pauline, and would have enjoyed her company, for she is as self-reliant and as energetic as Bradimante, for example, or as Marfisa. Most important of all, however—and this defines both *Orlando Furioso* and *Le Hussard sur le toit*—there breathes the same recipe, if not the same recommendation, for a life based upon love and loyal friendship through thick and thin; for courage, resourcefulness, and buoyant optimism in the face of adversities; for courtesy, assistance, respect, and honor between members of the opposite sex.

As Angelo becomes *Angélo*, then, and as he rides across plague-ridden Provençe in 1838, he represents not so much an epic hero as a "chevalier servant" (A., 140) to the married lady, Marquise Pauline de Théus. Angélo Pardi, Colonel of Hussars, is not a warrior but an émigré, not a leader but a gallant individual, neither a representative nor an ideal of any particular group of people, but a noble idealist virtually alone in a terrible land where, like Robinson Crusoe, he must survive by his own courage and wits. He is not an agent deputized by a king or sent by some group to attack a seemingly invincible enemy. Nor is he expendable either, as the epic hero often is. He is neither heir to a throne, nephew to a king, nor responsible for the public weal. He has escaped into

France because of a political assassination in Italy, but he no longer has any license to kill. Angélo cannot be seen as waging any combat against cholera in the abstract; he does attempt to save individuals from the disease. Giono has said that in *Le Hussard* he wished to place Angélo "aux prises avec des généralités passionnelles (choléra)" (P.A., 9). When he published such a premeditated statement, Giono seemed to be announcing *a posteriori* that in the novel he intended cholera as something more than a disease, that he saw it symbolically.

While Angélo Pardi is recognizably one and the same with the Angelo of the "premier état" (P.A., 7), none of the precisions given in the primitive version relating to his escape into France, his stay at Aix, or his need for liberty is essential to an appreciation of *Le Hussard sur le toit*. The stories are quite different, as are the two heroines, both named the Marquise Pauline de Théus. What was physical attraction in *Angelo* becomes "amour courtois" in *Le Hussard*. None of the other characters from *Angelo* appears prominently in the later novel, in which only one interpolated story is retained.[23] While Angélo himself remains "au comble du bonheur" (H., 398), the world in which he lives and the dangers he encounters are vastly more significant. His physical existence is, to be sure, still situated in the high Alps between France and Italy, mountains that are as powerfully present. In *Angelo*, however, the earth as described by the author Giono in 1934

---

[23] In *Angelo* (173-188) Pauline tells the old Marquise the story of her childhood, her rescue of the Marquis de Théus, their courtship, and their marriage. Pauline's husband, the Marquis de Théus, is a major character in *Angelo*, in which Angelo himself is in love with Pauline. She tells more or less the same story, but much abbreviated in *Le Hussard sur le toit* (357-360), but she tells it to Angelo. In this novel, Angelo and Pauline have never met before Chapter VI, and the Marquis de Théus is not a character.

lies under a "ciel d'azur" (A., 11), or under a rainy gray sky (A., 99) soon warmed by a "soleil de mai" (A., 55). The change from the beautiful sky of *Angelo* to the murderous chalk-white sky of *Le Hussard sur le toit* indicates again, as the fanciful title suggests, the complexity of a symbolic pattern.

It would seem that, as Giono meditated upon *Angelo*, he was satisfied with his hero, or that he still wished to offer his readers a positive and heroic view of man. He was also satisfied with the geographical theater of action, the Alpine region that he knew familiarly. Similarly, he was content with the imagined circumstances of Pauline de Théus, her childhood, her physician father, her love and marriage, and with the fact that she would meet Angelo. He was dissatisfied with the type of fiction he had at one time considered, an intrigue à la Stendhal's *Lucien Leuwen* involving love and a courtship hopefully leading to marriage, dissatisfied also with the test that Angelo underwent in the "première rédaction." A positive hero, so brave, so dashing, so naively young, so bent on liberty, merited a contest more challenging than seduction. Therefore Giono designed a significant world lined symbolically, where the problem *ad demonstrandum* is: can Angélo survive a passage through contagion and, although plagued by evils, menaced by enemies, attacked by creatures and by men, retain a joy in living and continue to honor the brave lady who has offered him her hospitality and her assistance?

Angélo's principal dangers stem from two immense unknowns: the white sky and the black death. The whiteness strikes brightly and hotly from a limitless cosmos upon a disease-ridden earth inhabited by men who desire death, by carnivorous animals and birds among which the hero and the lady pass virtually unscathed. Thus, *Le Hussard sur le toit* is a modern parable[24] serving both as a criticism of man and as an encouragement to him. There is, and most critics of this novel have agreed, a certain gaiety in this work and, despite the horrors of the plague, many pleasant days for Angélo and for Pauline. Meanwhile Giono, after eight years of reflection, develops his diagnosis of the nineteenth century; for the novel, though modern in its search for a fresh novelistic technique, deals only obliquely with the twentieth century.

Before proceeding to a progressive analysis of the symbolic pattern of this novel, where the chains of significance, unlike the novels of Stendhal, shift and deepen gradually before the delighted eye of the reader, we might consider briefly, in order to eliminate them as sources of inspiration, two earlier works of fiction that treated the plague before 1942, or before Giono completed "le travail des années" (P.A., 9) on *Le Hussard*. One is Defoe's *Journal of the Plague Year,* already mentioned, and the other is Alessandro Manzoni's *I Promessi sposi* (1825-1826), and in particular its Chapters XXXI-XXXVII. There are four major points of dissimilarity between the English novel and Giono's French work: (1) Defoe is discussing a largely imaginary plague,[25] while Giono is treating a real one that devastated Provence in 1838; (2) for artistic and historical as well as for linguistic reasons, Giono has preferred the noun "le choléra," to "la peste," which he barely

[24] See Louis MacNiece's theory of modern "double-level writing" from his *Varieties of Parable* (Cambridge University Press, 1965), p. 3. In other words, Giono's *Hussard sur le toit* is, in my opinion, because of its quest for novelistic innovation, to be affiliated less with much nineteenth-century fiction than with the fiction of Kafka and Beckett.

[25] In his Introduction to *Robinson Crusoe and A Journal of the Plague Year* (New York, 1948) Louis Kronenberger says of the latter work: "It is probably the greatest fake document of its length in all literature; and even for a writer who was always trying to make fiction sound like fact, it is a superb tour de force" (xiii).

uses throughout fourteen chapters, or 398 pages of his novel;[26] (3) Giono, admittedly writing creative fiction, nowhere seeks the objectivity of a journalist but rather relies as sole defense upon third-person narration by an omniscient, omnipresent narrator, himself, speaking consistently in the *passé défini*; and (4) Giono declines to share the sternly punitive thought underlying Defoe's statistics, namely, that a good plague now and again would supply a salutary lesson to dissenting man.[27] Giono's central concern is not history (although he displays an impressive knowledgeability concerning the nineteenth century and its plague), nor politics (although Angélo like many young men of that century is preoccupied with "liberté") nor psychology (since there is no character development in the novel). Thus, by eliminating the courtship motivation, and by subordinating history, politics, and psychology to a symbolic pattern, Giono took precautions not to remind his readers of *I Promessi sposi* with its *simplex* hero Renzo, the silk-weaver from Lecco. There are no elements characteristic of the picaresque novel in *Le Hussard sur le toit*. It is not primarily a travel book or simple

[26] Thus far I have been able to find the word "peste" in only three passages (267, 371, 373).

[27] The longest block of material where Defoe expresses what seems to be his motivating thought in writing this fiction consists of the two paragraphs beginning in the Kronenberger edition: "Here we may observe, and I hope it will not be amiss to take notice of it, that a near view of death would soon reconcile men of good principles one to another . . ." (538 ff.).

There is one case in Chapter VI of the *Hussard* where Angélo from his rooftops witnesses twenty people killing a cholera victim in the streets below him and then sees two of the murderers succumb to cholera. Angélo delights in their subsequent agony, but after 6 lines (117) devoted to Angélo's "amer plaisir," Giono quickly turns away from this too horrible irony. In other words, Giono deplores the plague, or seeks to practice, as we shall see, preventive medicine.

"roman d'aventures"[28] either because Angélo's trip home to Italy, or to the place from which he came, illustrates a further symbolism that matches the pace of the narrative; as they climb the Alps, Angélo and Pauline perform a difficult passage from first acquaintance to happiness, while Giono goes from the first word "aube," itself a whiteness, to the last word of the novel, "bonheur."

CHAPTER I of *Le Hussard sur le toit* opens upon Giono's usual circular world, or serves as an introduction in a circular way. Throughout one day, from morning to evening, various people in various situations in Provence are introduced: Angélo, first of all, a shy young Italian who, because he is a "soldat de métier" (15), prefers a morale of action. For him, the only way out is through the circle along a road personified (13, 15, 16, 25) because it is life. We meet an *aubergiste* waiting for the opportunity of becoming the King of Naples, a young Madame de Théus whose servant has just died suddenly, a naval inspector from Toulon, a Jewish physician in Marseilles who will evacuate his family but remain to treat an epidemic, and a monk whose way of life is an attainment of liberty. These potential characters with their "fulgurantes tranches de vie" (33) are menaced by the sky, by the sun, by insects, by plants (melons and tomatoes), and by other men. Man lives, "enfermé sous un globe de pendule," under a sky (14) that is "meurtrier" (15), under a "ciel" (16, 35) that is "gris" (29, and four times on 30), "blanc" (31), "de craie" (13, 14, 15) similar to "chaux vive" (31) in a world that is "barbare" (21, 27), and inhabited also by "ces bêtes qui étaient du

---

[28] The adventures of Angélo form, to be sure, the surface or narrative interest of the novel, for, as the author says: "Il y a eu beaucoup d'aventures au-dessus des villes méridionales . . ." (H., 128).

mauvais côté" (Chapter II, 44): "oiseaux" in "nuages" (45) or in "bourrasques" (43); "rats" (41, 52), "le chien" (42), "les cochons" (49). It is a world of "pestilence" (45), "choléra" (47, 49, 50) and "contagion" (58). By the time the "bon prince" (64, 84) Angélo, due to his "magnifiques bonds de chat" (59), arrives at Sisteron in Chapter III, among carnivorous foxes, "nuages de . . . grosses mouches" (60), and "chiens enragés" (60), men, this "canaillerie à deux pieds" (63), are dying from the plague, their faces marked "de tant de vices" (63). Why is this so? There is an "énorme plaisanterie . . . mêlée à l'univers" (67). Angélo suffers from the burning sky full of "oiseaux carnassiers malgré leurs roulades vermeils" (65), and from the "lumière du grand soleil blanc" (Chapter IV, 77). The cholera has reached epidemic proportions, but man's "fourberie" seemed to Angélo "plus inquiétant(e) que la mort" (Chapter V, 87).

By Chapter VI (96-150) Giono has established his principal themes: Angélo, cholera, animals, and the sky. It is also the "moment critique" (131). Driven by hunger, thirst, and by a murderous mob, Angélo takes refuge upon the rooftops of Manosque, Giono's native city, where he is attacked by a "monceau de corneilles" (119) and by "hirondelles" (130, 131, 133). Below him the cholera rages (99, 102, 107, 108, 114, etc.), is an "épidémie" (104) and a "contagion" (145, 149) among "cholériques" (149). This modification of the word "cholera" into "choleric," with its secondary or extended meaning of irascible, alerts the reader to the linguistic virtuosity to come. In this chapter where Angélo is, alas, only too briefly for the enchanted reader atop the roofs of Manosque, the grim accumulations are relieved by three whimsical passages: Angélo and the friendly gray cat (119-150), the "petite fille" seen tripping along the street in her Sunday dress (128-

130), and Angélo entering the "grenier" (138 ff.) full of treas-
ures from a gentler past. In this same chapter Angélo finally
meets Pauline, the young Madame de Théus whom Giono selected to be his heroine, as far as the reader of this one book
knows, from the various characters sketched briefly in Chapter I. From his rooftops Angélo is close to the white sky (118,
126, 141), to the white dawn (132), to the "étoiles" (110, 114),
to the murderous sun (116, 120, 125, 127, 133, 134, 138, 142),
and to a comet (132). A further suspicion, originally aroused
by the phrase "canaillerie à deux pieds"—that the frequency
of the animals signifies that Giono will equate them with people (126, 127)—also occurs in this masterful chapter.

In this city of Manosque there is no love, only a "corps social mourant" (167), afflicted by the "malédiction d'avant les
temps" (155), stricken not so much by cholera as with "la
colère de Dieu" (155). Once he descends from the rooftops,
Angélo (an angel, 158, 166) assists a nun to wash the dead for
burial. She is herself a bird (153), a lion (160), and a peacock (161). The "étoiles" are "éteintes" (151), but the
"aurore blanche" (151) presages a deadly "soleil blanc"
(170). By Chapter VII the view of man as an animal is well
established. People are dogs (183, 200), hares (184), eagles
(184), cats (186, 203), and insects (193). "L'homme est aussi
un microbe têtu" (172). "Les hommes ne valent pas grand-
chose" (192). Therefore the "maladie" (198, 200) rages under a furious sun (182), "un soleil fou" (176), as white as
plaster (182), where people are "silhouettes calcinées" (181).
Angélo searches for his valet Giuseppe, for whom "la mort est
un échec total" (230) under, in Chapter IX, "le ciel . . . blanc
de craie" (205), under an "ardent soleil blanc" (214) that
means death, or that brings "le mal" (224). Thus, the pattern
has gone from cholera to choleric, to malady, and now to "le

mal." In other words, Giono is proceeding very gradually from the concrete to the abstract, and associating with the abstract word "mal" another word: contagion (and contagious). Cholera has also become choler, and this choler has been associated with the sky and with God.

The coming happiness of Angélo and Pauline, prefigured by the colored sky during the rainstorm (219-221) of Chapter IX, a sky that is "azuré," "bleu de gentiane," "bleu sombre," "une teinte violette," "lie de vin," and "rouge comme un coquelicot," begins in Chapter X. An isolated "gentiment" (19) of Chapter I becomes in reference to Angélo a score of "le plus beau" (242), "gentil" (236, 245, 254, 265, 267), and "angélique." As the two friends approach Italy or "la terre promise" (244), the dawn is red (252), and the sun golden (236) and beautiful (243). Other men, however, continue to behave like animals.

At this point the author begins to circle cautiously around the problem of the symbolic pattern. At first he uses insinuation and adroit persuasion. What was the plague, after all? The plague was perhaps a revolution (281) or general injustice in the nineteenth century (286-87). The white sky (277, 279) was possibly only a pervasive sadness (276) in the year 1838. Now relatively safe in the high Alps, Angélo and Pauline see a sun in equilibrium (311), a blue sky, and a gray sky "pommelé de rose" (315).

In Chapter XII the author satisfies his reader's curiosity concerning Angélo and Pauline, or ties the threads of the intrigue (350, 361), and also, clearly now, alludes to the plague and to the sky in terms of a symbolism. Why do all these people die? They die, for one thing, because they want to die, Angélo learns from the clarinetist from Marseilles. This wandering musician speaks in accents very familiar to the readers

of Jean Giono, or with the voice of the author himself. This
is how "one" dies:

"One catches himself, all set like a grasshopper, to unspring
the leg muscles, so deathly eager is a man to vault towards
that tiny strip of unobstructed sky directly above the pavement. That's really it, don't you know, a man dies from all he
longs for. . . . It dawned upon him that cholera was more than
likely an *imagined* disease; that this was precisely what he
himself had been up to; that he had better get back on the
straight and narrow and dream up something less apt to
cause panic fear. . . . If you personally insist upon expiring,
then expire; if you insist upon passing on, by all means pass
on. . . . He had observed that in the piney woods, where the
scent of resin embraced sunshine to beget the hot breath of
an oven, that the cadavers he encountered (one of which was
that of a gamekeeper) suffered especially from romantic
agony: in their bearings a recognizable languor, along with
a certain melancholic outlook, the sort of superciliousness one
expects among the fashionable . . ." (334-35).

Thus in this passage, where the change of narrative focus
betrays the author's ironic voice, the last of the modifications
concerning the plague is stated for the first time: cholera in
the nineteenth century was the "mal du siècle." It is not a real
illness, although it was contagious, but it was rather an *invented* or an imaginary illness.

Further in this same chapter Angélo and Pauline journey
into "un ciel sale et sombre" (345), "un ciel couvert" (346),
observe the "travail noir du ciel" (346). The adjective "black"
is in this case used figuratively to recall the "énorme plaisanterie . . . mêlée à l'univers" of Chapter III. Concurrently the
former massive accumulations of "choléra" dwindle and are
replaced more and more frequently by "maladie" (341, 344,

345) because "le choléra fini, il restera les miroirs à affronter" (340). Death, in other words, will remain.[29] Both man and the sky are hostile to man.

The author's lesson by a first intervention in Chapter XII was not, however, sufficiently succinct; we shall hear a second time from Giono himself, represented by the character of an Alpine physician.[30] Whether man dies of "peste ou choléra," he says to Angélo and to Pauline, "les dieux en profitent" (371). Cities lack more than an adequate supply of "chlore" or of "chlorure" (369 ff.), "en tout cas de tout ce qu'il faut pour résister à une mouche, surtout quand cette mouche n'existe pas, comme c'est le cas"; chemistry will not solve their problems (370). It is even less likely (370, 375, 376) that medicine or surgery will see anything beyond the flesh they probe. The plague, an "épidemie de peur" (368), or a "mélancholie" (370) is other; it is "une maladie de grand fonds; il ne se transmet pas par contagion mais par *prosélytisme*" (376). Melancholy, the *mal du siècle,* makes certain societies resemble an assemblage of living dead, "un cimetière de surface" (370), driving "à des *démesures de néant* qui peuvent fort bien empuantir, désoeuvrer et, par conséquent faire périr tout un pays" (371). Cholera is nothing more than "*un sur-*

---

[29] That the mirror represents death to Giono seems very probable since it was so clearly represented by Cocteau in *Orphée,* as well as in the scenario of *Le Sang d'un poète,* as pointed out by Otis E. Fellows in a lecture, "L'Homme et ses miroirs," delivered in the summer of 1960 at the Maison Française of Columbia University. Professor Fellows recalled: ". . . et voici ce que le héros, Orphée, apprend: (Heurtebise) 'Les miroirs sont les portes par lesquelles la Mort va et vient. . . . Du reste, regardez-vous toute votre vie dans une glace et vous verrez la mort travailler comme des abeilles dans une ruche de verre. . . .'" (Scène vii from *Orphée,* 1927.)

[30] Marcel Arland also recognized Giono in this "gros homme à redingote" (*op.cit.,* see above, note 2).

saut d'orgueil" (377). Science can dissect a human body, telling us of what the person died, but neither how nor why. In the final analysis we human beings are ignorant: "Le globe terraqué roule, on ne sait pourquoi ni comment dans la solitude et les ténèbres" (378).

Therefore the narrator (the mountain doctor) wanted to describe how death approached, how finally "la conscience humaine sentait alors dépouillée de toutes ses joies" (379). This is how a person died: his joys fled like birds, first the migratory, then the others. His face became stupefied. What is the matter with him? "Il a qu'il crève" (379). Then fled the sedentary birds (the sedentary joys: "ordures . . . déchets . . . qu'on trouve sur place rien qu'en sautillant, . . ." [380]). "Le cholérique . . . est un impatient" (381) as he hastens towards the end of his "existence physiologique" (384). Soon the impatient patient sees clearly on both sides, into life and into death, as he chooses lucidly (384). Only one thing can incline a man to the side of life, one thing alone, and that is love (385). "Le meilleur remède serait d'être préféré" (382). What is cholera? It is "une nouvelle passion" (382) that came into the world around 1838; it is the desire for death. Is this the fault of the Alpine physician? No. *"Est-ce moi qui ai fait le monde?"* (383).

After this lecture from the country doctor, Angélo and Pauline set out the following morning on the last lap of their journey together. The sky is clear. It will be sunny for three days. Angélo is delighted with the "pureté du ciel" (387). Surrounded by camellia-colored mountains, they halt at noon in a "solitude ensoleillée" (389). The pure sky was treacherous, however, or had not vented all its evil. That night Angélo and Pauline wage their combat against cholera, and win. Why does Angélo win now when previously he had failed to

cure a person of cholera? He won because he had treated
Pauline with love, with tenderness, and with honor. Pauline
lives, and Angélo does not even suffer an attack of the plague.
Why? A person who practices courtesy forgets himself as he
cares for others; a true healer, "quelqu'un qui s'oublie"
(369-70), does not die either of real cholera or of the "mal
du siècle."

While Giono has, with the assistance of his *raisonneurs*,
made the symbolic meanings of the plague very clear, or
while he has used the plague as a conscious symbol, he has,
on the other hand, nowhere given such precisions about the
white sky that grows intense as the cholera rages, is relieved
by the rainstorm when Angélo finds his servant Giuseppe,
and whitens again but feebly in the rapid closing pages. As
the book ends, Angélo rides happily home, "au comble du
bonheur" (398), in fact. We do not know that any other male
character survives. Perhaps the narrator heard the story from
Angélo. There is, even in the final pages, no further clue as to
the origin or meaning of the evil white sky or of the furious
white sun that have bombarded Angélo with their deadly
white rays and stricken a whole countryside with their malediction. Where the cholera with all its variations upon this
theme is artfully disposed throughout the text until it is firmly
resolved, there is no conclusive explanation for the association of whiteness with evil. It may be therefore a case of pre-
conscious rather than of conscious symbolism.

Even if we did not recall, however, that Giono's "com-
pagnon étranger" from around 1930 was *Moby-Dick* (of
which he made what appears to have been the second French
translation, from November 16, 1936, to December 10, 1939,
and that he published in 1941, and that he subsequently composed his unconditional tribute to Herman Melville, *Pour
saluer Melville*, 1943), this whiteness first, and this sole sur-

vivor, secondly, speak loudly not of Albert Camus[31] but of Melville.

It seems very true, in fact, that there are specific indebtednesses to Melville in *Le Hussard sur le toit*, completed, as Giono tells us, in 1942 but published at the one-hundredth anniversary of *Moby-Dick*. Beginning with the least important influences, we recall that the last action in either novel takes place on a beautiful sunny day and begins around noon, and that in either case the conclusion is rapid. In both books whiteness is associated with the immensity of the cosmos, with the Deity and deities,[32] with fire or the sun, and with light, which itself is white, or "sans couleur. Si la lumière frappait directement la matière des choses, elle donnerait sa blancheur vide à tout, à la tulipe comme à la rose" (M.D., 203). Like the wind in the final pages of *Moby-Dick*, the white sky in Giono is incorporeally present: "les choses qui exaspèrent et outragent l'homme n'ont pas de corps; ..." (M.D., 537).

Giono's white sky like the white whale might also be "le Jugement Dernier et la vengeance de la foudre et la malice éternelle" (M.D., 545)—"tout ce qui est démoniaque dans la vie et dans la pensée (M.D., 192), a malediction from "puis-

[31] Since the problem of Camus and Giono remains troublesome, it seems important to recall the conclusions of W. M. Frohock (*Yale French Studies*, II, No. 2, 1949, pp. 91-99), who found that whenever Camus was dealing with characters' moods, or with anything outside his everyday experience, he followed Giono: "At such moments Giono is very much with him, through the similarity of the kind of association which they contrive with metaphors; in other words, there seems to be a marked similarity of poetic sensibility." In this study, published three years before *Le Hussard* was released, Professor Frohock included Camus's *La Peste*. There may be also a "Mediterranean" outlook common to Giono and to Camus, one due to climate and geography, an outlook that would then also include Georges Bernanos.

[32] The reader will recall the recent article on this subject, "Gnostic Mythos in *Moby-Dick*," by Thomas Vargish in *PMLA*, LXXXI, No. 3 (June 1966), pp. 272-77.

sances qui datent de toujours" (M.D., 192). In both great
novels the problem of good and evil in the universe is studied,
like black and white, and among the powers invoked are
Jehovah and the Old Testament (H., especially 155, but also
165, 244, 276, 371). Men are sick, and from their sickness
Ishmael also escaped, as Jean-Jacques Mayoux pointed out
in his penetrating study, *Melville par lui-même*.[33] This sickness is not of the body alone, for the same *orgueil* that Giono
attributed to men dying of the plague also appears in man as
Giono translates Chapter XLI entitled "Moby Dick." Melville's original has suffered here, but he had said: "This is
much; yet Ahab's larger, darker, deeper part remains un-
hinted . . . where far beneath the fantastic towers of man's
upper earth, his root of grandeur, his whole awful essence sits
in bearded state; an antique buried beneath antiquities, and
throned on torsoes! . . . Wind ye down there, ye prouder, sad-
der souls! question that proud, sad king! . . ." (M.D., 194).
Man's fear and his solitude are clearly shown in both novels
as we recall from the famous sentence in Chapter XLII of
Moby-Dick, "La Blancheur de la Baleine": "Et bien que nom-
bre d'aspects de ce monde visible semblent être formés par
l'amour, les sphères invisibles furent forgées dans de la peur"
(203). It would seem that much more than the whiteness, indeed a view of man and of his condition in the world, is common to Melville and to Giono. The latter has in his *Pour
saluer Melville* put the words into Melville's mouth to express
what according to Giono the American novelist meant in his
books. Giono has Melville say: "I spoke about the arrogance

[33] (Bourges, 1958), p. 87. See also Katherine Allen Clarke's "*Pour
saluer Melville*, Jean Giono's Prison Book," *French Review*, xxxv, No.
5 (April 1962), pp. 478-83. She notes that Giono and Melville have in
common their fascination with the "haunting charm of the sea," the
"same conception of heroism and war," and their preoccupation with
Leviathans.

Publisher's Note

THESE ACKNOWLEDGMENTS WERE INADVERTENTLY OMITTED

Grateful acknowledgment is made to the following agents, publishers, and editors for permission to quote, translate, and reproduce copyrighted and other published material: Editions Bernard Grasset, Editions Buchet / Chastel, Editions Gallimard, La Librairie Hachette, Les Guides Bleus, *La Revue de Littérature Comparée, The French Review, The Kentucky Romance Quarterly*, and *The Romanic Review*.

The author wishes also to thank Mademoiselle Aline Giono for her assistance, counsel, and support, and also to thank the librarians of the Doheny Library, University of Southern California for their helpfulness.

Grateful acknowledgment is also made for research support to the University of Southern California.

of the gods, if you want to know; I spoke about the ravings of weak men and the bitterness of failure. The loneliness of man, that's what I spoke about . . ." (77).

What is *Moby-Dick* to Giono? It is "ce livre-refuge où le monde entier peut abriter son désespoir et son envie de persister malgré les dieux" (p.s.m., 35). Such a reference to his own personal "désespoir" throws light upon the fictional production of Giono, who might otherwise be considered untouched by any such underlying feelings. We have seen from *Le Hussard sur le toit* why man needs a refuge on this "globe terraqué," which rolls through limitless space. More than any other specific indebtedness to Herman Melville, Giono seems to have adopted from the American novelist his treatment in depth of cholera, or what Léon Cellier very aptly called in *Moby-Dick* "la superposition de sens."[34] *Le Hussard sur le toit, roman courtois* in its structure, parable in its determination to propose an explanation of life, symbolist in its means to that end, was perhaps also meant to be a "livre-refuge" to readers in the twentieth century, for Angélo's journey with Pauline was a "combat avec joie" (20) against their shared adversities. Giono's solution of life, his encouragment to the reader, his positive thinking, or his own determination and "envie de persister" are clear, as they are not clear in *Moby-Dick*.

Thus in 1934, which marks the genesis of *Le Hussard sur le toit,* Giono meditated upon the nineteenth century, even to the extent of describing a character from *Angelo* as having a "tête légèrement épique" (A., 54), just as throughout the nineteenth century authors had meditated upon the remark made

[34] Cellier said in *L'Epopée romantique* (Paris, 1954): "De nos jours, un Melville dans *Moby Dick*, un Claudel dans le *Soulier de satin*, ont admirablement montré que la superposition de sens était conciliable avec le roman ou le drame" (15).

to Voltaire by Monsieur de Malézieu: "Les Français n'ont pas la tête épique."[35] Dealing with a century that had "discovered" approximately eighty French *chansons de geste* and the epics of Europe and of the Orient, that had also popularized Villon and the *macabre*, that had struggled so valiantly to produce epics that they had rendered "oiseuse toute discussion sur la forme et la technique" of a literary work, since "tout pour un romantique est épique,"[36] Giono chose to write instead of an epic a *roman courtois*, not only because he appreciated the narrative possibilities of a medieval romance, but also because, like Victor Hugo a champion of women, he approved certain human relationships perhaps best illustrated in that type of fiction. To novelists like Hugo and Giono, both fathers of daughters, the nineteenth century with a masterpiece like *Adolphe* reached an impasse concerning the position of women. Love, in other words, is a better solution than the battle of the sexes, or than war, or heroic contests. Advertently or inadvertently, Giono gave his hero both a name and a title famous in the nineteenth century, *Angelo*, thus paying homage to Victor Hugo, who in his poetry achieved the epic and whom Giono's narrator, the Alpine physician, is fond of citing (A., 371-73).

Most of all, Giono persisted in his personal conviction evident from his earliest writings: despite man's human condition, but most especially because of man's human condition, life can be joyous. As Giono's first *raisonneur* says in *Le Hussard sur le toit*, "La mort n'est pas tout; . . ." (336).

[35] See Voltaire's *Essai sur la poésie épique*, Vol. x of the *Oeuvres complètes* (Paris, 1823).

[36] See the concluding pages (78-79) of Cellier's Chapter III, "La Théorie de l'épopée nationale."

IV   The Epic Mode

Batailles dans la montagne (1937)

Batailles dans la montagne of 1937, Giono's last novel before
the war dropped its veil of silence over France, pictures a
world torn by Heraclitean strife. Battles reach all the way to
high heaven: "Le ciel était plein de grands gestes." Water
wreaks havoc with man, sweeps over tethered horses, drowns
cattle at their stanchions, uproots forests, and undermines
earth. Glacier and river thus strike terror, before gravity
causes a multi-colored vertigo. In such elemental chaos men
easily triumph over women—frail mice fallen into vats of
dough. Youth succumbs everywhere to toughened age.

White, bearded, patriarchal, and powerful, the old hero
Boromé, like a Biblical Jacob and an epic Charlemagne, overcomes the young hero. A giant begetter with twenty-eight
women of his own, thirty-seven children, and eighty servants
or migrant farm hands, Boromé is venerated, loved, and cherished like a dying king, or like God the Father. Continuing
to inhabit and make the world habitable, he narrates his life,
i.e., his series of battles won because he knew his force and
used it, because his heart wanted to possess all, and because
he recognized himself as quasi-divine, or as heroic.

This fearsome novel ends with a fragrant peace restored
to the mountain hamlet where Boromé lies enthroned upon
piles of white lambskins, his "barbe toute fleurie" (p. 355).[1]
Released from a flood that has driven the sixty survivors to

[1] Gallimard, 71st edition.

high ground during an unseasonable warm spell in late November, the villagers celebrate their miraculous "deliverance" by lighting all their ovens and baking bread.

In *Jean-le-bleu* of five years earlier, Giono had told the unforgettable story of "The Baker's Wife,"[2] which Marcel Pagnol adapted for the celebrated film of 1938. There also the old hero or baker, so superbly portrayed by Raimu, remains victorious after a struggle with a young shepherd over the possession of a heroine Aurélie. Both Boromé and the baker, as they age, presumably accumulate money, property, and strength while the youth in either case slips away, never to be heard of again. In this second treatment Giono has stated his conclusion: the old must deal only from power: "Considering this extreme strengthlessness of the young. Ask a young man about it, and you will find that he will not think of this characteristic, this characteristic strengthlessness he has, tending rather to think of strength, as if it were attributable to himself when, first of all, strength is not an attribute of the young; and when even believing that he is strong is in itself a gross error, for youth is above all a time of strengthlessness" (321-22). Whereas Marcel Pagnol sentimentalized the famous film version, or preferred to have us believe that Aurélie happily leaped again into the loving embraces of her aged husband and the protective villagers, Giono had ended his story with the resounding triumph of all men over her, as, baking bread, they celebrated their "victoire."[3] In such a manner the new heroine of *Batailles dans la montagne* is purveyed from hand to hand, another mouse half drowned in dough.

The equally fragile young hero of *Batailles* has lost the faunlike beauty of Aurélie's shepherd for a purity far surpass-

[2] *Jean-le-bleu* (Paris, 1932), pp. 173-90.
[3] *Ibid.*, p. 190.

ing that of traditional Tristans. Incorporeal as an angel, Saint-Jean enters the novel rather late as carpenter, builder of rafts, and savior, first associated with the heroine Sarah obliquely by means of a medieval *aubade*, or the dawn song of a lark.[4] Not until Chapter X, or his ascent of the magic mountain, does the narrative pursue his frail consciousness.

Saint-Jean builds a raft strong enough, indeed, to cross hell, he says (p. 112), and poles it into the jug-shaped coomb of Sourdie. Painfully conquering this uterine valley, he re-emerges as a sexual symbol, afterwards painfully associated with sticks of dynamite, fire from heaven, torches, lightning, knives, and hypodermic needles. Evanescent and volatile, this hero tends to vanish after his several voyages over water, or up precipices, into "pureté vide" (p. 269). Afflicted with vertigo as he looks down thin air from the cliffs of Verneresse to the flooded valley below, Saint-Jean suddenly comprehends existential anguish; to know life, he says, is to know "inquiétude" (p. 285). Thus, by 1937 in *Batailles dans la montagne*, Jean Giono at last openly succumbed to the emotional climate of a decade.

Although not yet a radical departure from the popular, successful pastoral novels that, propelled by André Gide, launched the novelistic career of Giono in 1929, *Batailles*, by its admission of unrest and by its heroic determination to enter the lists committed to the defense of youth and the furtherance of the hero, tokens the growing involvement of Giono in politics. When Saint-Jean enters the grotto to steal Jove's thunderbolts, he too intends to engage upon a "new life," he says, just as *Les Vraies richesses* of 1936, from which first political work the city of Manosque rechristened the lane leading from the city perimeter up to Jean Giono's house,

---

[4] The hero is not named until p. 105 of a 362-page novel, and also called only "Jean," or the author's name, on p. 294.

launched its author into a new or political role in France. As he wrote this epic novel of 1937, Giono was largely to replace fiction with polemics for a considerable period of time, near to ten years.

Returning to an epic form different from that employed in his Odyssean *Chant du monde* (1934),[5] Giono again employs on the eve of World War II that literary form almost from time immemorial concerned with the obligations of the human male: heroism, bravery, fidelity, reputation, and self-sacrifice. It is inherent and accepted *noblesse* that *obliges* Saint-Jean, somewhat bitterly nonetheless, to undertake his heroic triple feat: hell, mountain, and flood. His aim is humanitarian, his purpose is *délivrance*, or even *délivrement* (p. 350). Like any conscript he steps forward out of the ranks, or volunteers to suffer combats, to engage in war, to administer a community, to arbitrate, to tighten and develop his male friendships, and to name a second-in-command. Furthermore, and like all epic heroes, it would seem, he suffers excess, prone to the temptations of pride, as others to ambition, treachery, greed, and all the hideous punishments that will doubtless ensue as chastisement for the violence of necessary crimes. Saint-Jean will for the sake of his fellow man bear his stigmata upon his flesh forever, for, like the French Roland, Saint-Jean also sometimes resembles Christ, or functions as a *miles Christi*.

Rather than think of himself as the Savior, however, Saint-Jean understands the meaning of a suffering leading to sainthood (p. 296). Looking up at him as he scales the precipice

---

[5] See Hallam Walker's excellent "Myth in Giono's *Le Chant du monde, Symposium*, xv (Summer 1961), pp. 139-46. His greatest compliments to Giono are publicly to have recognized and then to have praised this novelist's "deep knowledge of mythic lore and the human creature" (p. 146).

or rows across the leaden waters of death, the girl Marie is sure that he must be some kind of god (p. 296). Better informed, however, and turning towards Christianity in 1937 also, the omniscient narrator, whose voice is only one of those entrusted with this novel, calls this hero more properly one of the Lord's archangels. In fact, the poor youth might well be sculpted stone caught kneeling inside some parish church as the narrator pauses to study him: "Saint-Jean knelt down, rested his hand on the earth, then looked up at them—like this. They were standing up, still caked with clay and rigid as church pillars. There he was, on his knees, neck bent, with his constant little smile of bitterness" (p. 332).

Like many time-honored heroes of epics, Saint-Jean springs from unknown parentage, arrives upon the scene like Perceval out of the forest, where at some earlier time—a year ago or fifteen years ago—he felt for Sarah an undeclared love. This young hero is blond and yellow-eyed, his hair and moustache as bright as the jonquils that the sailors in *Fragments d'un paradis* ached to see among the blue vastnesses of ocean. He has a habit of appearing to be looking elsewhere, at some other world. So evanescent is he, so like a ray of light, that Sarah sees him usually as a bird: "It was afterwards she saw this raft, which so resembled him. Oh! It seemed entirely he, this bird's silhouette and the same inclination to swoop about Villard-l'Eglise the way it did yesterday afternoon, this same nodding acquaintance with solitude, which was the essence of him" (p. 180). If he is a man, then Saint-Jean is Giono's first hero whom one may completely love—and thus a triumph in an unheroic century.

As a prose epic in French letters, *Batailles dans la montagne* seems to derive in largest part from the theories and fiction of Chateaubriand. In the hundreds of pages of notes and justifications for *Les Martyrs*, Chateaubriand derives his

mode from the famous Biblical epics by Dante, Tasso,
Camoëns, Milton, Voltaire, Klopstock and Gessner, specifying
that if one wished, as became the case with Giono, to treat
modern man, one was obliged to defy Boileau's injunction
against "le merveilleux chrétien": ". . . puisque la religion
chrétienne est aujourd'hui la religion des peuples civilisés de
l'Europe."⁶ Following a poetic tradition practiced so nobly by
Lamartine, Vigny, and Victor Hugo,⁷ Giono borrows their
angels and their flood images, agreeing, as Lamartine pointed
out in his "Réflexions sur Milton" or preface to Chateaubriand's prose translation of *Paradise Lost*, that the Christian
religion was "la plus pathétique et la plus sublime des
poésies."⁸

Once Giono's literary conventions are recognized, his ex-
cessive lyricism becomes not only pardonable but required
and exemplary, his apologies therefore unnecessary, and his
complaints that his books were attacked without having been
"read" more understandable.⁹ One does not need to profess
Christianity or attend services regularly to be a Christian,

⁶ See the notes to *Les Martyrs* from *Oeuvres complètes de Chateaubriand* (Paris, 1826), pp. 336-601, here p. 557.

⁷ See Léon Cellier's *L'Epopée romantique* (Paris, 1954), especially
pp. 78-79: "tout pour un romantique est épique." The Biblical epic
in French poetry also includes, of course, works by Du Bellay, Ronsard,
Du Bartas, Godeau, Saint-Amand, Père Lemoine, G. de Scudéry, Cha-
pelain, Desmarets de Saint-Sorlin, Coras, Lesforgues, Louis le Laboureur,
and Sainte-Garde. In fact, Chateaubriand's apology is not unique, particularly because of two works on aesthetics by the author of *Clovis*
(1657), Desmarets himself: *Discours pour prouver que les sujets
chrétiens sont les seuls propres à la poésie héroïque* (1675), and *Dé-
fense du poème héroïque* (1674).

⁸ *John Milton. Le Paradis perdu* (Paris, 1855), p. III.

⁹ Criticism of *Batailles* is resumed by Maxwell A. Smith in his *Jean
Giono* (New York, 1966), pp. 84-87, and notes, p. 180. Unfavorable
criticism came principally from Firmin Roz, Jacques Madaule, and
Robert Brasillach, from 1937-1943.

any more than Milton himself, for ultimately Giono's Biblical epic echoes *Paradise Lost,* just as Giono's personal rebelliousness in religion as in polemic, seems close to Milton's. Chateaubriand also noted:

"Milton no longer went to church, nor any longer indicated his religious beliefs: in *Paradise Lost* he states that prayer is the only practice favored by God."[10] A reading of *Paradise Lost,* like a second look at *Batailles,* convinces one that Giono, just as Chateaubriand decided for Milton, "flottait entre mille systèmes" of religion.

It is easy to imagine Giono anguished at the immanence of another world war, expecting an angered and grief-stricken Heaven to strike man down with thunderbolts and floods, imagining man fallen and lost like Milton's Adam whom Saint-Jean resembles, thereafter the loss of a pastoral world and the fall of Eve-Sarah to the lusty Boromé. To the modern reader, nevertheless, as to Michael narrating the flood story in *Paradise Lost* (Book xi, v. 700 ff.), one pardonable and exemplary youth survives catastrophe so that the Archangel reasons against despair:

> Farr less I now lament for one whole World (v. 874)
> Of wicked Sons destroyd, then I rejoyce
> For one Man found so perfet and so just,
> That God voutsafes to raise another World
> From him, and all his anger to forget . . .
> Such Grace shall one Man find in his sight, (v. 890)
> That he relents, not to blot out mankind,
> And makes a Cov'nant never to destroy
> The Earth again by flood, . . .

[10] "Etude historique et littéraire sur Milton de Chateaubriand" in the Chateaubriand translation, p. xxiv.

As we shall see, the victory of Boromé, which concludes the Giono novel, is not necessarily final, but probably valid only for a season.

That the prose novel could by virtue of its "epical characteristics" and "epic deliberation" ponderously and deliberately treat vast problems of supreme theological importance, and continue to probe life's unsolvable mysteries, thus striking roots deep into the artist's "philosophy of life" to present his boundless hope before the blackest of evils, such a Milton scholar as Marianna Woodhull foresaw in 1908: "The time is not ripe perhaps for the elevation of the novel into a paean of triumph of a worthy hero in the spiritual warfare common to nations and to humanity. Toward the ideal of such an epic we may be moving. . . ."[11]

Giono's background—alpine peaks and dark green coombs devastated by the thaw of the Treille Glacier from its shimmering magnitude at the apex of heaven—demonstrates not only the strife presented by Heraclitus but a universe of four separate elements distinguishable, theorized Empedocles, despite their harmonies and discords. Principal agitator therein, Saint-Jean vibrates as if agent for the very hand of God, which stays just short of total destruction. As is usual throughout Giono's writing, the view of nature is vitalistic and vibrant with God. The first element to be associated with the dizzy hero is water, and, as Gaston Bachelard noted, "L'être voué à l'eau est un être en vertige."[12] Saint-Jean's assignment first is to conquer water.

The first chapters therefore deal with mud, are muddy battles as one survivor struggles up mountains of sliding mud

[11] *The Epic of Paradise Lost* (New York, 1907, 1968), pp. 5-9, 15-25, 33, 44, especially p. 81, *et alia*.
[12] *L'Eau et les rêves* (Paris, 1942), p. 9.

where trees ride down like knights at Agincourt to fall prostrate and then be buried by succeeding ranks. At his high-altitude farm of Red Oak, Boromé fights a second and losing battle against a river of mud. Through Chapter I the odor of mud is alarming before the leaden sheet of water covering four mountain villages appears to the first chief narrator, a lay preacher with the ironically outlandish name of Clément Bourrache,[13] or "Pope" Borage. Narrating throughout Chapters II and then III, as if he were to be the hero of the novel and the focus of its world view, Bourrache wades cautiously into the mysterious silence of what has become a water-filled valley.

The pet mare and her darling colt float away dead on deep water from which dead men, long frozen in glacial ice, descend with their skins of ripe wine swept ashore past icebergs. Alone between bands of cloud, above and impervious to the voices or footsteps of men, the impersonal narrator (Chapter V) describes the glacier, this touch of blue not yet worn away in sky, flashing its green ice before rolling over backwards down a black rotation. Sight here has usurped sound. A crystal rainbow becomes a solid arch of thundering water, like the beating wings overhead of a column of birds. This a lone shepherd seeking higher pastures *would have seen*, had he sat there alone under the twilight of a tarred and empty sky. There *was* the sound of water-scarred granite precipices sliding down into ravines, towns buried under a lake, ice cracking down each glacial moraine. Anguished and

---

[13] Giono's particular genius shows very clearly here again in his characteristically marvelous choice of proper names: *une bourrache* (L. *borago*; Bot. *Borago officinalis*) is a feminine noun meaning borage or herb with diuretic and sudorific properties. The plant grows wild in uncultivated areas. The root *bourr(er)* means "to cram," "to stuff," as in "to cram your head with trash."

overcome by false ceilings of cloud, "one" still *might have glimpsed* the glacier's grip over all that mankind, and its "grand geste" (p. 158) in wrath. Even as the Biblical torrent ("Ebron" = Hebron) swirls its dead freight wrathfully into the rising lake, Saint-Jean plies his raft, establishes himself as victor over leaden death, and makes manifest the air-borne nature of man, creature of air.

The concurrent theme of air also commences in Chapter I, when the adolescent shepherdess Marie, initially the narrative focus, overlooks the Villard hamlets from her high pasture. A lone bird flies across the gulf of *Verneresse*,[14] a name sufficiently frightening, like all Gionoesque universes forged in fear. The epic similes of bird especially, and of wind, and world falling set the stage for another *Paradise Lost*. Chapter II reverses the airy view by looking up at God from below: "cette Verneresse presque perpendiculaire qui, d'en bas ressemble aux jambes de dieu assis sur son trône" (p. 60). The bird-in-air image recurs at critical moments until Sarah realizes, as we have already seen, that this swift-winged marvel is Saint-Jean: "cette forme d'oiseau," possessed of "cette espèce d'aisance dans la solitude" (p. 180).

The most lavishly extended similes establishing the climate of epic wonderment accumulate about air, sky (p. 53), silence (p. 72), waterfalls (p. 83), and the dawn song of a lark (p. 152).[15] During his ascent of the precipitous face, as the gulf beneath him whirled, spotted like a peacock's tail

[14] Finding no tranquillizing etymology, one ruminates such concoctions as "verna" (L. = slave, but of unclear, perhaps Etruscan origin), pagan goddess of slaves.

[15] W. D. Redfern points out in his *Private World of Jean Giono* (Durham, 1967), and from material in Giono's *Journal* (1936-1937) that Beethoven's Fourth Symphony is to be associated with this novel, just as his Sixth lent its form to Gide's *Symphonie pastorale*.

feathers, Saint-Jean felt the powerful suction of air: "L'air du gouffre . . . tirait vers lui" (p. 277) as if hooks in his head were prying him loose from the rock.[16] In Chapter XI, after truly epic crescendo, Saint-Jean becomes, in fact, a bird in flight (p. 318 ff.). Slender-necked, with feathered wings out-stretched, so thin that he is almost transparent, he rises through air with the splendid sweep of an archangel himself. It is now his face that glows with a yellow dawn of deliverance from evil. His lightning has blown up the dam and released the flood waters, and his splendid and hallowed wings will sweep away suffering and give man his daily bread. In the paragraph following "les ailes d'archange s'ouvrirent avec un bruit de tonnerre" (pp. 330-31), Giono has written lines that truly soar with Milton's in power and glory: "(the arch-angel's wings unfurled with a roll of thunder). Pinions of flame and floating dust, bronzy, shearing, whirling water palms, tapered to a raven's featheredge; and so very blue. . . ." The "great wings of the archangel," overcoming both earth and water, unfold in blue flames.

The element of fire most characteristically reveals Saint-Jean, however, and also, doubtless, the fiery as the fundamentally oneiric temperament of Jean Giono.[17] When in 1937-1938 he wrote his first long analysis of creativity, *The Psycho-analysis of Fire*, Gaston Bachelard drew from Jean Giono's current work, *Les Vraies richesses* (1937), one of his subsequent theories of aesthetics: that intellectuality is to be equated with fire, or that fire indicates the intellectual's com-

[16] *L'Air et les songes* (Paris, 1943) by Gaston Bachelard explains this vertigo by the poet's conquest of air. The aerial spirit of the ascensional or vertical poet overcomes the demon of gravity, for example.

[17] See Mary Ann Caws' *Surrealism and the Literary Imagination* (The Hague, 1966), where she relates Bachelard to Breton, and analyzes psycho-criticism.

plex, certainly the temperament most peculiar to this poet and here to his preferred hero.[18]

After he commences the ascent of the holy mountain, shaped like the body of God with a glacial hand, the inner logic of fire and this Promethean hero begin to predominate. After his eyes are bound to prevent his going blind, Saint-Jean crosses incandescent snowfields to enter the grotto; and it was the sight of a mountain grotto that seems to have furnished Giono's initial inspiration.[19] His ritual approach led him past the face of Verneresse, metal forests of icicle, beech and fir, and across snow. The prohibitions against handling fire (dynamite) accumulate, only Saint-Jean and the maiden Marie being able to warm it, or to cradle and touch it. Both will henceforth carry its wounds on their flesh, or the virgin constitutes a fresh sacrifice. In magic cauldrons it is brewed, coddled, and heated. During the inbound journey—phase 1, or the trip across water—Saint-Jean feels sexual desire for Sarah's daughter Marie, and on the outbound trip she rows a rigid, motionless, almost dead god. Upon reaching shore, she herself falls spent and used up, as Saint-Jean corroborates. *Pyrphoros*, he is now worshipped as a god by the male community, or by those other men bold enough to thrust females aside and join the torch-bearing argonauts. Before the explosions begin, Saint-Jean and his band of heroes abstain from food. After purification ceremonies, during which significantly only the very young aspirant sleeps out his novitiate, Saint-Jean lights the hidden fire of Paracelsus for communal healing and

[18] See *La Psychanalyse du feu* (Paris, 1938) and the English translation by Alan C. M. Ross, with preface by Northrop Frye (Boston, 1964), pp. 17-18. *Batailles dans la montagne* might well have furnished Bachelard a program for his succeeding studies of air, earth, and water.

[19] See Tréménis and its grotto, from Maxwell A. Smith's *Jean Giono* (New York, 1966), p. 85.

fresh life. Thus, as archangel, he intercedes personally to fulfill the plans of God.

After having, like the lark, arisen to heaven's gate, the god-like hero falls back upon muddy earth—where the book began and will end.[20] His flight was after all only a "vol à fleur de terre" (p. 325), at very low altitude. His function as healer was earth veterinarian, cow doctor, rock emptier. The whole of life boils down to living on earth: "C'est tout simplement une question de vie sur cette terre" (p. 353). The exhausted and emaciated hero resumes his dreams of power,[21] through the realization of which he will plant his newly purchased fields, build a house painted white and surround it with a white fence, raise a family, grow grain and red and white tubers, keep the bellies of his cows and his wife filled with young, and plow deep. Before this de-poetization of the hero, the reader would gladly have dropped the book (especially after a mystery in Chapter I is resolved on the last page in a withholding technique that Giono, will develop to its highest point in *Le Bonheur fou*, 1957) except for the parting words, which again recall Marie.

After the climax in Chapter XI, Giono had closed with a short final Chapter XII called "Avec Monsieur Boromé," in which the old hero easily persuades Saint-Jean to depart without the wife he longs for, Sarah. The only remaining consciousness and presence is precisely that through whose life the novel commenced; Giono has returned full circle to Em-

---

[20] Twenty years later, Giono, probably with the anger of wounded pride and rankling reviews of the novel still fresh in his mind, called it a muddy-styled work. See his famous comment in Claudine Chonez' *Giono par lui-même* (Paris, 1956), p. 61. Giono claimed that he no longer liked the book.

[21] Gaston Bachelard's *La Terre et les rêveries de la volonté* (Paris, 1948).

pedocles and the roots of things. More basic than victory and defeat, deeper even than Giono's picture of Saint-Jean as *homo faber* with heavy feet of clay, extends a mythology concerning the twelfth part of the year, December with winter coming on, the heavy snows long overdue: house, home, slumber, undergound, and hibernation.[22]

Actually two major problems remain to haunt the reader after he has read the novel: (1) what happens to Saint-Jean and Sarah, who clearly love each other? and (2) who and what is Marie? Wrestling to understand, the puzzled reader rehearses in his mind a calculated stream of allusions to femaleness and women. The first major association, which one might have missed in Giono's very early portrayal of Arsule in *Regain* (1930), associates woman and cow or horse. Strange as it may seem, Sarah herself, placid as a cow, working like a horse as Boromé's farm hand, pulling him down the mountain from Red Oak after he has broken his leg, is seven times called his horse, not only by the narrator, but also by villagers, who resent this treatment of her—albeit not enough to protest.[23] Paralleling such textual clarifications comes the desperately poignant story of Joseph Glomore and his mare, more loving and tender than his sniveling wife.[24]

This common idea that a woman resembles a work horse or a milch cow is preached by the evangelical parson, Clément Bourrache (pp. 202-29), who tells the story of a villager named Rachel. After this story Saint-Jean speaks up to note that the preacher has "no feeling for women" (p. 254).

[22] Gaston Bachelard's *La Terre et les rêveries du repos* (Paris, 1948).

[23] Pp. 48, 97, 98, 99, 101, 244. See also p. 336, where ten women hitch themselves up and pull Boromé like horses.

[24] See p. 126, for example. In this connection Giono has committed a very strange and for him quite unusual error, by calling Joseph's weeping wife Madeleine, and then forgetting and calling her Julia (p. 304). Other lapses occur on pp. 168, 317, and 320.

Then another villager with the Protestant name of Le Pâquier defends Rachel to his fellows, and to Saint-Jean, before he accuses the parson of procuring for Boromé's use not only Rachel but also Sarah (pp. 214-26). Agreeing, the villagers resent Bourrache not only for his words but for his actions, and furthermore for refusing on religious grounds to drink wine with them.

When such associations and contrary opinions are reinforced by the bull episode and by the other references to Saint-Jean and his cows, etc., the myth of Io comes eventually to mind.[25] Searching for identity, Sarah had fled into Egypt, where even as Saint-Jean asks Boromé to release her—for the two men settle this question face to face as in *Regain*—Sarah's veil has fallen over her face and she sleeps. Like Milton's Isis, she is a fallen angel, whose veil no one dares raise. Doubtless after her winter hibernation she will in springtime be "liberated" by Saint-Jean.

Largely by her name, then, and her temporary role as companion to a patriarch, "Jacob," who wrested with the angel, Sarah also belongs to the diffuse Biblical atmosphere of this epic novel. Similarly, the story of Boromé and Rachel recalls that of Hagar fleeing into the wilderness with her son. Allusions to flood occur at the outset, referring readers to Leviathan, Jonah, the "rose" garden of Eden (p. 31), the creation, a vengeful God (p. 175),[26] a cruel world (p. 225), and hark-

[25] Io belongs in the Prometheus legend according to Aeschylus, and otherwise her story is well told by Ovid in the *Metamorphoses*, I, v. 700 ff.

[26] It is very curious to compare Zola's "Hiver" from *Les Quatre journées de Jean Gourdon* (1866-1867) as he writes about a January flood of Giono's home river, the Durance. In this whining first-person account, the river becomes personified as a murderous female beast, like the medieval *guivre* or Grendel. Even more rewarding is a comparison of Giono and Faulkner, for the "Old Man" sequence from *The Wild Palms*, seeming to date from 1939, recalls the terrible 1927

ing back to the atmosphere of Chapter I, which restates Psalm 104. In his Preface to *Paradis perdu* Chateaubriand had also pointed out that the river descending from the throne of God, like Giono's Ebron from Verneresse, derives from Apocalypse (22:4): "And shows me the river of the water of life, shining like crystal, proceeding from the seat of God and the Lamb."[27]

Like Chateaubriand, Giono seems to have felt that angelology was "une des doctrines les plus belles, les plus consolantes, les plus *poétiques* du christianisme" (p. 564), and to have concurred that angels "are invisible friends whom God has sent us for our protection and our consolation here below."[28] According to Lamartine also, such an angel as Ithuriel functions as a heavenly guide and personal guardian, similar to a bird, "comme un aigle immense" with "ailes de feu." God also resembles a mountain—and in an epic:

> "The universe stands whole in the hollow of His hand;
> And life flowing forth eternal from His breast,
> Like rivers fed forever by a spring's enormous flow,
> Now departs and now returns to end where it begins."[29]

Various elements in Giono existed but very differently in Alfred de Vigny's *Le Déluge*: Pyrenees, Sara, the angel, the fall from innocence, the Protestant minister. The angel Saint-Jean does not particularly resemble any one of the four archangels of Judeo-Christian tradition, and yet, like Michael, he con-

---

floods in the United States. Here the approach of the waters, the river, the dynamite, adventures in a boat (raft), and the return to a *status quo*, the woman being consigned to limbo, to some degree resemble *Batailles*. In fact, when Maxwell A. Smith refers to Villard-l'Eglise as the "ark," he may also have been recalling Faulkner's Indian mound.

[27] *Op.cit.*, p. 44.   [28] *Idem*, p. 565 (my translation).

[29] "L'Ange. Fragment épique" (c. 1818-1819) from *Oeuvres poétiques complètes*, ed. M.-F. Guyard (Paris, 1963), pp. 72, 149, 151, 543.

quers a terrible monster; like Gabriel, he heralds the approach of winter; like Raphael, he is a healer; and like Uriel, he brings light. It is also true that Saint John the Divine appeared in *Paradiso* xxv as a bright light.

During the course of the novel, Saint-Jean functions very much like Milton's angels, or as ". . . rational agents above man and beneath God, who out of obedience or revolt or innate impulse invisibly controlled the events God left to them."[30] As in Milton, and also in Jean Calvin, an angel remains noble, capable of passing from being to non-being, but exalted mightily above men in his power. Although he may be represented—and Chateaubriand had traced Milton's representations to Italian painting, much as we seem to have found Giono's in church sculpture—outwardly as a man, he still should seem to strive for the entirely spiritual, or the "pureté vide" of Giono. As angels make love in Milton, so Saint-Jean feels love for Sarah and desire for Marie. According to angelological thinking as found in patristic and scholastic theology, Saint-Jean exists; he descends from the mountain in the flesh, "truly present in time and space to man's senses," and yet frail, tenuous, and quasi-immaterial.[31] Thus, the Puritan compromise of Milton is maintained.

We know from the outset that our major characters—and we may perhaps assume the same for the others—are not Catholics but "mountain Protestants," although the narrator suggests that distinctions between these two Christian persuasions be abolished as far as this story is concerned. Critics have been scandalized that Sarah reads the Bible aloud to her daughter in the evening, just previous to joining Boromé, who is her common-law husband, in his bed. Like any devout

[30] See Robert H. West's *Milton and the Angels* (Athens, Ga., 1955), p. 6 *et passim*.
[31] *Ibid.*, p. 137.

Protestant woman, however, Sarah draws from the Bible both strength and comfort, while doubtless not expecting it to change either the world or her role in society. Saint-Jean formally requests the ordained Protestant minister to marry Sarah and him.

What has puzzled and angered critics in this novel is the very successful portrayal of the deputized parson, Clément Bourrache. Apparently exorcized, W. D. Redfern had this to say in 1967: ". . . Bourrache . . . suffer(s) from a fixation on woe. Bourrache is a prurient prude, and foul-mouthed Bible-puncher; he speaks in a bizarre mixture of slang and wildly apocalyptic extravaganzas both for and against God."[32] What seems to occur in the novel is Giono's apprenticeship in the art of that persistent satire which will so clearly separate his postwar masterpieces from the early novels, with their paeans of praise for man and nature in sweet concord. Thus, like any uneducated lay preacher dependent upon Scripture for his chief source of inspiration and doctrine, and having assimilated it until he speaks or, as he says, "weeps on the summits" (p. 47), Bourrache thunders like an Old Testament prophet hauling man before the bar of God's judgment. His parable of God, the dough, and the angels has its basis in the Old and New Testaments, where people are both grass and bread, chaff on a summer threshing floor, threshed in wrath, and gathered like wheat.[33] When Reverend Mr. Charmoz asked him to preach to the people every day but Tuesday, or on the days when the ordained minister could not come to the hamlets, Bourrache at length admitted his unworthiness (p. 209).

Despite his own additions to Scripture, Bourrache is not al-

[32] *Op.cit.*, note 15, p. 114.
[33] Daniel 2:35; Matthew 3:12 and 13:33; Isaiah 21:10, 40:6, and 41:15; Jeremiah 51:33; Micah 4:13; Habakkuk 3:12; Numbers 14:19, for example.

ways ignorant, harsh to women, critical of morality, or stern and unfeeling. He fears God, whom he visualizes as an inscrutably mysterious warrior. When night falls and he stumbles into the flooded valley, he imagines himself lost among angels, the very word setting him off into incoherence, or poetry: "With angels, he said, who have wings that ripple like foliage in a forest and swords that glow like ripened wheat . . . But on his tongue welled a juice in which his words were drowned" (p. 93). Because he is ridiculous and unpopular, however, Bourrache is not chosen to be the hero, although he is allowed by the argonauts to join them in their torchlit procession across the flood.

Giono is ironic, doubtless, and, even worse, subversive, not only in his treatment of Bourrache, where he allows such profanations of the Bible and goes even so far as to permit this preacher to confuse Scripture with *Salammbô*,[34] but also subversive in his attempt to eliminate divisions within Christianity. As Jean Giono pointed out in conversation, however, he dealt in his fiction generally with Provence, aware that east of the Rhône lay this ancient Cisjurane Burgundy, and Holy Roman Empire. Thus, to recall that religious freedom was granted the schismatic Waldenses in 1848 and that modern Provence includes descendants of the twelfth-century Vaudois only refers the reader back again to the un-French names of our characters and to John Milton's defense of French Protestants. Protestantism, which Giono had good reason to know personally, stays very much alive in Provence today.

Batailles dans la montagne, while not committing its author to any religious creed or specific doctrine, does conform by the words and actions of its characters to certain tenets of

---

[34] "Il récitait à haute voix les histoires d'un pays où des cadavres de lions pourrissaient entre les vignes. . . ." (p. 326)

Protestantism: liberty in secular and religious matters, the authority of private judgment, the responsibility of the individual to God alone, religious toleration, a refusal of ceremonialism, the preference for simple ritual (a simple villager named Marie Dur volunteers to conduct a funeral service herself, if worse comes to worst), freedom of ministry, and fondness for the letter of the Bible as for Biblical exegesis. The Protestant characters in the novel seem quite at home in the high Alps near Villard with its foreign name, or in a Provence, which was, in point of fact, German before it became French.

The archangel Saint-Jean himself, it must be said in Giono's defense, is treated seriously and without intentional profanation or irony. Weary from ferrying souls across black water, he leans against a tree, listening incredulously to a lark celebrate this sorry, flooded dawn as joyously as any happier one. Was man really nothing at all on earth? he asks himself. Did free will not exist, or man's will? Had the world no sensitivity ("répondances") towards man? Meanwhile the bird continues to sing, until Saint-Jean understands: the lark extols love! With such tender scenes of great feeling before his mind, the reader may perhaps pardon Giono's anarchical bents. The lyrical passages of *Batailles dans la montagne* often seem undistinguishable from prayer, as the youth, i.e., the fragility of this sacrificial hero, strives to slip skyward from the bondage of flesh.

During his working hours in his study at Manosque, Jean Giono could raise his eyes from his table and see between him and the western window his statue of Saint George, he will inform us in *Noé*; as we shall see, Saint George will also, like Saint John, play an important part in Giono's fiction. In any case, prayers and Christian saints have always appeared in French epics, particularly those of the Middle Ages; one group celebrated the heroes of Orange and Narbonne: Saint Michael, Saint George, Saint Mercure, Saint Gabriel, and Saint Domistre.[35] Angels also function in the old French *chansons de geste,* where they are particularly attached to Charlemagne as to lesser heroes.[36] Such great poets seem to have bequeathed to Giono their belief in prayer, or in the efficacy of words and sermons, plus their demonstrations of an ascensional order rising from beasts through man, heroes, saints, and angels to God himself. The wonder of man, a creature so splendid that were the whole world joined against him and all other men, plus the uttermost blacknesses of sky, still one man's heart would pierce such difficulties like a hot knife, always being retempered, through snow. This is Boromé's conclusion at the end of his "Life Is a Battle" tirade (pp. 250-52): "Were the entire world to set to it, the entire world and every person in it, plus the darkest parcels of sky, the heart of man would still slice through all that like a red-hot blade through snow."

While Chapter V, "Le Glacier," contains perhaps the longest and most highly developed images of ice, sky, forests, waterfalls, crowned moon, and the play of living light and living shadow, it is rivalled by Chapter X, in Saint-Jean's ascent with Marie of the midnight forests, where magic doors open before their knock until they approach God, or finally emerge into the unendurable glare of cliff and snowfields. Conscious that the epic requires not only surpassing lyrical power from its poet but also a brilliant display of rhetoric, Giono describes the source of the Ebron, for example, by means of

[35] These appear in the *Chanson de Roland* and/or in *Aspremont,* for example.

[36] See Adolphe J. Dickman's *Le Rôle du surnaturel dans les chansons de geste* (Paris, 1926). The author counts 22 *chansons* in which angels figure.

a splendid *accumulatio*. The water trickled from the glacier, seeking channels through granite:

"It finds them, enters, pierces, splits, pushes, strikes, retreats, like the blood beating in a man's wrist, propels, splits, crushes, pierces, descends, remounts, twists, expands, bifurcates like the branches of an oak, twists, luffs, expands, ties knots, constructs a honeycomb, cracks open the cliff of Muzelliers, leaps into space like a crystalline arch" (p. 165).

Such staccato groupings of sibilants dramatize the force of water until it leaps in the last free transitive phrase down its waterfall in a manner that such other anthropomorphizing novelists as Balzac, Hugo, and their master Rabelais would recognize as the French language displayed to perfection. Nevertheless, the entire book strains towards the swift explosions of dynamite set off by Saint-Jean as his argonauts watch him from below; in that passage (p. 328 ff.) he becomes openly at last the archangel whose magnificent wide-sweeping wings "vont battre et emporter le malheur de tous au delà du ciel" (p. 329).

After many such frightening passages of explosion, vertigo upon precipices, darkness and swirling flood water, mountains sliding downhill, the mad bull running amok, and the dangers associated with all such cataclysms and perils, the novel ends with Saint-Jean looking in through a window at Sarah, and then seeing her last through the other veil of sleep. Softly he retires, taking summer with him, allowing King Winter to rule by virtue of his cold age, white curls, fur robes, while his adoring villagers rest indoors near their warm ovens. Summer's golden god had run after Sarah too late, had overstayed his term, must yield to crabbèd age. This contention between Summer and Winter underlies the novel, reaching back at least to such a medieval *tenson* as the famous Vergilian verses that Alcuin may have written for

Charlemagne at Tours, "Conflictus veris ac hiemis." Giono has only mistaken lark for cuckoo.

In a long series of metaphors, which proclaim Giono as a master of the stream of consciousness, Marie in Chapter I presents, as if in a dream such as generally prefigures the action of medieval fiction, the plan of the novel, its major themes, and its underlying mythology of the seasons. Here she explains cosmic and human strife (*batailles*), summer as represented by a rose garden blooming at winter's gate, the story of the dying mouse that she lifted from the vat of dough, the future forays of the bull enraged because of the flood, and her vision of a beautiful hero more powerful than death (pp. 30-36). It is she who first recognizes the dangers of mud and the fear of her flock of sheep. It is also she who remains standing outside Boromé's door, beyond his beam of lamplight, as Saint-Jean fades away into darkness.

In terms of the epic mode, the problem of Marie admits of further hypothetical solution. We need in actual fact know nothing about her origins, and Giono's condescensions—that she is Sarah's daughter, and fatherless, and that she is a pleasing virgin well into sexual maturity—probably suffice. As we see, she has by her dream prefigured the entire epic during the course of which she, as a fictional character, accompanied Saint-Jean and shared his problems while keeping her own counsel. Refusing everywhere an unequal role, she proves herself feminine, or less strong physically than the hero. The depth, duration, and scope of her consciousness, however, surpass that of any other character except the omniscient narrator's and her determination extends even beyond murder in her own defense. Hurling herself into the situation, she takes command and insists upon equality. Thinking, planning, watching, and dreaming, however, she usually remains above the action, overlooking the valley from above Red Oak, for example, or again acting as a queen when with the refugees at Villard-l'Eglise. In the final words as in the opening sentences only she and the author seem present.

It seems Giono the author who draws his material from Marie, rather than the other way about. It is Marie who enjoys the author's respect, as she lends him her eyes. His opening and closing words are by way of the invocation, prayer, and the farewell, traditional in epic poetry. Jean Giono henceforth will portray creation and his own creative and fabulatory function as a feminine being such as Marie and Julie. Marie is his personal Muse, or *anima*.

Deux cavaliers de l'orage (1965)

It seems possible to state without reservation that as a novelist Giono was interested in the abstraction of epic to the degree that from the publication in 1934 of *Le Chant du monde* to *Deux cavaliers de l'orage*,[1] published in one volume in 1965, he three times shaped and modeled epic material.[2] The more recent work in the epic mode reverses the pattern of *Batailles dans la montagne* by disclaiming an *anima naturaliter christiana*, as Tertullian termed it, proffering at

[1] Although the novel appeared in its present form in the Gallimard edition of 1965, to which our page references here will refer, its Chapter I was published in the *NRF* (December 1940), and it appeared serially between December 3, 1942, and March 18, 1943, in what Odile de Pomerai called "the notorious collaborationist paper of Alphonse de Chateaubriant" (*French Review*, Vol. 39, No. 1, October, 1965, p. 81). Giono's epic novels are, thus, less separated than originally appeared, covering almost in direct sequence the years 1934, 1937, 1940, 1942-1943. Having stated reservations, however, we leave for later treatment the one intervening novel: *Que ma joie demeure* (1935).

[2] Odile de Pomerai states unreservedly (p. 82): "This violent epic is of the same strain as *Batailles dans la montagne* and *Que ma joie demeure*. It has the same 'outsize' kind of subject. . . ."

best the words of Mark (9:23): "I do believe; Lord, help my unbelief!"

While not necessarily flaunting a world of men without women, as epics often do, *Deux cavaliers de l'orage* still follows what recalls Greek legends of their Older Heroes. The prose unfolds stark, denuded, and unharmonic, stripped of feminine lyricism, or softening, and virtually lacking in refined sensitivity. The real violence of being alive as a human being, of a physical body that, pierced or sliced, will noisily spurt blood and present its owner with grisly death, plus all the forms of savage violence to which a primitive society looks up in admiration have replaced Saint-Jean's wistful tendernesses. These later heroes prize physical prowess as in hard muscles, worship those most skilled in wrestling, horsemanship, wild yellings along the forest paths in the black of night. Who has not witnessed such men?

These heroes are warriors buffeted by cyclonic storms over stricken mountain passes, cast in the bronze of arrogance, striving for reputations of bloody daring, boldness, blows, and wiles. To them, life is a joyous contest of grunting strength, a warfare of men and horses and such largess as silver spurs and silk-tasseled crops. Aged and youthful, the chiefest of them are like certain primitive Greek heroes, male twins.

Deux cavaliers de l'orage begins by establishing in Chapter I, sometimes published separately as the "Histoire des Jason," an incredible genealogy, from an executioner named Jason, who set up his guillotine around 1893 in the High Country, through his son, who wandered for nine years until he wed, not Medea, but a giantess named most fantastically Ariane du Pavon. The bride's home farm boasted fifty peacocks. The Brunhilde-type maiden resisted, wrestled, and boxed her husband with arms, breasts, and thighs of iron. Able to do the hard labor of three big men and two mules, Ariane also vies with her groom in epic taunts, boastings, or "gabs." Three massive contests and three sons later, the pair own a mountain stronghold and engage in smuggling. After losing her husband and one son in World War I, Ariane remains the venerable widow of the isolated fastness as the story proper begins.

After having enjoyed himself immensely, much as Rabelais when creating Grandgousier and Gargamelle laughed hugely in mock-epic fashion, Giono quietens down to introduce his heroes in more sober guise, the "twin" or surviving sons of Ariane. At age twenty-six, young Jason rivals a bear in strength and a wolf in cunning, heavy and massive, weighing his two hundred pounds. His angelic youngest brother, whose name is Ange, but who is called "My Junior" ("Mon Cadet"), is then a blond child of seven. Chapter II begins the brothers' adventures from ages thirty-five and sixteen as horsemen together they set forth from High Country and Low Country, where speed, daring, and size are all second only to masculine pride.

The older hero and central character of Giono's pagan epic is Marceau Jason, called "Stud" ("l'Entier")—black curls, hairy body, a master of a man as horse trader, mule skinner, and father of five. The fact that Giono as super-narrator disassociates himself from Stud's admirers appears only through such slight indications as the varying colors of this hero's eyes —never the blue that Giono associates with creativity, but rather either gray (p. 39), small brown (p. 45), or little and acid-colored (p. 49).

"Stud" Jason is dominated by one overpowering passion, his physical love for "My Junior," whom he lifts tenderly to his first horse, whom he bathes with loving fingers, whose body he caresses admiringly, with whom he proudly rides, and whom he cherishes beyond the point of adulation. Jason's unnatural terror that he will at some time fail to protect Ange haunts him as much as his frantic desire to *give* the lad everything at every moment. This problem of wanting overwhelmingly to *give* to others had already been developed by Giono into those monsters of benefaction, M. and Mme Numance in *Les Ames fortes* (1949). There, the pregnant waif and barmaid Thérèse, upon whom the besotted elderly couple lavish their entire remaining fortune, kills not only them but presumably also her own husband. Even without such an example from Giono as a guide, however, the reader will by virtue of his own acute discomfort guess that Ange must either deliver himself one day from Jason or really succumb to suffocation, or worse.

Fine distinctions have been carefully drawn here by Giono to separate *Deux cavaliers de l'orage* from a tragic mode; for whatever pity the reader may instinctively wish to bestow upon Jason arises so mixed with repulsion and cold curiosity that he is content to watch the black-clad chorus weep as women may have keened circling Beowulf's funeral pyre on Hronesnesse. After passages recounting several mad gallops of Jason and Ange, the narrator informs us that their expeditions are hell-bent, as it were: "courses farouches à tombeau ouvert" (p. 44). Death and, whenever possible, magnificent funeral ceremonies by way of communal expiation usually reward the epic hero for his pains. This an old woman understands as, not even accusing the Christian God, who is apparently unknown to her, she indicts the author/creator of men: "Celui qui a mis deux hommes sur la terre s'est trompé" (pp. 70-71). At any moment, she adds, one of them is apt to find the other superfluous. If the twain meets, in other words, contrary to Rudyard Kipling, murder results.

Sharing the explanatory burden with Jason towards the

165

end of the terribly dramatic climax of Chapter III, "Les courses de Lachau" (p. 114 ff.), the narrator drives home his philosophy of man's nature. It is compounded of blood and domination, the physical violence of blood pounding through flesh, supervised by the head with its lightning thrust for power. The brain set on fire burns for the pleasure of killing; incendiarism delights the brain, and that, says Jason, is the sad truth (p. 115), because fire lights as it enlightens. Similarly, friendship delights the body—hearts, bowels, bellies, hands, feet.

Thus, the male friendships that rule the world serve to delight the flesh. Bending down, Jason drops on the kitchen floor over one hundred pounds of bleeding flesh wrapped in sacking. "Arrive le ruisseau de sang," comments the narrator, who has known since *Le Grand troupeau*, as we have seen, that the world is crazy for blood. The spilling of blood is our greatest theatrical event, he continues (p. 117 ff.), certainly attracting record attendance. Heroic players lavishly spill their own demonic blood and that of others indiscriminately: "Veterans of all the adventures here below. Men marked by the wind and the rain of this country to become its legends. Night riders, owners of the shadows under the chestnut trees, always ready to leap to the saddle at the first call of the open spaces, at the hour when a mellowness of the seasons unleashes demons in the hearts of solitary men" (p. 182). In the narrator's considered conclusion, such heroes leap to battle at the summons of their coursing blood, which is itself regulated by wind, rain, and, ironically, the "tenderness" of spring, for instance. Therefore the novel's title: the twin horsemen of the storm.

This third clearly heroic novel refers by its depiction of soldiery and combat to *Batailles dans la montagne*, in which struggles and contests commence in the hereditary times

when Ariane fought thrice and boasted three times. In her
deed of the three-gallon jug (p. 17) she also like Saint-Jean
before her vanquishes gendarmes. Stud Jason performs
a vastly more significant feat, however, by hoodwinking the
French army and delivering Ange from military service
(p. 35). During the races at Lachau, or central episode, he
slays the beast with one blow on its forehead. Chapter IV
commences the several grisly wrestling bouts, Jason against
such champions as Clef-des-Coeurs (p. 131 ff.) and Le Flam-
boyant (p. 171 ff.), which will terminate in the completely
hideous contests between himself and his brother Ange. In
order to prolong the reader's agony, Giono inserts other contests, such as Jason against diphtheria and Ange against the
flood waters and felled tree pinning Jason to the ground; in
fact, the last most awful contest occurs only in retrospect. To
have portrayed the final flesh-rending struggle to the death
between Jason and Ange, probably even Giono, aroused to
terrible wrath at mankind, found too strong for his stomach.
After the two practice bouts, first in the moonlit forest and
second on the threshing floor, Ange wins for the first time.

When one recalls the multiple allusions to Ange and the
symbols that accumulate about him page after page, one realizes after reflection that he and not Jason comes closer to being the author's choice. Throughout this novel, fire represents
Ange, because of his blond beauty, but also due to his fierce
powers of attraction, suction, seduction. Here again, however,
Giono himself seems troubled because he saw at first the eyes
of Ange as sharp black (p. 21), only to discover later that a
gentian blue shone off their tar-colored irises. How very terrible, Giono seems to feel (p. 42), when such eyes, so divinely
able to see, should be used to kill a poor blind animal in sport.
Jason had given Ange a whip with a leather tip as supple as
an adder, and he wore it habitually about him: "He was so

expert at handling it that one morning he killed a little badger, with one stroke of this leather thong, as it was trying blindly to disentangle itself from the early morning mists" (p. 42). Impassively the narrator about-faces to discuss the lovely, expensive, plaid saddle blanket that Jason also gave Ange, thus squelching the reader's reaction of sympathy for the badger; his surprise as Ange is revealed here for the first time in his true colors—and perhaps for the only time in the course of the novel—as the bloody killer he will become when grown to full manhood, i.e., adult heroism.

Handsome as a virile Greek hero, lavish in his giving of gifts as a medieval sovereign, golden as a pagan god, stiff as an emperor, Ange struts like a peacock or lounges as lasciviously as a dormouse sunning itself in summer. While still a youth his tiny muscles clung birdlike to slender ribs. Golden cockerel under a shimmering crown of oak leaves, he shone: "His blond locks smouldered about his head like a golden crested helmet; an oak tree's boughs, inlaid with liquid moonlight, formed his feathers" (p. 196). First in his heart surged, not love, but pride in his skills as horseman and reveller, as fierce tamer of mules and horses, and, finally, as champion athlete and champion wrestler over Jason, himself champion over all contenders. His revenge, because premeditated over a decade of silence, will fall from an even more devilish boot than from the unreflective, simply brutal savagery of Jason.

The twin heroes ride back and forth from the High Country during an unusually expanded period of time, the whole novel making the strangest use of duration, from 1893 to 1902-1903, to 1918, thence to Ange's military service in Briançon[3]—an event that coincides with Giono's own biography—and a year later to the horse races at Lachau, and the

[3] See Giono's own induction as recalled in his *Voyage en Italie* (Paris, 1953), Part I, pp. 15-17.

principal storm of the novel on a last Friday in October. During the last five chapters no years are mentioned, but the seasons delimit the action through the second storm of Chapter VI. In Chapter VII suddenly, in only twenty-four pages, Giono speeds through a summer season,[4] a rainy autumn of flood and mud, followed by the winter the story ends in Chapter VIII.

This relativity of time, either extended drowsily over long decades or compressed into a few pages, seems to represent Ange's life, of which childhood from his point of view passed so slowly, but which, once Ange awakened, plunged rapidly into the season of death. From his angle, the novel represents an *Entwickelnsroman* as Jason in true Spartan fashion labors to transform Ange into an athlete and wild mountain horseman.

Jason's role consists of prying Ange loose from one interior or another, such as first from the womb and shelter of his ancestress Ariane. Striding even into the bedroom where the newlyweds lie abed, Jason draws Ange from his wife's embrace, cheerfully offering to build for the abandoned Esther a fire on the hearth in her husband's place. Allowing Ange an allotted time with city prostitutes, Jason personally fetches him thence, just as he saves him from being swallowed by the armed services. Jason even cuts the cord between Ange and admiring ladies purchasing mules, and even from Esther's brother.

In educating "My Junior," Jason seems in sternly draconian fashion to be drawing the youth from various insides out into exteriorities, as if manhood occurred on some periphery beyond the calm wombs and darknesses of interiors. Reluctantly always, Ange languorously leaves bed and beautiful wife

---

[4] Granted such a season is very short, lasting only one month in the High Country, says Giono in *Ennemonde* (1968), p. 47.

to join a world of athletes and night riders, a world of beasts, brutes, contests, drinking, low company, and carousings. Therefore once Ange stands firm and fights Jason, he finds such peace in the hope of freedom that he destroys what has robbed him heretofore of tranquillity, or he castrates "Stud" Jason, the latter in return destroying Ange's interiority, or cutting open his abdominal cavity and releasing his insides. Ange has been irretrievably lost from his first crime—the death of the badger accomplished as and because Jason so wished.

The coaxing of "My Junior" from his warm, firelit interiors into such cold desolations as stormy forests and flooded uplands figures only one opposition among those erected by the movement and structure of this novel. Other antinomies— town vs. country, mountain vs. plain, storm vs. peace, male vs. female, child vs. man, interiority and femininity vs. exteriority and masculinity—characterize Giono's latter epic. Despite its many horrors, the novel haunts the reader because of its apparently chaotic but in actuality very careful composition, and even because of its dynamic atmosphere of tension and heroism, all the "splendour," as D. H. Lawrence said, for which the human heart thirsts.[5]

While agreeing in 1965 that *Deux cavaliers de l'orage* constituted an epic, François Nourissier found no resemblance between the "giant" Jason and the Greek argonaut and searcher for the Golden Fleece.[6] However, on second thought, the two Jasons have, in addition to their elemental savagery, certain traits in common, both born into accursed lives of some antiquity. Both die wandering and wretched deaths as befits men only slightly removed from centaurs,

---

[5] See *Apocalypse* of 1931 (New York, 1966), p. 31.
[6] "*Deux cavaliers de l'orage*, roman de Jean Giono," *Les Nouvelles Littéraires* (Nov. 25, 1965), No. 1,995.

bears, wolves, and boars. Both appear convincingly with masses of black curls, with huge muscles, and noble or "ducal" (Jason) mien. Both wrestle with heroes of great renown and travel extensively with many boon companions. Perhaps also, in Giono's transcription, Ange represents the treasured Golden Fleece.

Very celebrated inseparables, who specifically feasted upon meat to increase their physical force, or athlete-gods, one of whose altars stood at Olympia near the starting gate of the horse races and whose temples graced the ancient Mediterranean as far west as Marseilles, were the Spartan Tyndarids, Attic Dioskouroi, or Roman Castor and Pollux. "So deep was the impression of these ideal figures upon the soul of pre-Christian paganism," said Lewis Richard Farnell, "that they were able in some measure to survive its downfall."[7] Descended perhaps originally in the pre-Dorian era from the Achaean royal family of Sparta, these heroes of dual nature, celestial and chthonian, appear to recur anew in Ange and Jason. Riders on white horses, condemned to spend their lives alternately, as do our brothers, in the High Country (Olympus) and the Low Country (Lachau = Hades), these tutelary gods originate, if classical scholars have read Homer and Pindar correctly, from an aniconic period of primitive fetichism.[8] At Rome first the Dioscuri were patrons of the *equites* or *chevaliers*.

Ange and Jason seem incarnations of these great twin brethren, who were actually siblings rather than twins, Castor a mortal son of Tyndareus, and Pollux divine because sired by Jove. As Tyndaridae they received in antiquity

[7] *Greek Hero Cults and Ideas of Immortality* (Oxford, 1921), Chapter VIII, p. 228.

[8] The Dioscuri are often compared with Sanskrit twins (Açvins, or Aśvins), Amphion and Zethus of Thebes, the Phrygian cabiri of Samothrace, the Gemini, etc.

heroic honors, while as Dioscuri they were paid divine tribute, the one returning to earth while the other (Jason) departed into the snowy heights alone. Ange represents the
golden-helmeted horse tamer Castor, never able to rise beyond his own mortality; Jason is the quasi-divine pugilist
Pollux.

In his highly imaginative *Apocalypse,* D. H. Lawrence likewise dreamed of these Twins as belonging "to a very old cult
which apparently was common to all ancient European peoples; but . . . heavenly twins, belonging to the sky." He saw
them further as the two witnesses in Revelation, or as "the
olive trees of the underworld," perhaps also as the French
scholars visualize their epic heroes, Roland and Olivier:
"They were often panthers, leopards, gryphons, earth and
night creatures, jealous ones. . . . In the same way they are the
secret lords of sex, for it was early recognized that sex is a
holding of two things asunder, that birth may come through
between them."[9] Lawrence further saw that such twin heroes
were mounted on fiery steeds pounding and laughing through
the storms like powerful centaurs celebrated in southern
France by such a medieval epic as *La Mort Aymeri de Narbonne*: "How the horse dominated the mind of the early
races, especially of the Mediterranean! You were a lord if you
had a horse. Far back, far back in our dark soul the horse
prances. He is a dominant symbol: he gives us lordship: he
links us, the first palpable and throbbing link with the ruddy-
glowing Almighty of potence: he is the beginning even of our
godhead in the flesh. As a symbol he roams the dark underworld meadows of the soul."[10] Are not his death blow to the
horse, and the feasting on the fabulous race horse, signs that

[9] D. H. Lawrence's *Apocalypse,* pp. 126, 129.

[10] *Ibid.,* pp. 97-98. See also "Angel Horses" and Lord Macaulay's
verses on the Dioscuri in M. Oldfield Howey's *The Horse in Magic
and Myth* (New York, 1958), pp. 24-25.

Jason must soon leave his earthly godhead and stagger alone up the trackless snowy summit, where, agonized, he will eventually win through to his heavenly father?

The dying hero proceeds from his ancestral home up this magical, snowy, and unexplored mountain, where the villagers will find him dead. All other journeys, whether to the induction center at Briançon or to Lachau, the circular hell in the Low Country, start from and return to the castle hamlet, or "ancien château paysan" (p. 113). The fortune-teller Delphine recounts to the heroes' wives two nighttime descents into the "red" city of the plain, while Jason's wife Valérie narrates her daytime trip there when, lost from her new husband, she danced with the amorous stranger. The women marvel at this city, which by its color and its Porte Saulnerie strongly resembles Giono's Manosque. It is a city of the combats common to a mercantile civilization, and alien to the High Country, a place of desired encounters, a battleground where such as drunken harvesters once a year quarrel and destroy in their haste to squander their season's wages.

The Jason "castle," with its walls so thick that entire staircases and landings wind comfortably within their black thicknesses, perches on a mountainside high above coombs of bronze and bronze forests assaulted by icy blasts (p. 39). Devilishly savage, it haughtily breasts the worst winds, summoning its wildly heroic sons back to their lair: "Revoir les forêts sombres et le froid bien-aimé de leur terre sous le vent" (p. 38). Without *Ennemonde et autres caractères* (1969) one could not place precisely this fictional *Haut Pays*, or High Country.

In an accompanying statement printed on the fly-leaf of *Ennemonde*, Giono points out that the wrestler "Clé-des-coeurs[11] avait passé furtivement à travers les *Deux Cavaliers*

---

[11] Spelled *Clef-des-Coeurs* in *Deux cavaliers*.

de l'orage," and, in fact, his editorial note printed on the earlier novel announces the later *Ennemonde.*[12] Although Giono said that *Ennemonde* resulted from or continued the earlier novel—i.e., that the two were originally two, not one—a reader may feel that a reediting or fusion of the two texts in some Faulknerian manner of alternation would result in one epic novel far superior to either text as presently separate.

In Part I of the 1969 novel, the Ennemonde story begins: "Les routes font prudemment le tour du Haut Pays"[13] itself characterized by "le vent, le froid, la neige, la solitude, la peur . . . la peur endémique" (E., 23) on the parts of its more unheroic inhabitants. Thus, at once, the same High Country traversed so often along two of its transverse routes by Jason and Ange now receives direct attention, the latter work being called "cette Histoire et Geógraphie du Haut Pays" (E., 32), underneath which there lies "plus aucune image de civilisation." This addition or elaboration of historical and geographical material, particularly when it is largely mythological, as here, enhances and authenticates the epic feeling of *Deux cavaliers.*

Ennemonde situates the High Country as extending between Mt. Ventoux on the west and the Lure chain on the east,[14] bounded on the north by the high pass called Croix de l'Homme Mort, and on the south by the town of Séderon. Or, we are picturing the actual 15-to-20-kilometer distance north-south between Jabron Valley and main highway number 100, and a 60-kilometer distance east-west from the valley separating Ventoux and Lure to Sisteron, the fantastically picturesque gateway to the Durance River valley. In this area, says

[12] Capitalized "Deux cavaliers de l'orage" on its fly-leaf.
[13] Page numbers in *Ennemonde* (Paris, 1969) will appear henceforth as here: E, p. 9.
[14] 6,273 and 5,994 feet in altitude respectively.

Ennemonde, there are two towns,[15] two villages,[16] six hamlets of less than twenty persons each, and approximately fifty farms. One of these towns may be entered by the Soubeyran Gate,[17] also like the city of Manosque.

The High Country from some distance appears as a white crest between Mt. Embrun and Queyras (E., 38), or when seen in the far distance from Sainte-Baume as a small white triangle set on the northern range. It is always white in any case, repeats Giono, more so in summer even than in winter (E., 39). These sparsely settled regions contain people who cordially hate each other and also generally frequent each other, as we realize from the twinship of Ange and Jason. All men feel to some degree an existential anguish, specifies Giono, even when, as he still believes, they stem from an essence preceding their existence (E., 139): "Ils remplacent les angoisses de la civilisation par les angoisses du monde primitif" (E., 62). Heroes such as Clef-des-Coeurs, who devotes his waking hours to Greco-Roman wrestling and to making love to Ennemonde, live peacefully and die like Hemingway's Robert Jordan from causes beyond their control (E., 96).

Besides continuing the associated theme of blond hero and the peacock, as in Saint-Jean and Ange Jason, for in *Ennemonde* "la mort a les couleurs du paon" (E., 130 ff.), Giono helps us understand why the pet peacock rode on Ange's saddle like Death itself, as brilliant with bursting feathered flames as was the end for Giono's Bobi.[18] In the Camargue

[15] Such as Sault, a road junction with a population of 718, and/or Noyers-sur-Jabron on the north slope of Lure, population 100.

[16] Such as Aurel, Barret de Lioure, Montbrun les Baronnies(?).

[17] Giono, having never been one to let pass an occasion for a good joke, and given his jests at mercantilism, may be twitting his French readers about the French politician Baron de Soubeyran (1829-1897), under charges of grand larceny when he died.

[18] *Que ma joie demeure* (1935).

story, Part II of *Ennemonde,* heroic combat is joined between the huge adder and the crested secretary bird, which, arriving like dawn, a walking vulture, stalked its breakfast and "vit en pleine Iliade" (E., 144).

L'Iris de Suse (1970) may also take place in some faintly cannibalistic High Country, although allusions to Toulon and to a Villard, which seem rather to indicate the Villars of Puget-Théniers with its ruins of one of the many Grimaldi castles, probably sets it in the Alpes Maritimes. Here reoccur the same magically arresting descriptions of "our" high mountains and high pastures as in *Batailles dans la montagne* and the same mountain climbing represented as ascending one after another through "vestibules sombres."[19] As in *Deux cavaliers de l'orage* Giono has required a sonorous progression of storms.[20] When their automobile jumps the road, sails out past the parapet, and bounces down the mountain in flames, the noble lovers of *L'Iris de Suse* die at what is presumably the same high pass, the *Col de la Croix.*[21]

Esther des Jacomets and Ange are newlyweds in *Deux cavaliers de l'orage,* with the young bride resembling a Gionoesque dream of feminine beauty—blue-black hair, generous and sensuous body, keen perceptions, and powerful desires for tenderness, fulfillment, and liberation. In fact, Ange has freed Esther (Aurélie) from her father's too rigid supervision, allowed her literally to let down her hair, and then dropped her unprepared into the society of the Jason women, wife and mother, and the old witch Delphine. Giono honors Esther by allowing her a share of the narrative responsibility, shifting gradually from third to first person in order together to watch Ange and Jason disappear into the forest that cloudy

[19] *Iris de Suse,* p. 48.
[20] *Idem,* pp. 106 ff., 203-06, for example.
[21] *Idem,* p. 221.

last Friday in October. Indulging her stream of consciousness (p. 53 ff.), the super-narrator bows to Esther as he had dignified the bovine Sarah in *Batailles dans la montagne*; in both cases these heroines are reminiscent of Scott's Rebecca, recounting warfare to a person inside the room with her.

The long central section of *Deux cavaliers*, "Les courses de Lachau" (pp. 45-131), is approached by two short rising actions and followed by three short combat chapters of sustained tension ended by the choric finale, or "Choeur." Almost again in dramatic form, as if Giono had once cast this material for the stage, the central block splits into scenes: (a) the departure of heroes from Ange's house, and (b) the reunion of the women and children at the Jason castle-farm. Working from the second interior, a kitchen with staircases leading down into the stables and up into bedrooms, with a roaring fire in the hearth and a cold, foggy darkness outside, the narrator summons in set order his entrances or additions to the Jason women, Ariane, Jason's wife Valérie, and the bride Esther: Delphine, the children, the older boy Jules, Jason, Ange. The latest arrival, or younger hero is clearly designated as the target: "Just as they discovered the thing, the blond My Junior enters. He had just enough time to open and close the door: he is so blond and fair that he stood there marked against the night. And here inside, the reflected rays of firelight strike, mantle and envelop him as if he alone inside the house were the only one alive" (p. 118).

The combined maleficent forces of weather, darkness, and the future accumulate after the disappearance of the twins, the older drawing the younger down the mountain slopes into the circular red city of Lachau, where horses always race on that particular Friday. Oracular wisdom and ceremonies of purification and augury commence at the arrival of the old woman Delphine, a high priestess from afar, specialized in her secular life in the preparation of pork and pork products. At the Jason farm a pig has just been butchered and its carcass, laid out on the kitchen table, is being dressed, cut, and tried out by the women.[22] According to the rules of female hierarchies, during such ceremonies as the preparation of pork for the winter season—and whether in rural France or the backwoods of Vermont—age not only takes precedence, due to its experience and its manifest proof of physical superiority, but also freely indulges in its prerogatives and priorities: the right to speak first, to eat, and to drink even immoderately; the right to be respected and obeyed; the right to officiate, command, and interpret. Thus, Giono descends for this kitchen ceremony, during which the five huddled and drooling children, the youngest a mere toddler and nursling, are peremptorily thrust out of doors and told to remain in school for four (long) hours, or until 5 p.m., into the root level of his primitive society, to the very place and time where culture is transmitted. Although no longer a virgin, Esther is still accomplishing the difficult first month of her wedlock, and evidence indicates that she has not as yet conceived.

In her first pronouncement Delphine delivers herself of prime wisdom: that in the world "women have only women" (p. 58). In other words, once the men have left, the four adult women understand each other and communicate *as do all women* instantly, or see instantly into each other's hearts and thoughts, all barriers dropped. In the savage odor of raw flesh that permeates their kingdom, they bring in the basin of

---

[22] Readers of Giono will recall, for example, the magnificently barbaric death ceremony and atonement to the pig in *Rondeur des jours,* where Giono speaks of the pig-sticker of Vachères, that splendid mountain village perched high on a rock pinnacle. See "L'Eau vive," *Livre de Poche,* p. 27 ff.

blood. It is good blood. Twirling a heather twig in it, Delphine flicks one drop on Esther's palm, closes the girl's hand, opens it, and examines the blot. Quickly she orders Esther to rub her hand on her (Delphine's) apron. Despite repeated queries, Delphine never reveals Esther's fortune, so the chapter closes in horrifying suspense. Old Ariane, second in rank to the seer, agrees peripherally that she has never understood at all what men were thinking or doing. They advise Esther tangentially that, despite her illusions to the contrary, marriage has made her henceforth totally and irrevocably alone forever: "what we love, my girl, has to be sought and has to be found all by ourselves. No one seeks it for you, no one finds it for you" (p. 62). To women, men are always closed books, and the more hermetic the more they read ill, adds Ariane, considering the especial loneliness of people. The peacocks did not sing at dawn of this day, she notes, which means that the day has not properly begun: "'Le jour d'aujourd'hui n'a pas été annoncé'" (p. 73).

Being about the same age as Delphine, Ariane also can pontificate to the younger women on the subject of the sexes, one of them inside and the other outside life: "On the one side there are those who are inside life, and on the other side are ourselves, we women." It is easy to criticize men, she adds, without understanding—and no woman can understand or know—what they face, which may be what makes them so mean and so oblique in all their dealings and methods. The easiest of all is to criticize one's own husband. She and Delphine were taught, *forced* even, to speak only good of their husbands, as they were prepared for lives as their servants: "In my day, in Delphine's day, they had taught us to speak for. They had forced us to speak for. And all our lives we were obliging."

Indulging her dark thoughts in ever-darkening weather, Delphine speaks of reading the future in the entrails of animals, especially in those of rabbits, concluding that a satisfactory life consists of having learned to want what your fortune has wanted. The future, she adds, may be defined as the sum of all the things of which you have not yet thought. Looking in a man's entrails, this cave where death lurks, one would learn too much. It is she who stipulates that two men on earth are one too many. In a sense of heightening anxiety the women hear Delphine accuse Ariane of two sins, pride and the desire to dominate. Where will the curse fall? While Valérie hunts for her children, she understands, finding them huddled in the cold on the doorstep, that the curse will strike Ariane's children.

In what is for Giono's fiction a rare treatment of children, the reader must see the origins of behavior through categorization into males and females. The former are expressly not picked up by the mothers, not suckled and not fed, but, in fact, accused of voyeurism, left out in the cold as guardians and as responsible for the behavior of all, sent on errands where Jules is attacked physically and coldly received thereafter, without a word of either thanks or sympathy. The females, on the contrary, are cuddled, suckled by Esther (*sic*), and admitted with open arms into the female community. Beyond the male children, or outsiders, are the adult males, or outriders. Thus, the interiority-exteriority antinomy is reinforced through this female complicity.

The rising fear of the women, who are except for childless Esther vulnerable only through their children, grows as Delphine and Ariane prepare to see what will make them curse life itself. During this waiting period Delphine recounts to Esther marvelous stories, such as how she and her husband transported their wounded son down the mountain to Lachau one dark night, followed by Valérie's account of her sole contact with urban life. When Jason enters, he speaks the same words to Ariane that Delphine has already uttered concerning blood, fire, and her will to dominate. Thus, both male and female, old Ariane serves as the key to the novel, she a last daughter unwanted by her parents, who thus became a man to please them before they gave her to Jason, whom she had to serve as a woman. After Jason narrates his heroic adventure in Lachau, he ridicules the idea that he could sleep now.

The conscience of the women serving their spiritual needs, Delphine functions like the Pythia at Delphi,[23] washing, purifying, prophecying imperturbably. In her cave of Trophonius she revives ghosts with blood from her *mensa delphica*, sacrifices a pig, twirls heather in lieu of Apollo's laurel, all before the chestnut tree beyond the door. Without the sacred tree, without mephitic vapors rising from Hades below the forest path, Giono could hardly have conveyed Homer's savage animism. Up the mountain through the bronze gates Plutarch speaks of in *De Iside et Osiride*, the Delphine oracle divines by fire, by blood, by darkness, by maddening fog and cloud that drenches hearts in fear. As at Dodona and as at Delphi itself there will be human sacrifices upon this mountain, in-

---

[23] See *Essays Classical* by F. W. H. Myers (London, 1883), pp. 1-105, for the best treatment I have seen on Greek oracles. See also H. W. Parke's *Greek Oracles* (London, 1967) and his *Oracles of Zeus* (Oxford, 1967). Among the essays published by the Bibliothèque des Etudes Françaises d'Athènes et de Rome, see Pierre Amandry's *La Mantique apollinienne à Delphes* (Paris, 1950), Part I, Chapter IV, p. 42 ff., and Part II generally, but especially Chapter XIII on the possible significance of the tripod. Perhaps it is Giono's table.

See also *The Greeks and the Irrational* by E. R. Dodds (Berkeley and Los Angeles, 1951), especially Appendix II on Theurgy.

In his *Divinae Institutiones*, Liber I, Capitulum VI, Lactantius classes the Delphic as fourth among the ten Sibyls of antiquity. Giono seems admirably, however, to have preferred her, as being by far the most intriguing and mysterious.

cluding the awful deed of Jason with the pruning hook, or castration knife.

No one will deny that the epic tone has changed over the years from the Christian *Batailles dans la montagne* to *Deux cavaliers de l'orage*, nor fail to admire Giono's innovations in the latter book: antecedents of the hero, world of women, pathetic children, extension of time, and the author's new point of view towards youth—no longer considered innocent, fragile, and victimized. Mutilated by the blond youngster whom he worships above his own life, and then having killed this same beloved brother, Jason is found dead on the snowy wastes of the mountain. In his frozen mouth is a piece of bread that he had neither time nor strength to eat before he died. For a dying hero, there is no peace. Mourning, black-clad villagers will bury their dead. Here also the bread signifies warfare's cessation, sometimes called "peace."

When in 1938 Christian Michelfelder published *Jean Giono et les religions de la terre*, the first book devoted entirely to this then young author who had just published *Batailles dans la montagne*, he was struck by Giono's great piety as in such a belief as that death is a return to a mountain. Giono used to say, in fact, "I do not say that rock is dead. Nothing is dead. Death does not exist."[24]

---

[24] As quoted by Michelfelder from *Le Chant du monde* (p. 181).

v   The Tragic Mode

Un Roi sans divertissement (1947)

World War II came to an end for Giono not earlier than 1947 when La Table Ronde in Paris broke an embargo against the novelist by publishing his immediately famous chronicle *Un Roi sans divertissement*. During the preceding ten-year period Giono had to some degree put aside fiction[1] for political action: *Refus d'obéissance* (1937), or the refusal to bear arms, for which he suffered[2] his first rigorous imprisonment in Marseilles, chained leg and wrist, and the resultant paresis; and *Lettre aux paysans sur la pauvreté et la paix* (1938), where he tells women how to stop war by a method different from that of Aristophanes. Aside from his marvelous voyage fragment, as we have already seen, plus *Moby Dick* and *Pour saluer Melville* of 1943, Giono maintained a silence or was unable to write and publish novels for this period of ten years. Meanwhile, he joined the national committee of surrealism, or André Breton's FIARI; refusing after imprisonment to join the Comité National des Ecrivains, he was blacklisted by them on September 9, 1944. In *Les Lettres Françaises* of October 4, 1944, Tristan Tzara attacked Giono,[3] accusing him of fascism. In 1944-1945 the novelist was imprisoned for a sec-

[1] I am disinclined to neglect W. M. Frohock's observation in *Style and Temper* (Cambridge, 1967) that during his lifetime Giono suffered "periods of reclusion" (p. xv).

[2] In *Jean Giono et les techniques du roman* (Berkeley-Los Angeles, 1961) Pierre R. Robert also feels in *Un Roi sans divertissement* another expression of "angoisse moderne" (p. 79).

[3] "Un Romancier de la lâcheté," No. 24, NYP.

ond time. Therefore both the surrealist *Noé* (1947) and the tragical *Roi sans divertissement* stem from the war years, from the pain of deprivation, hunger, humiliation, and loneliness. Rather than succumb to his whirlpool of troubles, however, Giono sank under them until he touched rock bottom; only then, with strength renewed and novelistic techniques enriched by maturation,[4] did he rise a world master, pioneering what his heirs after 1950 would be calling a new realism.[5]

It is largely thanks to this noble *Roi sans divertissement*, with its moral universe framed by Pascal, that a whole new group of French critics condescended to Giono, along with steadfast André Gide (again in 1948, and it was through Gide's efforts that Giono's first novel was published twenty years earlier): Marcel Arland, Maurice Nadeau, Pierre de Boisdeffre, Robert Kanters, René Lalou, Gaëtan Picon, Claudine Chonez, Paul Morand, Jacques Pugnet, and Gabriel Marcel; among such ever faithful champions as Henri Peyre, W. M. Frohock, Maxwell A. Smith, Henry Miller, Stephen Ullmann, and Katherine A. Clark.

For this return to fiction in 1947, now writing in techniques soon to be exploited by the "modern" novelists, Giono chose a subject suitable to the tragic mode, due to his personal tragedies, doubtless, to the fresh tragedies of Europeans and Americans by the millions, but, perhaps also, however, because nothing in all literature so raises the spirit of man and woman alike as a study of tragic crime, remorse and atonement. Therefore, despite his "second manner," underneath this tragic story of Captain Langlois lies Giono's old hope, sustained from his early pastoral days of the 1920's and 1930's,

[4] See André Rousseaux's memorable assessment, "Jean Giono, seconde manière," *Le Figaro littéraire* (March 7, 1953), p. 2.

[5] See Robert Poulet's "Giono à l'avant-garde," *Carrefour* (16ᵉ année, Feb. 4, 1959), No. 751, p. 13.

that somehow, as Victor Hugo had once managed to breathe courage into the defeated French people, he too might in some fashion serve those beside whom in all conscience he had refused militarily again to serve.

Like all masterpieces of world fiction, the opening paragraphs of *Un Roi sans divertissement* strike the reader direct blows, Giono punching rapidly after "Frédéric a la scierie sur la route d'Avers": he inherited from his father, grandfather, great grandfather, the whole family, where the sawmill was, at the angle, hairpin turn, edge of the road. Then tangentially he launches forth into a maniacally detailed description of a beech tree, eternally young god like Apollo, all of which for neither rhyme nor apparent reason leads us into concerns for justice and beauty. The third paragraph quite unnerves the reader with what will be rapid, dizzying alternations of fragmented pasts and presents, recreations, testimony, contradictory evidence from hateful survivors, where the only unknown one among them, the truly silent chronicler and author of the book, will unravel a riddle as maddening as that posed by the sphinx, or ferret out truths from witnesses, sources, and his surrogate storytellers.

In modern fashion, devoid of divisions other than frequent pauses in the text, this novel falls nevertheless into two halves, each containing three forward progressions despite confused reconstructions of events occurring principally in 1843-1844, 1846, 1867-1868, and the present, or 1884. The three sections of Part 1 settle into place fairly easily, each one commencing and recommencing apparently pointless details about Frédéric and his sawmill.[6] Eventually, the reader working earnestly

[6] Page numbers henceforth will refer, as here, to the Gallimard edition, labeled *Chroniques* 1, of 228 pp., signed "Manosque, 1er sept.-10 oct. 46." In Part 1, then, I see 3 sections: (1) pp. 9-30, (2) pp. 30-56, and (3) pp. 56-81.

meanwhile, all will acquire coherence as the beech tree, and not the sawmill necessarily, contains the solution to the first riddles.

Allowing fiction priority over history when problems in epistemology beset snowbound mountaineers, the narrator recalls a December of 1843 when he was only a child in a world of falling snowflakes over the twenty or twenty-five fast-disappearing houses. Lashed by cruel-faced high priests of the feathered serpent of yore, the villagers huddle, cowering, in their square rooms so much less comforting than the rounded rock caves of stone-age man, but equally afraid, while some god or demi-god (p. 22) whisks away plump Marie Chazottes from her own yard at 3 p.m., almost hauls off Georges Ravanel, and savagely cuts to ribbons a living pig in the farmyard. Snow continues to fall as brave Bergues tracks the killer into the clouds, below which the same old, eternal threats to man prowl, dealing fear to all alike, as they undergo fifteen hours of darkness for a few daylight hours, or until spring raises the cloud cover. I think, the narrator ventures parenthetically, of Perceval hypnotized before drops of blood from the wild goose on the snow. And, in fact, for any literate reader of our century, if snow falls on black earth below drops of red blood, can the Grail castle and Perceval be far behind? They never found Marie, concludes the teller.

Time may be chronicled from one Frédéric (1844) to another (1884), and foul mud from the sawmill be piled below the beech tree; unnatural modern man will worship in his own way either the golden bulls of Mithra or the "hêtre divin" (p. 32). In fact, camping *now* at the high pass, the silent one describes autumnal ashes (p. 35) wearing feathers like bloody Aztecs, flashing lightning from steel plates of warrior priests, flouncing hangmen's capes, Borgia's berets, bronze as Indians reddening the western sky for sacrifice. *Then* near maples bloody as butchers, the godly beech seemed in autumn less tree than green snakes, crimson hair, golden fillets, crystal dust, tall flame. Supernatural dancers shrouded in brilliant scarves poised despite drunken limbs at the tip, where gods take flight. Such beauty hypnotizes like Perceval's goose blood on snow (p. 37) while the narrator's refrain lulls the reader:

"Settled upon the gradins of the mountain, the forests finally sat silently looking at it (the beech tree).

"Settled in full sacerdotal attire upon the gradins of the amphitheater of the mountains, the forests no longer dared stir" (p. 37).

Having subsequently studied genealogies of the victims, who now include the tracker Bergues and Anselmie's husband, and having also examined portraits, the narrator can conclude that what the victims shared was good blood and succulent flesh (but this is no chronicle of cannibalism, p. 46!): "Beauty has served us with a warning: . . . man cannot live in a world where the exquisite elegance of a guinea-hen's plumage is considered superfluous" (p. 47). Under cloud and snow falling uninterruptedly for twenty days, some thirsty Quetzacoatl, specifies the narrator, demands victims, or some Abraham offers up Isaacs among the villagers. Section II leads us through chronicled *thens* and *nows* until after murders 2 and 3 the antagonist, Captain Langlois, arrives with his policemen to investigate and to seek the murderer; his hostess, the old prostitute called Saucisse, opens her inn. For one Christmas eve the golden splendor of monstrances diverts the murderer briefly.

Beneath the scrutiny of the hero-detective Langlois, Frédéric II of the sawmill, repairing an antique clock decorated with the face of a shepherdess, discovers high on the beech tree the body of Dorothée, her Dresden-china face white and pink in sacrificial death. Anticipating in chains of narrative futures what Frédéric will tell after his pursuit of the murderous demi-god across an Alpine summit into virginal snowfields of a New World, going ashore like an explorer into the strange Aztec-sounding village of Chichiliane, the narrator approaches the solution to the four murders. Hot in pursuit, the beloved Captain Langlois surprisingly neglects obtaining a warrant for an arrest, and he also fails to provide a witness. Even worse, for he is our leader and hero, he threatens the local landlord with Cayenne, and commandeers the city hall in the name of King Louis-Philippe. So rapidly have our futures become staggering presents, the reader's heart almost bursts at the conclusion to Part I, where, claiming accident, Langlois himself commits the tragic act of disgrace and horror by firing both pistols point-blank into the supposed murderer's abdomen.

Having been led up the narrator's garden path into believing that the novel concerned the identity of this murderer, the aristocratic M. V. of Chichiliane, only to discover his error, the reader carefully restates here the problem of Langlois. With aged villagers, now one and now another, narrating years later in their vulgar speech, all revolves about a metamorphosed Captain returned into permanent retirement near the seat of his crime, his stony face betraying his suffering. Introducing the final new characters, including Mme Tim of the castle and the royal procurator, who also loves and shields his former officer Langlois, the hero organizes a wolf hunt. Finally, in the Val de Chalamont, Langlois again faces the old wolf backed by the beaters and the din of their cresselles up against a granite cliff. Again he shoots his suddenly pitiful victim in the belly.

Twenty years later (section v, pp. 135-73), the narrator remembers how as a lad tending cows he and his chums persuaded Saucisse and Langlois's widow Delphine to accompany them from their bungalow built by the Captain before his marriage up under the apple trees. Thus, at age eighty Saucisse assumes the narrator's role to recount the slow development of her special awareness, the knowledge (pp. 151-52) that what Langlois did was, in fact, too bad! Where Langlois's affirmation that all men resemble each other solves nothing, his journey in the rain to study M. V.'s portrait and perhaps aid his widow and orphan in some slight way, while Saucisse, like Alain Robbe-Grillet after her, hypnotically takes inventory of the room (pp. 164-65) so as not to condemn her hero, forces Saucisse into knowledge. The châtelaine Mme Tim will eventually concur, after having strained also to know.

The final section recalls a time ten years earlier (1857-1858) when the procurator, Saucisse, Mme Tim, and Langlois danced an anguished quadrille. One after another, diversions failed: an invitation to the castle of Saint-Baudille, an ascension of its staircases in search of "celui qui a le remède" (p. 189), even putting a false soliloquy into Langlois's mouth. That fall he built his bungalow fronted by a labyrinth of hedges and sought as his bride a young whore who would not enclose him as M. V. was cloistered by his gray wife. Another square forms with the anguished hero as one side. On or around October 20, when the first snow fell, Langlois himself contemplated, on the pure snow, drops of red blood from a butchered goose, and later that night blew himself up with dynamite.

Veteran of the Moroccan campaign and/or of the Mexican campaign, like Monsieur Joseph soon to play hero in *Le Moulin de Pologne*, the romantic hero Langlois with his fine mustache and shiny black hair sleek on his temples was "un sacré lascar" (p. 40) whom all the men and boys in the village instantly recognized as their ideal of kingship. Hanging on his every breath, they trusted him as he theorized: the murderer was not a cannibal, and yet Langlois could "smell" the corpses. It is finally Langlois who recalls Pascal's theory of *divertissement* (p. 54), to which the narrator returns in the closing words of the novel: "Qui a dit: *'Un roi sans divertissement est un homme plein de misères?'*"

Characteristically, once Giono set down such a representation of the world, he continued to defend his conception, so that one meets with neither surprise nor dismay Pascal's idea developed in Giono's history of King Francis I, or *Le Désastre de Pavie* (1963). This French king of the sixteenth century, entirely self-centered as Giono understood him, sought not to construct but rather to amuse, distract, *divert* himself.[7] Thus, Langlois's attempts to become interested in others, to profit from his sojourn in the castle—always from Perceval's time at least the place where knowledge is revealed—to construct something other than his house and labyrinth, fail to draw him out of the charmed circle of his own egotism. Such a man loved to pass under death's nose with gallant gestures, and the journals called him when he fell "crowned with death" (p., 35). His *art de vivre* masked an appetite for death, for like all sensualists he reveled in desperate straits and abysses (p., 36, 64). Therefore at Amboise Castle this French king rode Polish horses, and hunted wolves until he could enjoy Bayard's favorite sport: hunting men (p., 66).

Paraphrasing Von Clausewitz, Giono continues in *Le Désastre de Pavie* to redefine war as a continuation of diversion by other means, a purpose served in some centuries, to be sure, by a fury for building (p., 77). The heaviest burden

---

[7] See the Gallimard edition of *Le Désastre de Pavie*, pp. 33-34. Subsequent page references to this book will be prefaced by p.

of the human condition is *ennui* (P., 89). From time hanging heavy on his hands, man becomes an inventor, a discoverer, and a believer in progress. Notwithstanding, blood and the trappings of death remain his chief *divertissement*. "La nature de l'homme est violente, que l'exercice de sa violence le distrait, . . ." (P., 92). In combat, whether against wolves or men, kings like Francis and Langlois meet their destiny (P., 218). They differ somewhat, of course, because of their centuries, men in the twentieth having been afraid for about one hundred fifty years (P., 18).

Just as courtiers and wars struggled to turn King Francis I away from his contemplation of his royalty, so the royal procurator, Saucisse, and Mme Tim labored to keep Langlois from falling into a trance, or being hypnotized by drops of red blood on snow. Thus, Giono quoted Pascal correctly from *Divertissement*: "Let the experiment be made: allow a king to be left quite alone, without any gratification of his senses, without any occupation for his mind, without company, thus able at his leisure to turn his thoughts upon himself; and it will become apparent that a king without diversion is a man sunk into wretchedness."[8] Pascal's very words, then, were adopted by Giono into the tragedy of Langlois.[9]

[8] See the *Pensées* of Blaise Pascal, ed. Brunschvicg, introduction and notes by C. M. Granges (Paris, 1964), No. 142, p. 114.

[9] In his recent book on tragedy, Geoffrey Brereton does not necessarily view Pascal's vision as in itself tragic. See in particular III, 8, p. 167, from Brereton's *Principles of Tragedy. A Rational Examination of the Tragic Concept in Life and Literature* (Coral Gables, 1968). Brereton's definition of tragedy, on the other hand, complements Giono's novel: "A tragedy is a final and impressive disaster due to an unforeseen or unrealised failure involving people who command respect and sympathy. It often entails an ironical change of fortune and usually conveys a strong impression of waste. It is always accompanied by misery and emotional distress" (p. 20).

Langlois himself agreed with Pascal—as Giono disagreed with his own emulator Albert Camus[10]—that we can understand the human heart, that there are among us *no strangers* (p. 148). How else could Langlois have guessed that the beauty of the monstrances on Christmas eve would keep the murderer among them from sacrificing to Apollo another choice victim? Therein lies the novel's sum of wisdom, which Giono himself explained to an American visitor, Professor Maxwell A. Smith,[11] as years later he carefully explained it to me, adding that to understand the novel one need not become a specialist in Pascal. When Langlois discovered in himself, said Giono, the same evil as in the murderer, he lost the desire to live. Furthermore, consonant with his credo, Giono will, after having exhausted his taste for the tragical, hunt for reasons why man should, despite his evil nature, continue to desire to live—ergo, *Le Hussard sur le toit* (1951), for instance.

"Man says," said Langlois, "that life is extremely short . . ." (p. 209), and yet Saucisse raved about Langlois' flair for living: " 'Ah! le bel homme! Et qui savait vivre! L'idiot!' " (p. 182). Ah, there was a man! (p. 113). Even after his crime, when his black eyes bored through people without ever seeing them any more, when he was so sad that he "engendered melancholy" (p. 147), and never smiled, the three companions watched over him and doted. "Black tiger" that he was on his tall black horse, and "supernatural" (p. 212) in his monachal, martial, and Byronic elegance, Langlois was beloved by both Saucisse and Mme Tim. Beside him, a person felt like someone! (p. 216). Why? Because Langlois, who could not even save himself, had paradoxically but by general

---

[10] Maxwell A. Smith calls "Langlois . . . therefore . . . an anti-Meursault." See his *Giono* (New York, 1966), p. 133.

[11] *Idem.*

consent "ainsi remède à tout" (p. 215): the tragic catharsis in operation.

In part also, Langlois's charm stems from the fact that he is several times equated with Perceval and furthermore enveloped with the attendant symbolic topology. The legend of Perceval, according to Jessie L. Weston,[12] took root also in Giono's Alps, where, as we have already seen, vestiges of gnosticism still survive. Langlois himself comes from Chrétien de Troyes's "li gallois"; he is the Britisher and a bondsman like the medieval Lancelot,[13] like him fated never to see the Grail in life, and like him monachal. The quadrille and square relationship stressed in the final section of Giono's novel refers also to the square medieval castle of ritual,[14] and both dance and labyrinth to the spiral castle of Welsh legend.[15] In gnostic terminology, of which the Perceval legend seems the very essence,[16] Langlois's soul in bondage (as symbolized by the house and the labyrinth) and his material or earthly bent to evil (as represented by the drops of blood), would re-become light as he put an end to his sufferings on earth. As in the various Perceval versions, weeping women must have surrounded the dead king. Giono's use of black and white relates more closely, it would seem, to Wolfram Von Eschenbach's *Parzival,* which commences with a disquisition on this contrast, and therefore also to Kafka's *Das Schloss,* black castle and heavy snow falling.

[12] *From Ritual to Romance* (Cambridge, 1920), but see here the New York, 1957, edition, p. 190.

[13] Lancelot < ille ancillus.

[14] *Perceval* (v. 3,086); Lorris's *Roman de la rose* (vv. 1,279-1,438), Meung's continuation (vv. 3,797-4,058).

[15] See Robert Graves' *The White Goddess* (New York, 1948), Chapter VI, p. 76 ff.

[16] See Leonardi Olschi's *The Grail Castle and Its Mysteries,* trans. J. A. Scott (Berkeley and Los Angeles, 1966), pp. 9-36 *et passim.*

One must not dwell on Gothic times, however, insists the narrator, for already one's own square century intrudes: "Déjà, on ne peut ignorer son siècle nulle part. Il faut préférer la peur à la voûte" (p. 28). Within the first thirty pages Giono demonstrates brilliantly his juxtapositions of pasts and presents, the chronology that made this novel so sensationally "modern" in 1947. Although maddeningly narrated in the present tense, the first past is that of Frédéric, his sawmill opposite the divine beech tree with its perennially youthful blond grace of Apollo, sum of all beauty. This present is the past of 1843. Out of this past, some months later, rode Captain Langlois, returned from active military service in "modern times" addressed, specifies the narrator, to the demands of liberty like the heroes of those days: Maréchal Prim and Giuseppe Garibaldi.[17]

Switching times from a fictional present (1843), when snow fell for days, to a time actually present for the narrator in 1884, when snow has also silently been falling for many days, Giono gives Alain Robbe-Grillet both his subject and his method used with such consummate artistry in the opening pages of *Dans le labyrinthe* (1959). In the latter past-become-present, the narrator speaks of the V. family at Chichiliane, where no one ever goes, and one male V. reading Nerval's *Sylvie*, who was probably a relative of the murderer M. V., but in any case physically very strong like him, "un malade, un fou" of 1843. In this frame of reference the narra-

---

[17] It is fascinating to realize how the same books of history inspired both *Un Roi sans divertissement* and *Le Moulin de Pologne*. Here Giono has equated Langlois with both Juan Prim y Prats (1814-1870), who returned to Spain from exile in 1843 and who visited both Puerto Rico and Mexico in the New World, and Giuseppe Garibaldi (1807-1882), who in 1843 was in the New World, where he visited Brazil and Uruguay.

tor is a grown man speaking of Percevals and quests, whereas in 1843 he was a mere child.

Each reader will, like each critic whom we have mentioned, prefer his own favorite pages, but to my mind the passage narrated from the point of view of the villagers in 1843, when the narrator was a young child, appears particularly admirable (pp. 25-27, ending with a parenthesis directed at the reader, pp. 27-28). Instead of the more familiar "vous" used by the mature narrator in conformity with the style of Saucisse, here the more reticent "on" conveys a sense of family intimacy of which the child will in phrases whisper only so much, for once more we have entered really sacred ground. We have moved from Bergues tracking the murderer on snowshoes to the warm farm kitchen whence "one" can look out over the "extraordinarily white desert"—white all the way to the black wood:

"Dusk is falling. A barely perceptible breeze, which we cannot hear, rises. What we can hear sounds like a hand brushing against the shutter, or the door, or the wall; the sound of a moan, or of a shrill whistle whimpering, or the opposite. A noise in the attic.

"We listen. Father stops sucking on his pipe. Mother freezes, holding in her upraised palm the salt which she had been about to drop into the soup kettle" (p. 25).

The voice might have come from *Jean le bleu* (1932) as he stood beside his father, protected by him from the world, helped by him to grow unafraid enough to duplicate its fearfulness. To the narrator this descent into inanimation has cancelled time; from its depths he must, in order horizontally to pursue his fabulation, swim towards the surface, as it were: "Mais il fallait remonter" (p. 28).

This restitution of time from mechanical to a human dimension, so closely associated with the essays of Alain Robbe-

Grillet, plus Giono's new attention to narrative focus, which he will bring to perfection in *Le Moulin de Pologne*, might indeed have derived, as Maxwell A. Smith noted in this connection, from the novels of William Faulkner.[18] Many of the comments that Jean-Paul Sartre made concerning *Light in August* (1932) might have been intended for Langlois: ". . . c'est le monde de l'ennui. . . . Le véritable drame est derrière . . . l'ennui. Son héros est insaisissable. . . ." His actions appear like so many "fulgurations indescriptibles"—"sa *nature*" can be understood only on the "magique" level.[19] In 1939 Sartre discussed *The Sound and the Fury* (1929), particularly from the point of view of time.

Faulkner in this influential novel,[20] said Sartre, broke or decapitated time, scattering its pieces about for the reader to reconstruct as best he could. Bearing in mind that only present time is most properly catastrophic enough to shake the reader to his foundations, the American novelist had shown how to plunge his reader headlong into an "être présent." Of all times, the past is most surreal in the Faulkner novel, but the future inexistent. Through this cloudy irrationality events blaze like "constellations affectives."[21] While Giono certainly read Sartre's essays, he also pointed out to me in the course of our conversations in August 1970 that he not only acknowledged his debt to William Faulkner but insisted upon it as his most extensive.

Thus manipulating levels of time and abrogating his au-

[18] See Note 10.

[19] Written by Sartre in February 1938, and reprinted in *Situations I* (Paris, 1947), pp. 9-11.

[20] "The greatest literary development in France between 1929 and 1939 was the discovery of Faulkner, Dos Passos, Hemingway, Caldwell, Steinbeck," repeated Sartre in "American Novelists in French Eyes," *Atlantic Monthly*, 178 (August 1946), p. 114.

[21] See *Situations I*, p. 70 ff.

thor's outmoded right to authority, Giono hesitated, and probably quite rightly, to insist upon a solid, mythological sub-stratum for *Un Roi sans divertissement.* In other words, he at no point handled his mythical material openly by disquisition and comment in the way that Henry de Montherlant had treated Mithraism in *Les Bestiaires* (1934), for example. Therefore the nascent poetry of Giono's treatment rises freely from the reader, soliciting, as in the most admirable modern novels, the latter's pleased participation. Below the allusions to castle and Perceval lie Giono's half-expressed suggestions, mere will-of-the-wisps drawing from the reader long-forgotten texts of Plato, Apollodorus, Ovid.[22]

Evoking specifically for the reader only Apollo Citharoedus,[23] Giono links him with the beech tree from which, the reader may add, wreaths were made for victors in the Pythian games. The tree itself, originally from the tertiary flora of Arctic regions, merely suggests to the reader not only a precinct and adjunct of worship, but also inevitably some ultra-frozen north. Snow falling throughout Part 1 of the book, and at its finale, further suggests this to be the land of the legendary Apolline peoples, or Hyperboreans, where, Giono is implying, Apollo spent his winters, a shepherd god among pastors and flocks. M. V. dedicates offerings, *Graeco sacro*, to the Olympian god in the daytime, as apparently the ritual stipulated, perhaps at the mid-winter solstice, or some yearly offering, as at Delos, perhaps on this particular year, like the Stepteria. Or, M. V. is himself Apollo.

The sacred tree, recalling like *Deux cavaliers de l'orage* Homeric times, stands inside and yet outside the village, or like Apollo's temple at Rome, *intra pomerium.* Here also

---

[22] More specifically, and among others, doubtless, Ovid's *Metamorphoses*, 1, 200 ff.; Apollodorus 3, 96 ff.; Plato's *Republic* or Resp., 565d.
[23] The statue in the National Museum in Naples, I believe.

Apollo is not merely a sun god, but a chthonian lord of winter reigning over his own wild, desolate country.

The thought of wolves, the wolf hunt, and the putting to death of the wolf after a long pagan ceremony that involves as active participants not only the two women dressed in all their finery for the occasion but also the entire adult male community further flow swiftly into the mythological undercurrent. Barbarously Langlois has killed M. V., who like a wolf silently butchered his victims, and he will also explode the belly of the old wolf, which with equal fearlessness proudly rises to meet him. Both wolves are so far willing sacrifices to Apollo, as in the best rituals, and all participants have blood on their hands and in their eyeballs. When in ancient times on another remote mountain King Lycaon of Arcadia killed a wolf, or perhaps a token Zeus Lykaios, this son of Priam became himself a wolf.[24] And thus, Langlois *versipellis* feels his hair grow gray and his thoughts unable to dismiss a nature become more and more canine as it ceased through one great error to be nobly human.

In cabalistic terms Langlois leaves the right path to descend into the Kingdom of Cain, becoming prince of poison, Adam Belial, whose wife is the temple harlot and whose friend is another old whore. Because the good tree has borne bad fruit, Langlois constructs for himself an ecclesiastical maze for penitential purposes. Deeper and deeper, now always after nightfall, he strolls through his labyrinth of human suffering, after other magical labyrinths, such as the quadrille and the four-sided relationship, have proved futile, where he ultimately fails to catch the reverse spiral and follow it back out to salvation. Counting perhaps upon some belief that his soul will be allotted two other lifetimes during which to resist evil,

[24] See R. P. Eckels's *Greek Wolf-Lore* (Philadelphia, 1937), p. 32 ff., in particular.

he opts for the cabalistic four, or fire. This must represent his victory over winter and his final forgetfulness that he alone first shed the blood of Hyacinthus on the earth. *And* that others followed.

While Giono was known widely as a classicist for all the years of his lifetime, he probably had not read "Adonis"[25] by the American poet Hilda Doolittle, and yet he saw Apollo and the tree much as this contemporary saw Adonis:

II

Not the gold on the temple-front
where you stand,
is as gold as this,
not the gold that fastens your sandal,
nor the gold reft
through your chiselled locks
is as gold as this last year's leaf...

each of us like you
has died once.
each of us like you
stands apart, like you
fit to be worshipped.

The death of Langlois, the exploding of his head, which lighted up the dark evening sky above his maze, brought Giono's novel to what the narrator calls "la conclusion tragique" (p. 96), and one must concur that *Un Roi sans divertissement* rises to all the lordliness and purification of tragedy.

A RECURRENT feature in prose fiction, it would seem, is the tragic mode, observable as well in eighteenth-century Gothic

[25] See the *Collected Poems of Hilda Doolittle* (New York, c. 1925), pp. 68-69.

fiction[26] as in many modern novels, which may mean, as is the case for Giono's *Moulin de Pologne*, as we shall shortly see, both the use of a five-part structure corresponding to the acts of a tragic drama and the founding of the work upon a tragic view of the world. Thus, critics speak commonly of "tragic novels" by Stendhal, Melville, Hawthorne, Flaubert, Tolstoy, Hardy, Conrad, Camus, and Malraux.[27] In our century, in fact, the Racine-type tragedy, based, as in the case of *Phèdre*, upon the woman-monster or female dragon as she derives from Greek mythology via medieval clericalism, was written over and again in the 1920's and 1930's by François Mauriac. The particular and very different instances of tragedy that occur in Giono's tragic novels of 1947 and 1952 apply not only to these particular post-war works but to the mass realization of modern readers that we live in tragic times.

A struggle similar to that evident in Langlois, who eventually succumbs to "Tragic Resignation and Sacrifice" of himself, had also appeared in T. S. Eliot's *Murder in the Cathedral* (1935) and would recur in Boris Pasternak's *Doctor Zhivago* (1957): "The rhythm of tragedy ... is a rhythm of sacrifice. A man is disintegrated by suffering, and is led to death, but the action is more than personal. . . . Indeed, in our world, resignation to general guilt has become an order of life, or its shadow."[28] Langlois has assumed guilt for the isolated community, whose members avidly over the decades

---

[26] Horace Walpole's *The Castle of Otranto* (London, 1764) was so analyzed, for example, by K. K. Mehotra's *Horace Walpole and the English Novel* (Oxford, 1934). Mehotra points out that the action of this early Gothic novel takes place in five days. See pp. 6, 17, 83, *et passim*.

[27] See Clifford Leech's *Tragedy* (London, 1969), p. 31 ff.

[28] See Raymond Williams' *Modern Tragedy* (London, 1966), pp. 156 and 158, where Eliot's "the world must be dreamed in winter," is quoted from *Murder in the Cathedral*.

tell and retell his story, assuring themselves and reassuring their youngsters that he died for them all, just as the artistic Julie in *Le Moulin de Pologne* will inevitably be sacrificed, and the others purified. Thus, tragedy grips us all by the throat, for "we see that what is at stake here is always man's entire existence, that there is no question of compromise, no evasion of hostile powers, no turning aside of man's unconquerable will. . . ."[29]

In the old days of his glorious triumph as captain, detective, hero, and protector of the community, King Langlois towered, a pillar of strength, holding off mystery, darkness, evil, and death.[30] Then, whether through his own free will or whether by the will of Apollo, like Orestes, Oedipus, Heracles, Macbeth, and Othello he committed the terrible act of murder,[31] thus having to face "unaccommodated, alone . . . (the) mysterious, demonic forces in his own nature and outside, and the irreducible facts of suffering and death."[32] Like Job, Prometheus, Lear, and Ahab he stands in a *bound-*

---

[29] See Albin Lesky's *Greek Tragedy*, trans. H. A. Frankfort (London, 1965), p. 45. Lesky says further: "As an expression of man's profound reflection on the problems of his existence, it has a timeless validity" (p. 208).

[30] Very much in these terms, Charles I. Glicksberg speaks of modern tragedies in *The Tragic Vision in Twentieth-Century Literature*, preface by Harry T. Moore (Carbondale, 1963), p. xvi.

[31] See "The Question of Free Will," or Chapter 15, from Oscar Mandel's *A Definition of Tragedy* (New York, 1961). Langlois satisfied the definition: "A protagonist who commands our earnest good will is impelled in a given world by a purpose, or undertakes an action, of a certain seriousness and magnitude; and by that very purpose or action, subject to that same given world, necessarily and inevitably meets with grave spiritual or physical suffering" (p. 20). Similarly, he satisfies Geoffrey Brereton's *Principles of Tragedy* (see note 9).

[32] See Richard B. Sewall's *The Vision of Tragedy* (New Haven and London, 1959), p. 5.

ary-situation, and "at the limits of his sovereignty."[33] Like
Medea's and like Clytemnestra's, his is a fine nature gone
wrong[34] when it applies to M. V. the *lex talionis*.

In depicting his tragic hero, Giono has advanced beyond
the epic mode, for his reader felt only pity for Jason dying
upon his wintry mountain crest, whereas, because of the suffering of Langlois, one feels both pity and fear. Why control
and why mock our natural feelings of pity and sympathy?
Giono always asked. Is not the reader's contemplation of
Langlois salutary, close, true, and personal? Are not the former's concerns also with remedies lest he incur a similar fate?
All readers fall into Perceval's trance as they with Langlois
pursue ontological questions, striving to see daylight beyond
the mysteries of being.[35] Happily for them, Langlois's guilt is
an internal punishment due him by *ius naturale*, even though
ius civile had condoned the murder, and it remains untrans-
ferable to the royal procurator, or to Mme Tim, or to Saucisse. Like Oedipus, he solved the murder, but ironically justice was not even-handed:

> Apollo, friends, Apollo, he it was
> That brought these ills to pass;
> But the right hand that dealt the blow
> Was mine, none other.[36]

By a syllogistic reduction characteristic of the irony inherent
in tragedy, we see that Langlois has murdered a defenseless

[33] *Ibid.*, Sewall paraphrasing Karl Jaspers, p. 5.

[34] *Ibid.*, p. 49.

[35] See the development of these thoughts in D. D. Raphael's *The
Paradox of Tragedy* (Bloomington, 1959), as in the earlier *Tragedy: A
View of Life* (Ithaca, 1956) by Henry Alonzo Myers, who concluded:
"Since it is positive and affirmative, great tragedy satisfies our deepest
rational and moral inclinations" (p. 155).

[36] Oedipus after blinding himself, as quoted by Laura Jepsen in
Ethical Aspects of Tragedy (Gainesville, 1953), p. 45.

man and a trapped beast. He who murders is a criminal, bringing disgrace upon the law he represents. Langlois is therefore doomed to punishment.

Had Giono dealt only with *muthos, Un Roi sans divertissement* would have resembled a puzzle, or have been a mystery, a detective story. By probing character (*ethos*), the author provided the Oedipal and lofty hero, who knots the *desis* of Greek tragedy. Langlois himself also supplies the depth of thought from the modern philosopher Pascal, or the requisite *dianoia*. The *opsis* of the tragedy rests upon its rugged mountain scenery, the stark beauty of white snow deserts against black woods and sheer cliff faces, the whole bloodied by the sacrificial ashes and beeches. The chief narrator's descriptions of such beauties outside and the fearful peace inside his home supply Aristotle's requirement of song. His voice, in contrast to the untutored, savage diction of Saucisse and the natives, provides heights and valleys for a study of Giono's invariably complicated *lexis*. Thus the novel satisfies also the *Poetics VI*.

As Aristotle explained, we have in Langlois a man of strong character and eminent situation in his world who through *hamartia* turned to vice. It proved impossible for him, knowing what was correct, long to do evil. We pity him inasmuch as he did not deserve to fall, and we fear because he is a man like ourselves—just as more than once he observed was the case for M. V. The *metabasis* of Langlois occurs almost without warning; it is not so much a change from good to evil as a sudden reversal of everyone's confidence in him, a *peripeteia*. Part II of the novel, as we have decided to divide it, operates the *anagnorisis*, the hero's silent realization of his evil deeds. The death of Langlois solves the second or greater riddle of the book, the metaphysical problem of evil and of an arbitrary justice. His fall most fortunately for us all confirms the moral universe. With great irony, the lawman becomes morally an outlaw and, since a corrupt society fails to deal morally with him, takes the law for a last time into his own hands. As in *Oedipus Rex*, the king himself must punish Langlois, for they also are double. "A tragedy," says Richmond Y. Hathorn, "is a work of literature which has as its chief emphasis the revelation of mystery": "The solver of all problems is himself the problem beyond all solution. What appeared to Oedipus as a riddle—Man—is in reality a mystery—Myself."[37] Choragos:

> This is the king who solved the famous riddle
> And towered up, most powerful of men.
> No mortal eyes but looked on him with envy,
> Yet in the end ruin swept over him.[38]

Un Roi sans divertissement demonstrates finally what Dorothea Krook in 1969 established as "the universal elements of tragedy," or "the fundamental, universal elements of tragedy": (1) *"the act of shame or horror."* (2) "the *suffering* itself. This is properly tragic if and only if it generates knowledge ... into ... the ... human condition." (3) *"knowl-*

[37] See Richmond Y. Hathorn's *Tragedy, Myth, and Mystery* (Bloomington, 1962), p. 223 and p. 95. See also for a superior discussion of *Oedipus Rex*, p. 33 ff. See also "Sophocles' *Oedipus*" by Bernard Knox from *Tragic Themes in Western Literature*, ed. Cleanth Brooks (New Haven and London, 1955), pp. 7-29.

For recent bibliographies of tragedy, see Clifford Leech's book (Note 27), pp. 82-86; Roger L. Cox's *Between Heaven and Earth, Shakespeare, Dostoevsky, and the Meaning of Christian Tragedy* (New York, 1969), pp. 249-52; and for Greek drama, Shakespeare, and also general tragedy, see Alfred Cary Schlesinger's *Boundaries of Dionysus* (Cambridge, 1963), pp. 133-35.

[38] *Oedipus Rex*, trans. Dudley Fitts and Robert Fitzgerald (New York, 1939), p. 78.

edge . . . , or reaffirmation, of the dignity of the human spirit.
. . . ." (4) "affirmation or reaffirmation. . . ."[39]

As Krook points out, the knowledge need not be explicitly
the hero's nor the affirmation his, as is the case in this Giono
novel. Like Jocasta, both Mme Tim and Saucisse accept a
lawless universe, but, like Oedipus, Langlois rises above their
slave morality.

Le Moulin de Pologne (1952)

Le Moulin de Pologne, labeled "roman" instead of "chronique"
like the six novels that preceded it in the postwar years, falls
into what we have agreed may rightly be called Giono's
"seconde manière."[1]

As he completes the reading of this difficult and vaguely

---

[39] See Dorothea Krook's *Elements of Tragedy* (New Haven and
London, 1969), pp. 2, 8, 9, 25-26, *et passim*.

[1] The term "seconde manière" comes from *Giono par lui-même* (Le
Seuil, 1956, p. 107), by Claudine Chonez, who furthermore states that
Giono himself spoke mildly of his postwar fiction, claiming "qu'il n'y
a pas changement brusque, mais une évolution dont les causes remon-
tent très haut." The critic Pierre de Boisdeffre in Chapter IV of *Une
Histoire vivante de la littérature aujourd'hui*, Paris, 1958 (p. 249),
calling Giono "un des plus vivants écrivains de notre temps" (p. 251),
arbitrarily refers to this change in manner as "la métamorphose
stendhalienne" (p. 249). Even more recently, Gaëtan Picon spoke of a
"métamorphose décisive" in his *Panorama de la nouvelle littérature
française*, Paris, 1960 (Part II, "La Génération de 1930," p. 80). After
this transformation, according to Picon, Giono ceased moralizing and
consequently allowed his imagination more freedom to create myths.
In assessing Giono's importance in our century, Picon said (p. 81):
"Seul peut-être de tous les grands écrivains de sa génération, Giono
est parvenu à donner à son oeuvre des prolongements imprévus. Plus
puissante que jamais coule la sève de l'imagination. Et elle s'accompagne d'une audace technique et d'une maîtrise croissantes."

Gothic tale of sacrificial offering and death, the reader feels like a foremost juror summoned by an angry Giono to determine the guilt or innocence of a faceless witness in a murder trial, where the judge has died and where there never were advocates, actual evidence, or reliable testimony. If in such a case the juror hands down a verdict of guilty, he has realized that the tale told him by the anonymous witness was a murderer's rationalization, or that, in other words, there was neither morality nor fairness in his account.

It is therefore inappropriate to discuss the story told in *Le Moulin de Pologne* before ascertaining who is telling it, from what point of view it is told, what its basis in fact is, and what the role of the witness was. All that can be said about the story, before such questions are answered, is that it involves a series of exterior conflicts, resulting usually in death, between members of the Coste family and "destiny" until only an artist remains alive. After her disappearance, only the narrator remains to complete his testimony. Upon closing the book, the reader realizes that the narrator's was the sole testimony, that he was the witness whom the reader must exonerate or inculpate. Even after his case has been weighed and the juror's verdict pronounced, there will remain, as far as the *Moulin de Pologne* is concerned, the questions of the tale and its significance, and the further complication of the literary mode explicitly and implicitly invoked in this *a priori* innocent but finally furiously angry novel.

Henri Peyre, justly and unequivocally saluting Jean Giono in 1955 as "one of the finest masters of contemporary French prose," was perhaps the first to pierce the author's intent by seeing that in *Le Moulin de Pologne* the story itself "appears gratuitous."[2] In his chapter on Giono's narration, Pierre R.

[2] See *The Contemporary French Novel* (New York, 1955), pp. 145 and 154.

Robert in 1961, wondering if this particular novel was a completely satisfactory experiment, pointed out that there was more than one narrative focus, one of which became in time "le personnage central"[3] of the work.

It seems worthwhile to reexamine first the narrative technique of this novel in order to demonstrate the ingeniousness of the author by an analysis of this one very narrow facet of what will remain, even after continued inspection, an extremely complicated book. Before commencing this deliberation of evidence, the juror notes that his preliminary findings corroborate a statement by Claudine Chonez[4] to the effect that Jean Giono worked assiduously upon this book, so that whatever can be discovered in it was placed there by him with malice aforethought, to be discovered.

The first chapter of the novel, which begins reasonably enough with traditional statements in the third person past definite, as if Giono himself were telling the story, plunges the reader into details concerning the *Moulin de Pologne*, this "château de la Belle au bois dormant"[5] from which the book takes its title, and concerning M. Joseph, a mysterious man of about forty newly arrived in the small city:

"Despite his aura of mystery, he did not disturb us. This is quite difficult to explain. To tell the truth, he did disturb us. But not to the point of fear. When I noticed this, I was really much more astonished to see that evildoing was not being practised against him. Well, not really" (p. 13).

[3] Two very interesting pages are devoted to *Le Moulin de Pologne* in *Jean Giono et les techniques du roman* (University of California Press, 1961). See Chapter 1, *La Narration*, pp. 17-19.

[4] See *Giono par lui-même*, p. 59.

[5] P. 79. All page numbers refer to the 48th edition of Gallimard (Paris, 1952). This book appears also in the *Livre de Poche* series, and in English translated by Peter de Mendelssohn under the title *The Malediction* (New York, 1955).

Thus, on the seventh page of the novel, emerges unexpectedly[6] the unknown narrator who will refer to himself throughout as "je," and who slides on the scene so inconspicuously that the casual reader may not even have noticed a change from the third-person pronoun. Immediately following this reference, the reader is *on purpose* distracted by a vigorous discussion of trivia, in this case, of the rival musical societies which "nous" have in town. Three pages later, however, "je" reappears, this time as one of the hostile collectivity attempting to disarm and destroy the hero, M. Joseph.

It is not until page seventeen that the reader gleans the first concrete information concerning the narrator: "je" is a man, first of all, a fatuous, self-important personage, who draws sharp class distinctions: "I cannot boast that I belonged to the fashionable set, but my strict regard for the truth obliges me to declare that the high society of our small city has never spurned my humble self. And this particular high society was born to the purple" (pp. 17-18). The narrator is proud to be a confidant of the "gros bonnet," M. de K. . . ; both lead public opinion against their judge, M. Joseph.[7] "Je ne suis pas un esprit pénétrant et universel comme M. de K. . . ," says the hypocritical narrator (p. 26). Nor is he to be classed with "ces gens du commun sans imagination"; he belongs to "des meilleurs entre nous."

By the end of Chapter I, the reader, struggling to understand the who, what, and why of this work, perceives that the past tense is appropriate to the narrative since "je" is reconstructing incidents "avec le recul du temps." Reviewing

---

[6] See *Jean Giono et les techniques du roman*, p. 18.

[7] M. Joseph may perhaps also be classed along with Giono's Angélo and Camus's Dr. Rieux, since he is, in the words of Léon-François Hoffmann, a modern hero "qui par son action personnelle, peut contrecarrer les forces obscures de l'inconscient collectif." (*La Peste à Barcelone*, Princeton University, Paris, 1964, p. 85.)

from memory, "je" frankly evokes what happened long before, sometimes inventing a scene he claims to have witnessed
as he huddled close to M. de K. . . at the other end of an
esplanade. By the end of the chapter, the stunned reader
finds himself actually hearing a reconstruction rigged by the
arch-enemy of M. Joseph, the only character thus far for
whom admiration is felt. Such is the fearful reality of these
literary characters, however shadowy they remain, that a
stroll through Manosque today is apt to reveal them and their
"promenade" along the city's western perimeter.

After having brought the reader to "la nuit du scandale"
(p. 34), the narrator explains in Chapter II that he must
make a long detour (into what will be for the reader pluperfect time). This regression, during which the fearful reader
is following as closely upon the track of the narrator as upon
that of the five generations of the Coste family, destroyed by
their "destin, cependant défié" (p. 46) until only the artistic
Julie remains alive, occupies approximately one-third of the
book. Through these historical tragedies the reader must rely
upon the narrator, who now freely admits that he has his information from "notoriété publique," from "semble-t-il," and
from "disait-on," and furthermore, that, having subsequently
lived (?) in the *château*, he can imagine Coste there on a giv-
en day in November: "Je connais assez maintenant les personnages du drame pour imaginer sans trop y mettre du mien
leurs conversations et leurs gestes" (p. 40). Occasionally the
narrator reveals more of himself: "La vie des autres, avec ses
vicissitudes, ses malheurs, ses défaites, est extrêmement agré-
able à regarder." What is agreeable to the narrator is immediately explained; he enjoys observing in the lives of others "de
belles haines, de splendides méchancetés, d'égoïsmes, d'ambi-
tions" (p. 58). After the tragic death of Coste, the narrator
apologizes to the reader (p. 61) for what will be an accumu-

lation of "malheurs," asks the reader *not to laugh*, and explains that his only pretension is to a knowledge of the human heart, since he is neither artist, creator of art, nor a useless art critic: "Je me borne à dire ce que je sais de source certaine et le plus simplement du monde."

After such a falsehood, or such irony on Giono's part, the ugly narrator continues dispassionately to recount the tragic and sudden deaths of Coste's granddaughter, of his daughter, and then, with arrogance, the madness of her husband: "J'ai trouvé des signes de dérangement chez lui bien longtemps à l'avance."

When he became interested in the Coste story, says the narrator, his research led him to the old issues of two newspapers, where he found articles and "dessins horribles" concerning the deaths of Coste's second daughter Clara, who was "carbonisée" along with her husband, her two sons, and such innocent travelers as Dumont d'Urville.[8] The collectivity, he says, as he finds an excuse for them, was by this time terrified of the Costes since their destiny could also strike by-

---

[8] Jules-Sébastien-César Dumont d'Urville (1790-1842), a famous antarctic explorer, perished, as Giono's narrator says, in the train wreck of Versailles. We have thus one date for our story, which could set the arrival of Coste and his daughters in the town as much as twenty years earlier. Giono would have us imagine Coste as an *émigré* returning from Mexico to France around 1820. This date is historically understandable, corresponding then to the period of revolution in Mexico that culminated in a short-lived empire (1821-1823). Even the name "Coste" is reminiscent of the Mexican priest, revolutionary, and national hero, Hidalgo y Costilla (1753-1811). Coste was supposed a Jesuit, and it is also possible that Coste's death by tetanus poisoning, his "rire tétanique," is an attempt on Giono's part to suggest the call to arms of Hidalgo y Costilla, the *grito de dolores*. A further similarity is the description of Coste and his daughters, who seem intended as Creoles like the Mexican revolutionary. M. Joseph also came from Mexico and is associated with Pancho Villa (see pp. 14-15). Other names of characters recall the First Empire in France.

standers. When accusations are leveled, says the narrator (p. 75), "je sais qu'il ne faut jamais dire non. Il n'y a pas d'innocents." Therefore, continuing his research, he decides that the old housekeeper Hortense perhaps loved Jacques: "I have never been impeded by love: I do not know what love is. . . . It appears that love is a gift of oneself. Egoism in its pure state wears the same face as love, then. That's why they say that Miss Hortense died of love and that her death was chalked up to Jacques's account" (pp. 91-92).

Jacques's children were Jean and Julie, whom the narrator knew personally; he has thus brought the reader up to present time and to first-hand knowledge. When Julie was ten years old, the narrator was "a very small young man, with his own way to make at that time. I had already filed people into their two quite distinct categories: those who could be of some use to me, and those who were of no utter use to me." "Je" saw Julie being carried home from her tormentors at school; once an "adorable petite fille étonnée," also called "la morte," she finally fell ill. One side of her face became paralyzed and hideous, while the other side remained beautiful. Julie was "un ogre de musique," a fact that the narrator twists because he is proudly not artistic, or "nul en musique" himself: "Je participais à la chose plus par politique que par passion personnelle."[9] The town ("nous") hated the creative Julie, whom they loaded with their guilt; their hatred, shared by the narrator, fed them during lean times, since man does not live by bread alone. Like the others, the narrator *hoped* to see the artist "disparaître en charbons dans les ténèbres" (p. 114). As Chapter II ends, the narrator has

[9] P. 105. The reader arrives at the narrator's age at this point. Julie is thirty at the death of her parents, and she is six years younger than Jean, who is the same age as the narrator. At thirty-six, then, the narrator is "une jeune homme qui promettait" (p. 110).

returned to "la nuit du scandale," where Julie *unfortunately* did not disappear forever, "à l'encontre de l'espérance générale."

In the dramatic climax to this book, what is sardonically termed the "bal de l'amitié" (p. 117)—where the collective hatred of the town is unleashed against their sacrifice, Julie —Giono's scorching irony merits Léon-François Hoffmann's judgment of "un réalisme impitoyable."[10] The scene of the festivities, or mass hypnosis, is the Casino, situated next to the local *slaughter house.* After having applied himself assiduously to nonessentials, which hypnotize the reader and divert his attention from the mass violence and murderous intent of the local dancers, the narrator describes from close proximity the scapegoat Julie at the ball, her flight to M. Joseph, and the latter's mastery as he rescues her. By Chapter IV, this intended sacrificial offering is the cherished wife of M. Joseph, who has undertaken her combat with "fate." The narrator has been bought, or temporarily enlisted as their agent:

"In admiration I whistled a tribute to M. Joseph, for his consummate skill. I took off my hat to him. That's what you could call a first-rate performance.

"You can believe it or not, but, as I mulled over my approaching appointment, the fact that I was going to be dealing with such supreme skill, and at the same time with such a winner, warmed and comforted me. I am myself very hard to beat. I believe that what chills me the most is mediocrity" (p. 171).

Although Chapter V is an artistic triumph in that it succeeds almost totally in persuading the reader that the modern artist Julie is henceforth safe and will continue so, and although Chapter VI, despite the death of M. Joseph and the incipient insanity that only the narrator suspects in his son,

[10] See *La Peste à Barcelone,* p. 81.

lulls the reader and causes him to believe in the narrator's decency, there are enough clues in the final chapter to revive the reader's suspicions and enable him to clarify the finale according to what he has learned about human beings in the first four chapters.

The verdict is finally that "je" stands guilty of Julie's death, "par des biais." By delaying her in his room, he killed her by intent: "Si les intentions tuaient, nos salles à manger, nos chambres à coucher, nos rues seraient jonchées de morts comme au temps de la peste" (p. 85). After her flight, it was the narrator who tapped along the pavement, *hoping* to find her body. Destroying slowly the one artistic person in the community was a joy that he savored "dans les lenteurs" (p. 6); for, as the reader recalls, the narrator chose a slow revenge. Once M. Joseph was dead, and the narrator was the only person in town whom M. Joseph had to "buy," "je" could use "des atouts pour gagner" (p. 15) and "la force des choses."

The whole town hated Julie, not because of any share in any Coste destiny, but *because as an artist she* was dangerous, because she *charmed others*: "Si je disais qui j'ai vu, aussi subjugués, je ferais comprendre les autres raisons que nous avions tous de haïr et de brocarder cette jeune fille" (p. 106). Julie "n'offrait que *des places au Paradis*" (p. 140). Therefore "je" *helped* this other Pied Piper commit suicide, just as the townspeople had decided she should, the evening of the ball. A master stroke, on the part of Giono, is Julie's half lucidity when she inquires abruptly of the narrator if he will betray her.

After having returned to the first three chapters in order to understand the final or seventh chapter, and after having established the guilt, the reader can list, with the view of contrasting him to the author, the character traits of "je." He is, first of all, a narcissistic man like Montherlant's Costals, not content to record, for example, that he smiled, but impelled to say: "je me contentai de sourire finement" (p. 123). He admired M. Joseph only because he was an antagonist "de taille," showed some admiration for Pierre and Lucien because he alone detected their weakness, but, particularly, he disliked women. The vulgarity of his language throughout the book (the anonymous letters were "ordurières à souhait," p. 74) is most pronounced in his descriptions of women, as: "Son énorme poitrine surplombait le vide et, à force de compression et de retenue sans défaut, elle avait fait passer son ventre dans ses fesses" (p. 31). He is callous, as in his account of Coste's tragic death: "La mort de Coste fit un certain bruit" (p. 61). More than callousness, however, his prime characteristic is sadism. He dwells with delight upon the deaths of heroes: Dumont d'Urville "perdait sa graisse comme un rôti tombé de sa broche" (p. 72). His malignancy is often betrayed by a single word: the château was so near the promenade that one could "cracher sur la toiture" (pp. 35, 105).

Despite the detailed and consistent character of the evil narrator imagined[11] by Giono, there remain minor flaws in Giono's concept of him, or certain involuntary resemblances to the author himself. The first seems of least significance and the most understandable: the narrator is like Montherlant's hero an author, and one whom M. de K. . . considers inferior to Victor Hugo (p. 163). In other words, Giono sees this enemy as a poet. Like Giono, he is a spectator of human relations, with "l'ouïe fine" (p. 159) and eyes "exercés et sagaces"

---

[11] Jacques Pugnet first came to this conclusion when he said of Giono's characters that "leur comportement est moins observé qu'imaginé." *Jean Giono* (Paris, 1955), p. 69.

(p. 144).[12] In one respect, finally, it is impossible not to see Giono in the narrator, and that is in his use of imagery derived from country life and animals, despite the vulgarity with which Giono has disguised it. Although "je" is a city dweller, he observes that Sophie walks "comme les canards" (p. 29); that the girls at the ball assume "des immobilités de biches entendant le cor" (p. 129); that Hortense wanted "le posséder comme un taon possède un boeuf" (p. 89); that M. Joseph "récoltait beaucoup de saluts" (p. 33); and again that Hortense was a "femme forte comme un cheval . . . mangeant de la viande saignante, buvant sec, se crottant sans souci et portant ostensiblement du toc par esprit combatif" (p. 37).

The narrator, carefully imagined so that he is unlike Giono in his contempt for women, still resembles him in the way he plays with words and in his exploration of their precise meanings, since common words such as "hope" and "promise" either take on a new and sinister connotation as they come from his pen, or are susceptible of redefinition: "je parle de passion maternelle (loin de moi de parler d'amour maternel) . . ." (p. 91). It is in respect to language that Giono was originally classed by Jacques Pugnet as a modern novelist: "Nous ne pouvons refuser à Giono, un des créateurs de notre langage, le titre de contemporain."[13]

Although Giono has made a valiant attempt to ensure that no critic will identify him as the loathsome narrator, stipulating, for instance, that "je" disliked music when it is a well-known fact that the author of *Que ma joie demeure* (1935)[14]

[12] See *Style in the French Novel* by Stephen Ullman (Cambridge, 1957), pp. 217-31, where the imagery characteristic of Giono is studied, via *Regain*.

[13] See *Jean Giono*, p. 132.

[14] This novel of Giono, called "epic" by Henri Peyre (p. 136), takes its title from the Bach chorale, *Jesu, joy of man's desiring*.

is particularly fond of it, he may be equated, however, with the heroine Julie.

It is Julie, the artist, the person offered as a sacrifice by the community, who has the super-narrator's sympathy, and who appears to be Giono's projection of himself, much as the *persona* Marie was himself in *Batailles dans la montagne*. Just as the reader knows that Julie's face was only half beautiful, so one may recall with Henri Peyre the memorable sentence he quoted from Giono's autobiographical *Jean le bleu* (1932): "The tragic thing about our lives is that we are nothing but halves."[15] Just as Jean (Giono) viewed the world in blue, as we shall see, so does Julie: "The officers of the law took charge at the Mill of Poland. . . . With Julie, they had come across someone to whom they could talk, or more precisely, someone to whom they could not talk. She entertained them on the subject of the world of blue, where they were out of their depth" (p. 108). It is, as already seen, Giono and Julie who are fond of music, and Julie who like *Jean le bleu*, Noé, and Ulysse caused a "scandale" (p. 104) by singing at "une certaine messe de Pâques" (p. 103) "un *alleluia* ou un *In dulcis jubilo*. . . ." The narrator concludes: "Nous sommes des chrétiens, bien sûr, mais il ne faut jamais trop demander à personne" (p. 104). That the frail artist is expendable in our twentieth century must be attributed to "la comédie" of life itself; that "nous" righteously expect to be excused for this persecution is implied in the narrator's question (p. 139): "Qui n'a pas ses désespoirs?"

Aside from certain intrusions on the part of the author, *Le Moulin de Pologne* is a novel ostensibly written by an anonymous or auxiliary narrator. The book remains memorable as an interesting experiment in modern fiction, and a strong

[15] See *The Contemporary French Novel*, p. 136.

chastisement of the reader on moral grounds, meriting Gaëtan Picon's praise for technical audacity first of all because of its narrator. It is his telling of the story, his selection of incident and detail, his excitement at the sight and the thought of violent death, and his methodical indictment of the artist that reveal him as the villain.

After due deliberation, the reader firmly hands down the verdict of guilty, notwithstanding the narrator's plea of extenuating circumstances as he ends his tale (p. 235): "Et moi qui clopinais péniblement derrière elle. (Ai-je dit que je suis bossu?)."

AFTER having examined the curious and sophisticated narrative procedures of this novel, we may turn to our question proper, its literary mode. *Le Moulin de Pologne* is certainly described on its title page as "roman," but Giono perhaps, as he composed it, visualized it less as fiction than as drama, and most specifically as an English or Elizabethan tragedy.[16] Despite the precision given on the title page, we are informed in the text that the work is not a "roman" but a "drame," more properly a "faux drame,"[17] since it can be read only as prose fiction. Nevertheless, the life portrayed in this work is "tragique," the people represented are "acteurs" or "personnages," and the fabulous eighteenth-century estate called the Mill of Poland is a "théâtre."[18] In addition to these textual precisions, Giono further presents us with four epigraphs that, while elucidating the significance of the novel, narrowly relate it to four tragedies written and produced in England during the reigns of Elizabeth I and James I. *Le Moulin de*

[16] The title of the book also relates it to Gothic fiction and its castles, but then again, Gothic fiction is often derived from Shakespeare.

[17] *Le Moulin*, pp. 40, 233.

[18] *Ibid.*, pp. 22, 40, 58, 68, 76, 83, 157.

Pologne closely resembles, as we shall see, because of its subject matter, its structure, its characters, and its story elements, a traditional, five-act tragedy.

While we are familiar with novels heavily indebted to tragedies,[19] and also familiar with fiction that would be far less
effective without the dramatic preparation of its epigraphs—
a notable precedent is Pushkin's *Queen of Spades*[20]—we must
admire the practiced and subtle artistry of Jean Giono, who
in this modern French novel captured the glamour of a literary
mode perfected in England by William Shakespeare.[21]

Even a bare outline of the plot alerts us to resemblances
with tragedy since the story involves a heroine who is the
plaything of chance, herself helpless and innocent, but curiously and mysteriously unfortunate.[22] Acting with "une

[19] In his *Histoire de la littérature française* (Paris, 1912), Gustave
Lanson found the *Princesse de Clèves* "une transposition du tragique
cornélien dans le roman" (p. 490). In France, the connection between fiction and tragedy is commonly made, as by Maurice Rat
in his preface to the *Théâtre complet* of Racine (Paris, 1960),
where he discusses the influence of Racine upon Laclos, quoting also
Jean Giraudoux to that effect. In his *Imaginaire* (Paris, 1940) Sartre
also believes: "Lire un roman, c'est prendre une attitude générale de
la conscience: cette attitude ressemble grossièrement à celle d'un spec-
tateur, qui, au théâtre, voit le rideau se lever . . ." (pp. 87-88).

[20] The Pushkin work comes to mind not only because of its epigraphs
but also because of the similar use of fairytale for the impersonal,
amoral, and cold narrative tone of both works. Giono begins with a
"jadis" reminiscent of "Il était une fois . . . ," which Pushkin has
duplicated with the Russian "Once upon a time. . . ."

[21] Among many valuable studies, see H. E. Fansler's *The Evolution
of Technic in Elizabethan Tragedy* (New York, 1921); Janet Spens'
Elizabethan Drama (London, 1922); Lady Bess Campbell's *Shake-
speare's Tragic Heroes. Slaves of Passion* (Cambridge, 1930); John
Lawlor's *The Tragic Sense in Shakespeare* (London, 1960); Clarence
Valentine Boyer's *The Villain as Hero in Elizabethan Tragedy* (New
York and London, 1914); and especially Fredson Thayer Bowers'
Elizabethan Revenge Tragedy. 1587-1642 (Princeton, 1940).

[22] For a history of tragedy, a definition of English tragedy, and a

logique stupéfiante,"[23] fate dangles its sword of Damocles above this tragic young woman for whom we therefore feel all the pity, pain, and fear we experience in the theater for the unmerited misfortune of the tragic victim. After Julie's disappearance, or suicide, or death, and as this novel closes, we feel, just as after a Shakespearean tragedy, sorrow for Julie, fear of the patient malevolence of the narrator, anger because of the persecutions of society, and a pervasive sympathy for the suffering of all such artistic persons. Thus, in another Giono novel, the ancient catharsis of tragedy is again effectually achieved.

From generation to generation Julie's family has waged its unsuccessful combat with destiny until only she remains alive. At this point the narrator reveals himself not as her legal agent alone, but as the sole observer, a sage spirit of evil, a super-immoralist and self-appointed instrument of her destiny. Giono terms this conflict with a malignant fate from the name of Julie's ancestor, "la bataille des Coste," or the "bagarre-Coste," "ce combat" with fortune into which the heroine is drawn until she arrives finally at the very "centre du destin."[24] Julie is not ordinary, but like every "victime" of tragedy, "exceptionnelle," likened to a bird hypnotized by the serpent-like narrator, who will purvey to her his services, that sole "marchandise gratuite"—death itself.[25] Julie's end will come, not from water like that of Rousseau's Julie, but from a rope in the attic. As she is the pitiful victim, so the narrator is the antagonist of tragedy, and M. Joseph the valiant protagonist.

discussion of the Shakespearean or *modern* conception, see Ashley H. Thorndike's *Tragedy* (Boston and New York, 1908), pp. 1-18, *et passim*.

[23] *Le Moulin*, p. 232.

[24] *Ibid.*, pp. 51, 144, 52-53, 70-71.

[25] *Ibid.*, pp. 112, 35, 137, 140.

In structure also, as well as in theme, *Le Moulin de Pologne* bears a strong similarity to a tragedy, or to what T. W. Baldwin called in 1947 the "Terentian five-act formula."[26] Giono's expository Parts I and II present the major characters and recount the past tragedies of the Coste family. Part III, or the weird ball scene, where Julie is willed by the townspeople to commit suicide, corresponds to Act II or to the beginning of the action. The epitasis of Act III coincides with Part IV, where combat is joined in the confrontation of the narrator by M. Joseph. Act IV, during which the conflict reaches its desperate state, is represented in the Giono novel by Parts V and VI, where the death of M. Joseph and the incipient insanity of his son, observed by the narrator alone, warn the reader that presently Julie will be defenseless. The catastrophe of Act V occurs swiftly in the last eight pages of Part VII, just as the crisis-deed falls in the last scenes of *Othello* and of *Hamlet*.

Such an arbitrary division of this pseudo-Gothic novel into five acts—and Walpole's prototypical *Castle of Otranto* has also been so divided—finds further justification in the five changes of scene or five places where the action occurs. The protasis falls into an apparently compact area adjacent to the lodgings of M. Joseph, the streets of the small city, and an esplanade from which one overlooks the Mill of Poland. Since Part II of the novel is purely expository, no place mentioned is actually visualized. Act II is, as we have already seen, the second major area of action, which extends from the ballroom through the streets of the city to M. Joseph's lodgings again. Act III occurs in the narrator's room, and Parts V and VI of the novel (Act IV) at the Mill. Julie arrives in the last scene at the narrator's new residence, from which he and she walk to

[26] *Shakespeare's Five-Act Structure* (University of Illinois, 1947), p. 497.

the livery stable. It is presumably the same livery stable from which M. Joseph and Julie departed after the ball, and therefore within walking distance of both M. Joseph's lodgings and the Mill of Poland. However, Giono, or the narrator, describes his house as being fifty "kilomètres d'ici,"[27] the only slip of the pen, it seems, which Giono has made. Fifty kilometers is much too far for Julie to have walked, or for the two of them to have walked to the livery stable. The "ici" probably refers to Giono's own study and to his method of composition, which he has described so vividly, as we have seen, in the first fifty pages of *Noé* (1947). The author observes, then, neither unity of time nor of place, only that of action, as Shakespeare did, for example, in *Othello*.

Not only is *Othello* (Act V, Scene ii) invoked by Giono for his Part vii, or Act V, but also Shakespeare's *Henry IV* (Second Part, Act IV, Scene iv) for Part v, *The Changeling* by Thomas Middleton and William Rowley (Act V, Scene i) for Part i, and *The Atheist's Tragedy* by Cyril Tourneur (Act II, Scene i) for Part iv.[28] These epigraphs, and the particular

[27] *Le Moulin*, p. 227.

[28] For an exact situation of these epigraphs, see *The Works of William Shakespeare*, Stratford Town Edition (Oxford, 1938): *Othello* (vv. 361-62, p. 857), *King Henry the Fourth Part II* (vv. 313-15, p. 477). For *The Changeling*, see the edition of N. W. Bawcutt (London, 1958), v. 91, p. 95; *The Atheist's Tragedy*, ed. Irving Ribner (London, 1964), vv. 73-76, p. 31.

Giono's evocation of Elizabethan drama coincided with a strong interest in contemporary France, as one sees from consulting issues of *Le Figaro Littéraire*: *The Changeling*, playing at the Théâtre Récamier under the title *Les Amants maléfiques*, issue of Sept. 23-29, 1964, p. 12. Cyril Tourneur's *La Tragédie du venguer* was presented at the Périgord Festival, as reported in *Figaro* by Jean Prasteau, issue of August 19-25, 1964, p. 10. For *Tamerlan*, see Jacques Lemarchand's article, issue of July 15-21, 1965, p. 12. For another statement concerning Shakespeare in modern times, see also Jean Chalon's interview with Yvette Etiévant, issue of August 12-18, 1965, p. 11.

words quoted, serve two primary functions, that of comment upon the similarity of situation between the novel and the tragedy so that the reader adds to Giono's conceptualizations the wealth of the English masterpieces thus elicited, and also that of clarification of the catastrophe by these inferences of the parallelisms of character.

Giono's prime problem in composing this novel, it seems, was to admit the reader only very slowly into a guarded secret, which could be pierced by careful reading, by the assistance of literary association, and finally by deduction after the book was closed. The secret was, of course, the utter unreliability and then the criminal action of the narrator, whom Giono discredited only very gradually, and never completely. The catastasis-catastrophe, the death of Julie, does not actually occur in the book or on stage, as it were, but in the mind of the reader; it is therefore all the more frightening.

The first epigraph quoted by Giono on the opening page of his novel is one verse that he identifies as coming from *The Changeling*: "A wondrous necessary man, my lord." Since this expository section of the novel describes the arrival of M. Joseph, the reader assumes *a priori* that the "necessary man" is, indeed, the hero M. Joseph. A recollection of this English tragedy, however, demonstrates the falsity of such an assumption. In this play, after Beatrice and her villainous lover De Flores have set fire to the maid's chamber, Beatrice's father Vermandero comments, speaking of De Flores (v. 91):

<blockquote>
That fellow's good on all occasions.
Beatrice.   A wondrous necessary man, my lord.
Vermandero. He both a ready wit, he's worth 'em
           all, sir;
           Dog at a house of fire; I'd ha' seen
           him sing'd ere now: ...
</blockquote>

The "necessary man" is the low-born murderer De Flores, who forces his attentions upon the high-born heroine Beatrice. De Flores is a changeling in the sense of an inferior, a substitute, or an unreliable person.[29] He also describes himself as having a "swine-deformity" (Act II, Scene 1), and he betrays Beatrice, just as Julie asks the narrator[30] if he will betray her. Thus, the first epigraph refers to the narrator and not to M. Joseph. He is the "dog" at a "house of fire," which is our *Moulin*. Because the reader is fascinated by the Prince-Charming entrance of M. Joseph, he thinks of him as being the center of attention in the introductory section of the novel. There is another hero, however. The narrator had also introduced himself by the first "je," placed inconspicuously on the seventh page of the novel, as we have seen, and he also was doubly the "necessary" man: the antagonist, and the (auxiliary) author. We are therefore to supply for the narrator precisions established concerning the vile changeling De Flores.

The second citation from an English tragedy aptly occurs before Giono's Part IV:

> Walking next day upon the fatal shore,   v. 73
> Among the slaughter'd bodies of their men
> Which the full-stomach'd sea had cast upon
> The sands, . . .

verses that Giono identifies for the reader as coming from *The Atheist's Tragedy*. These verses patently remind the reader that Part IV of the novel takes place on the "next day" after the ball, and that M. Joseph, now master of the Mill of Poland, has vanquished Julie's enemies. There are, however, other secondary implications of perhaps greater import.

[29] See *The Changeling*, Act II, Scene 1.
[30] *Le Moulin*, p. 232: " 'Vous ne me tromperiez pas?' dit-elle."

These verses, spoken by the murdering Borachio, tool of his fiendish master D'Amville, are a perfect example of the villainous and unreliable narrator since Borachio's entire story of Charlemont's death is false. As D'Amville replies to his valet, he might be describing Giono's narrator (v. 110):

> Thou art a screech-owl and dost come i'night
> To be the cursed messenger of death.

We may therefore add Borachio to De Flores as a second literary antecedent of the narrator, and further realize that we are dealing, in this complex novel, with a "revenge" tragedy.

Giono's Part v, which recounts an era of relative serenity after the wedding of M. Joseph and Julie, opens with verses from Shakespeare's *Henry IV*. Although Giono has quoted only a few words from the last monologue of the dying king as he passes on his crown and kingdom to his profligate heir (v. 313):

> God knows, my son,
> By what by-paths and indirect crook'd ways
> I met this crown; ...

he might also have had in mind succeeding verses to the effect that King Henry saw his reign as one chapter or scene (as in Giono), that he knew his enemies "have but their stings and teeth newly ta'en out," and that he died hoping that his son might succeed him in peace. In any case, the epigraph that Giono selected implies the kingship of M. Joseph, reminds the reader of his dubious antecedents and of the unorthodox circumstances under which, the night of the ball, he acquired both the hand of Julie and her domain. Because of the narrator, M. Joseph's head always lay uneasily, as King Henry also said: "Uneasy lies the head that wears a crown."[31]

---

[31] *Henry IV*, Part ii, Act III, Scene i, v. 31.

The fourth excerpt from an Elizabethan play recalled by Giono, and this time in French rather than in English, is the passage from *Othello, The Moor of Venice*, where Cassio says as Othello falls dying upon the body of Desdemona (v. 361):

> This did I fear, but thought he had no weapon;
> For he was great of heart . . .

Coming as they do before the short catastrophe of *Le Moulin de Pologne*, these lines gives us a final clue as to the narrator, the victim, and the protagonist: Iago, Desdemona, and the aged Othello himself. Like this almost unbearably tragic play, Giono's novel horrifies because of its many violent deaths. It also contains, like the Shakespearean play, frequent references to destiny, to fate, and to a curse similar to a plague. Equally conspicuous parallels, however, refer to the characterization of Iago, the most unreliable of speakers, and to Desdemona, the most helpless of victims. Like Iago, our narrator has no knowledge of love, a great greed for money; and, like the narrator, he pretends to be a faithful servant to his master Othello. The Shakespearean play ends in suicide like Giono's novel.[32] The main difference is that in the latter the villain, cleverly remaining within the law, goes unpunished.

It is interesting to note that Giono has omitted one Shakespearean play, *Richard III*, which would seem indicated in view of the fact that the narrator is a hunchback. It seems logical to believe that Giono, inasmuch as he did not choose to refer his reader to this early play, did not see his narrator as the violent and passionate English king of drama. Actually, Richard III is a character quite dissimilar both to De Flores and to Borachio, and even more unlike Iago, as Andrew Cecil Bradley demonstrated: "Richard III, for example, beside be-

[32] For an excellent interpretation of *Othello*, still see Andrew Cecil Bradley's *Shakespearean Tragedy* (London, 1904), pp. 176-233.

ing less subtly conceived, is a far greater figure (than Iago) and less repellent. . . . Nor is he so negative as Iago; he has strong passions, he has admirations, and his conscience disturbs him. There is a glory of power about him"[33]

Aside from the four references to Elizabethan tragedies that we have already reviewed, there are three other epigraphs in the Giono novel, the first two of which in Parts II and III are anonymous French and Italian proverbs. The former provides the apology for Giono's regression of Part II during which he details the hereditary curse of the Coste family, or their "vieux sac" of "soucis." The well-known Italian proverb of Part III ("Herba voglio non existe ne anche nel giardino del re"), standing as it does before the episode of the ball where the townspeople believe that they have succeeded in driving Julie to suicide, is the type of admonition a parent might make to a willful child, or, in this case, the super-narrator Giono to his creation Julie (Giono). Although this victim will find refuge, so to speak, in the king's garden, or in the arms of M. Joseph, that refuge is not what she really desires. Thus, Giono foreshadows the catastrophe upon which our eyes are set from the opening pages. The interpretation of the proverb's significance is further reinforced by the last epigraph.

At the opening of his Part VI, very near the finale of the novel, Giono places the following: "Préparez tout pour une grande fête. Da Ponte—Mozart: *Don Juan*." Here are Don Giovanni's words as he opens *Scena* XIII of the eighteenth-century opera: "Sia preparato tutto a una gran festa."[34] Subsequent allusions in the text confirm this fore-shadowing: that

[33] *Ibid.*, p. 207.
[34] See *Don Giovanni* (1787), book by Lorenzo da Ponte, Metropolitan Opera House, Grand Opera Libretto (New York, undated), p. 20.

Julie is attracted, even during the lifetime of M. Joseph, to her fate by some living power of evil, the narrator himself, who could not possess her in life. Giono's reason for having chosen the *Don Giovanni* of Lorenzo da Ponte rather than some other version of this legend—such as the *Don Juan* of Molière, for example—seems to be that in da Ponte as in Giono, the legend is interpreted as being not solely the tragedy of Don Juan himself, but also that of Julie, or of Elvira, or of Zerlina.[35] As Giono says: "Julie herself was at stake, she who weary of warfare had surrendered herself to

[35] This conclusion is also substantiated by the beautiful arias composed by Mozart for Elvira and Zerlina, for example. In this connection, it may perhaps be recalled that E. T. A. Hoffmann, an earlier Mozart enthusiast, focused attention more on Doña Anna than upon the male hero in his *Don Juan, Fabelhafte Begebenheit*, etc. The *Don Juan* of Molière seems, on the other hand, predominantly the hero's play, although Giono's emphasis upon the narrator's nocturnal prowlings does bring to mind Sganarelle's reference to the *loup-garou*. See p. 761, Act I, Scene 1 of *Don Juan* in the *Théâtre complet de Molière*, Vol. 1, ed. Robert Jouanny (Paris, undated). It might also be argued that Giono's narrator is *doucereux* like Molière's *Don Juan* of Act V, and also that Giono derived his notion of a hunchbacked Don Juan from the opinion of some that Molière used as his model the Prince de Conti (Armand de Bourbon, 1629-1666), whose grandson, Louis-François-Joseph, before his internment at Marseilles, was connected with the Kingdom of Poland. Molière's patron, the Prince de Conti, was deformed, as Jouanny says in his notice to the play (p. 710) and as La Rochefoucauld knew (p. 83 of his *Mémoires*), *Oeuvres complètes de La Rochefoucauld*, ed. L. Martin-Chauffier (Paris, 1950).

Two modern French plays based upon the Don Juan legend, *L'Homme et ses fantômes* of Henri-René Lenormand (4 acts, prose, Paris, 1924) and *Don Juan* by Henry de Montherlant (3 acts, prose, Paris, 1956), on the contrary, focus their attention primarily on the hero. The latter play, however, associates this legend with the problem of the artist in the modern world, an association that underlies Giono's sympathetic treatment of Julie. For two current revivals of the Don Juan legend, André Maurois' adaptation of Shaw, and Tirso de Molina's *Don Juan*, see *Le Figaro littéraire* (October 14-20, 1965), p. 13, and July 1-7, 1965, p. 14 respectively.

public scorn, abandoning her person so generously that no amount of support could ever help her withstand the irresistible Don Juan from hell."[36] The narrator thus becomes the jeering Don Giovanni of "Deh vieni alla finestra, / O mio tesoro."[37] It is also interesting to note the prominence in both da Ponte[38] and Giono of the masked ball, in the palace of Don Giovanni in the former case, and appropriately near the local slaughter house in the latter. The festival referred to in the epigraph, however, is Julie's rendezvous with her seducer, the "Don Juan des ténèbres."

From the various epigraphs we have learned, then, a great deal more about the characters and the situations of *Le Moulin de Pologne*. Julie is also the helpless victim of her own tragic proclivities; for this novel, like a good Elizabethan tragedy, is based upon character: "Destiny is merely the intelligence operative within objects, which bow down before the secret desires of him who, while appearing subservient to them, in actuality provokes, incites, and courts them."[39] She is fatally lured as were Zerlina, Donna Anna, and Donna Elvira. Most particularly, however, she resembles, in her incapacity to resist, the infinitely pitiful and also very lovely Desdemona. M. Joseph, like Othello, is majestic, grand, and a highly romantic figure who appears as if marvelously from some western wonderland. Like Othello he has led a charmed

---

[36] See *Le Moulin*, p. 213.

[37] See *Don Giovanni*, Act II, Scene iii, p. 32.

[38] In the original book the ball scene of *Don Giovanni* involves all the major characters and, comprising Scenes 13, 16, and 17, brings Act I of this two-act opera to a magnificent conclusion. As presented at the Metropolitan Opera House in New York, the ball occurs in Scenes 4 and 5 and requires twenty-two minutes of stage time. Giono places an equal prominence upon the ball scene in *Le Moulin*, and it also occurs, as in the opera, at the end of the first half of the book.

[39] See *Le Moulin*, p. 218.

life and like him he is old and unsuspecting. M. Joseph has also, towards the end of his life, some of the pathetic dignity of King Henry IV as Shakespeare chose to portray him. Like that King Henry of drama, he marvels at the vicissitudes that led him to his royal estate, and like him has a son of questionable stability.

Concerning the narrator, Giono allows us to glean only the barest hints, since the idea is that we must not guess his real nature until after the last page. Dressed in black, this hunchback who nimbly scaled the wall outside M. Joseph's lodgings the night of the ball runs through the night like Don Juan the werewolf, imparting news of Julie's whereabouts like Borachio the screech owl. Under a semblance of honesty, like "honest" De Flores and "honest" Iago, he represents the overpowering forces of evil. Like them, he artfully misrepresents reality. Like them, and like Don Juan, he cannot experience love, and like Molière's hero also, his religion is the arithmetic of money. Wordlessly he summons Julie through the night as Don Giovanni sang to Elvira: "Discendi, O gioja bella!"[40]

Jean Giono, in *Le Moulin de Pologne*, published for his readers another splendid work for which we are vastly indebted. He again, while generously offering both entertainment and instruction, demonstrated the depth of his knowledge of the human heart and the mastery he held magically over his own art. By recreating Desdemona, Iago, De Flores; Don Juan and Borachio; King Henry and Othello, he acknowledged and reasserted the power of his masters and ours, as well as the permanent continuity of letters that knows no barriers of time or place. In writing fiction that is more nearly tragedy, he showed not only his versatility but also a hesitation concerning *genres* that is typical of so many French

[40] See *Don Giovanni*, Act II, Scene II, p. 30.

writers who were both novelists and dramatists. Thus, the English blood tragedy, perfected in London in the sixteenth century, curiously underwent in 1952 modernization in a French Alpine city, as Jean Giono, characterizing his enemies, defended himself and all artists.

Mort d'un personnage (1949)

In *Mort d'un personnage* (1949),[1] where a first-person narrator tells of the aging and of the death of his grandmother, Giono performs a double feat: making an attractive old woman the central character of a novel, and recounting at considerable length the death of a mother. As he admitted to Claudine Chonez and to others,[2] his heroine for this novel, the Marchioness Pauline de Théus, whose youthful gallantry we have admired in *Le Hussard sur le toit*, having since that time loved Angélo Pardi and lost him, represents Giono's own mother Pauline, whom he nursed during her last illness. This Madame Giono died after her son's return from his first internment in Marseilles.[3] The novel takes place, like much of *Noé*, which it follows, in that city, along its streets, on the way to and from school, and at a home for the indigent blind.

The novel replies in its title as in its philosophy to Jules Romains's *Mort de quelqu'un* (1911), for the old Marquise remains from the dramatic confrontation occurring at the end of Chapter I, at which moment the boy narrator, her unnamed grandson, first sees her awesome and noble presence looming above him, to the last rasping breath of air that she takes into her lungs, the central character, the life and breath of the novel, its focus, its charm, and its dark mystery. Far

[1] Editions Bernard Grasset (1949), 5 chapters, 183 pp.
[2] *Giono par lui-même* (Paris, 1959), p. 30, for example, and especially Maxwell A. Smith's *Jean Giono* (New York, 1966), p. 159, and p. 156 ff.
[3] January 9, 1946.

from ever having been a nobody, she lives doubly as a literary character and as a personage. In fact, as the narrator confesses for his fictional grandmother, Giono might have admitted for his own mother: that he made her as he wanted her to be and to have been, particularly when she lay dying.

In her grandson, first as a schoolboy returning from his day school, and then as a young man returning from his travels, the grandmother Pauline sees despite her better sense two lives and two persons: first, a reincarnation, as it were, of her beloved young lover Angélo Pardi resurrected marvelously from the dead in a second, new, and child's body, and then another, special individual whom she thrice mysteriously identifies and designates: " 'Maybe so,' she said, after having stared at me for a long time. And she drew with her horny fingernail a ring around my forehead and my eyes" (p. 25). Thus, despite Giono's many allusions to his father, as we saw in his apocalypse text called "Le Grand théâtre," and despite the overwhelming biographical evidence to substantiate their similar philosophical, anarchical, and Protestant leanings, it appears finally here that Giono's quiet mother was, after all, the Jocasta-type woman who bore and fostered a creative artist. Here, after *Un Roi sans divertissement*, the Oedipus legend surfaces again in Giono's fiction.

Mort d'un personnage belongs with *Jean le bleu* (1932) as an autobiographical novel. But because it was written in Giono's maturity, it lowers barriers to treat, albeit in a fashion sufficiently veiled to protect the author's privacy and personal dignity, the lower depths of his creative impulses. There is no doubt that the child narrating the early pages of *Mort d'un personnage*, becoming the mature man who cradles in his arms the skeletal body of Pauline during her last night of awful agony, loved this old woman so passionately that he fiercely disputed with death over her poor bones. He functioned when a boy much as modern psychologists describe persons of "high creative accomplishments," whether male or female: "This precocious ability to charm and perform for adults is a direct outgrowth of the need to please the mother in the fused, symbiotic interaction characteristic of Jocasta-mothering. The continually escalating demands of the Jocasta mother in her lover's dialogue with the child seem to lead to precocious development and to create force-fields of personality that must perform and be recognized."[4]

Commenting upon the four post-war novels that were published in 1947 and 1949, *Un Roi sans divertissement, Noé, Mort d'un personnage,* and *Les Ames fortes,* Maurice Nadeau, critic of surrealism, remarked that both Pauline de Théus and her grandson Angélo Pardi thrust themselves through life as if each had, as was true in Giono's case, a mission to perform. All were strong-souled persons in that literary family: "It would seem as if in this world they had been entrusted with the accomplishment of a 'mission.' . . . They advance, thus, in their separate directions somewhat like blind persons set on rails so that they cannot stop themselves from arriving eventually at their destinations; these are, to coin a phrase, 'alive souls.' "[5] Thus, the grandmother and grandson walked together through the busy city streets of Marseilles, stopping before street hawkers and store windows, or rather she pushed along the child with a hand of iron (p. 37) and a superhuman force. She was, in her absence, all fist, step, heart, and smoke. Rearing up each time just short of death's shadows, calling desperately in total silence to her lost lover, she bore her grandson before her on her fist like a young falcon. While

[4] "Mrs. Oedipus Has Daughters, Too" by Matthew Besdine from *Psychology Today* (March 1971), p. 64.

[5] "Un Nouveau Giono," *Mercure de France,* CCCVII, No. 1,040 (April 1, 1950), pp. 693-97, and here pp. 694-95; reprinted in *Littérature présente* (1952), pp. 135-41.

others dragged their feet along solid pavements or firm earth, she threatened to drop into an abyss that only she could have found on some polished dance floor. When at night she prowled the house calling "Angélo!" the blind servant girl whispered to the child not to answer. Fiercely obstinate in her quest, the grandmother passed seventy-five, seventy-eight, eighty, and ninety-five years.

Since he was flesh of her flesh, "puisque j'étais né d'elle" (p. 120), why should the narrator not remember intermittently how he trudged along beside her, how he heard her seeking her lover, how he watched her totter over the downdraughts into hell, and how he rode beside her? When he was sick, she ordered him to vomit, so badly did the city turn her stomach. As earlier in *Noé*, the narrator repeats a train ride from Marseilles to Aix, this time bound for his grandmother's ancestral estate of La Valette. There in "la solitude désespérée des collines" (p. 64) a bargain is struck with the notary public of Vauvenargues, whom this time the super-narrator Giono is able to pass off without his customary acrimony. Like Ulysses at the gates of hell, the grandmother will use the gold coins from the sale of her property to purchase her entrance into the valley of the shadow. Her son agrees with a pride characteristic of such an indomitable being that the grandson, specially marked on eyes and forehead, will have no need for dross. His father, says the child narrator, resembled Saint Francis of Assisi. The dead Angélo Pardi was St. George. His mother, said Jean Giono in *Provence*, dedicated him to the Virgin, or first dispatched him out into the world: "My first trip took place in 1911. My mother dispatched me on the *dawn* pilgrimage to Moustiers-Sainte-Marie. Prior to that occasion, I had seen only the olive groves about Manosque."[6]

[6] See *Les Albums des Guides Bleus* (Paris, 1954), p. 5.

Cuddling close to her warm body in bed, the boy narrator used the blind servant girl Caille as his mother, for his grandmother herself resembled one born blind and without a soul. Every time the youngster ran towards the blind girl, his motion set vibrating the winds of her soul, so that lights flashed on in the milky sapphire of her blind eyes, so that words still unspoken took shape upon her lips, until answering chords twanged across the distance that closed between their straining bodies (p. 102). And yet, he approached his grandmother. She touched him, set him upon her knees, scolded him, looked towards him out of eyes as green as ocean water, and yet she never saw him, for to her he was forever a nothing and a nobody. Much as he strove, he could not spring into life in her eyes. There was absolutely no way for him ever to exist in her eyes, because behind her eyes she herself did not exist.

The narrator's anguish at not being taken to her bosom rises in concentric circles outwards as he reels tragically before the impossibility of being loved by this Jocasta-mother, who automatically casts him out again and again, away from herself:

"Not a thing existing upon this earth could live again within my grandmother, on the far side of her eyes: neither the city with its trout flanks flecked with the moving green, pink, and blue shimmerings of its tiles, its zinc, its glass, and its smoke; neither the amphitheater of limestone hills, nor the far distant golden villages hung like bucklers in front of the rostra of rocks, neither the sea which panted against its fretted promontories like the soft underbelly of some gigantic lizard, nor the countryside, sweeping off into the distance, loaded with copses, aqueducts, stands of cypress, olive groves, meadows, cover growth, and the hastening flocks of white mountains which, far beyond our circuit of hills, flocked

rounding off in the direction of Aix and the Alps. Not a thing. She could be tenanted only by herself, never by any picture, never by the consolation of a color, of a sound, of an odor, which by adding its own modulation to the modulation of one's blood can elevate and uphold as if one were a vessel under full sail; never by an association of ideas that enlightens, until enchanted one steps forward. She was blind in her heart" (p. 103).

Deprived of his mother's love, the narrator sought, as she thrust him away from her and out into the world, his triple consolation, as he called it: color, sound, and odor. Thus, here in Chapter IV (p. 103) he restated his structural pattern recalled from *Jean le bleu* (1932) and again established for this novel in Chapter I. When he was eight years old, says the narrator on the opening page, he was walked to school every day by their servant, Poor Girl. As he was held by her hand, he reveled every morning in the odors (pp. 10-11), in the sounds (p. 13), and in the colors, especially the blacks and whites—for this is an Angélo Pardi speaking—of Marseilles. Dressed in a romantic sailor suit in the corsair-city of Lord Byron, he corresponds to the photograph reproduced by Claudine Chonez in her *Giono par lui-même* (p. 29), where the boy Giono, eight years old in 1903, stands with downcast eyes looking at another world and holding his hoop in his left hand only because the photographer or his mother has thrust it there to give him some support. Still disconsolate, he poses for his first communion at age ten, in the book of Chonez opposite his mother Pauline Giono from a photograph designated *circa* 1895 but probably earlier, judging from the smallness of her waist. As the narrator claims, her eyes seem vacant indeed, and her heart-shaped face and delicate bones are his own. Quite truthfully the narrator claims never to have known his mother: "Seul, j'étais vêtu en lord écossais" (and the ten-year-old's resemblance to Thomas Gainsborough's *The Blue Boy* is striking, as Giono also thought) "car je n'ai pas connu ma mère et j'étais habillé ..." (p. 12).

On at least three occasions in *Mort d'un personnage* the narrator brings his grandmother Pauline to life from a photograph, or from a painting real or imaginary. We first see her at the close of Chapter I (p. 24) when after having advanced —(1) myself, (2) Poor Girl, (3) the morning trip to school with its odors, sounds, and colors—towards the noon-hour recess, the narrator retraces his steps homeward beside Poor Girl, now reeling intoxicated, (3) the evening trip from school with its colors, odors, and sounds, (2) Poor Girl, and (1) Grandmother. Climbing the hill with Poor Girl, the narrator first sees her seated like a poor woman, which in real life, of course, his mother was. As he approaches, she rises, growing taller and taller above him, and becoming, the more closely he can see her, more and more richly costumed. Jet sparkles against her brilliantined white hair, but her face itself flows backwards into the shadows, lighted only on the tip of the nose or the fold of the lips. Splendidly the black silk taffeta of her rustling skirts quivers over her impatient limbs. Thus, she greets her grandson, the future creator of fiction:

" 'What is your name, little boy?' she asked, when I had climbed up to her.

" 'Angélo Pardi,' I answered.

" 'That's a lie!' she said violently. It was my grandmother."

Thus, Giono has his mother, or grandmother, first label him as a feigner, a reconstructor of reality,[7] while on another level she reproaches him seemingly for not being, but for pretending to be, her lost lover. In *Le Bonheur fou* (1957), Angélo

[7] And so W. D. Redfern begins his *The Private World of Jean Giono* (Durham, 1967): "Jean Giono was born . . . a liar. . . . It entails either twisting the truth, or fabricating from scratch" (p. 1).

Pardi, dressed splendidly in black velvet, leaves his mother Pauline to *descend* the staircase of their Italian castle of La Brenta.

Another time the young narrator sees her standing in black against a white, limitless, barren space into which the light from her eyes flows outward in a straight line touching nothing into infinity, as in the work of Giono's friend, Bernard Buffet.

In what is visually the most interesting representation of the grandmother, Giono uses a technique of surrealist collage, or what the narrator terms a "superposition" (p. 120). In Chapter IV the narrator, still a pre-adolescent boy, observes his grandmother at an afternoon party among a throng of lovely young girls dressed in "immaculate white organdy" (p. 119). Through a strange, visual delusion the grandmother's head appears above the body of a lovely girl or "furtively" blooms upon another's body in all the exceptional blaze of its own lost youth. Seen with her own head, the pretty girl relapses into an ordinary person, but the grandmother, even after returning to her own black redingote, still emprisons about her person rays of her "gloire attachante." Imagining "la parole blanche des jeunes filles" (p. 125), and their world of folly, dreams, hope, desires, sufferings, joys, and waiting, the narrator understands why they all clung around his grandmother in that black and white drawing room: to them, she was passion incarnate.

Another time the narrator, seeing her beside a tree, understood how terrestrial she really was (p. 109 ff.). Again, he saw her standing in a meadow where the family had gone in their buggy. The grandmother, as usual, was dressed in closely tailored, body-fitted, all black clothing. She had picked for herself a bouquet of summer flowers, pink daisies[8] and yellow

[8] "English" daisies, or *pâquerettes*.

buttercups. Her gestures recaptured the "gaucherie adorable" of girls' bodies, and of their winsome ways as she turned the flowers around before her face and caressed them with her bare fingertips, holding them in her black lace gloves. Even then, she seemed to moan: "Thus, doubtless without wishing to do so, she offered the agonizing spectacle of her beauty in the sunlight, while, irresistibly seized by the hips, she was being borne away along the paths of the underworld" (p. 110). Thus, from the earliest pages, and before Giono begins to wring our hearts in Chapter V with the death of this aged beauty, we have as readers known that we had entered here through the portals of a passionate love, admitted into the sanctum of such a love story as rarely read before.

For the last fifty or so pages, the skeletal-like remains of a once proud beauty fall by default to the narrator, now a grown man returning from an ocean voyage to Valparaiso, as if he had once signed on for the voyage to Antarctica as recounted in *Fragments d'un paradis*. Instead of his lovely marchioness, he finds a cachectic, cadaverous crone—blind, deaf, immobile, her head permanently sunken on her chest. She has lost control of her functions. No one wishes to care for her, even for money. Whoever exposes himself to such disgust must do so for love alone.

What is love? the narrator reasons against his loathing. Is it picture-postcard sentimentality, bridal veils, orange blossoms? Is it loving the beloved for one's own satisfaction? Can not the narrator love his grandmother truly and only for herself, by providing her with food, water, soap, care, and cleanliness? Overcoming his revulsions one by one, he undertakes to exercise his utter love, even to the point of looking at her lolling and obscene tongue, even to the point of washing all her body.

Then when only her head and her digestive system remain

to some degree under her control, she still provides her grandson with sheer joy, so comical is she in defending herself against everyone else, all stronger than herself. Craftily she makes known her likes and dislikes, refusing vegetables, sucking happily away on olive oil, meats, cakes, and candies. Patiently her grandson feeds her wine and coffee in a teaspoon. Hungrily he watches her alone, in black, where she always desired to be, whence she bends her ears to sounds from the other side, calls through imperceptible fissures (p. 141), and drinks the burning breath of him whom she lost. Despite his continued efforts to hold her back, he sees her rush irrevocably towards her lover as towards earth and matter. When newly cleaned and changed and combed, she sits in her chair, sometimes she confidently stretches out her bony fingers towards her grandson, somehow knowing that it is he, knowing that he is there, and furthermore certain that he will fill her hand with her favorite candy. Then the narrator cries, overcome with ecstasy: "Je n'avais jamais éprouvé une joie si complète" (p. 152). Then, momentarily at least, he feels that truly he is loved by her whose great admirer he has always been.

Even then, however, she finds someone who loves her old bones more than he does: herself. Thus, angrily, she tucks in her fragile elbows when he carries her from room to room, her chair lifted up to his chest and borne before him. Covered as formerly with the magnificence of her beauty, he says (p. 154), she could afford "storms and love." As brutally angry as a Persian queen, he adds, and mummified also, she now trusts no one.

Then in her final days grandmother has her last love affair with the one person who always sees her only clean, washed, combed, and gentle—the laundress Catherine. These pages (160-67) probe the human condition so deftly, with such memorable sureness, with such tremendous sympathy that no person who has ever been critically ill and entirely dependent can ever forget. Demandingly, grandmother summons the kindly, generous Catherine from her washtubs and like a small child nestles against the warmth and life so ready to be shared from her breasts. Warmed against the creeping cold of death, the old crone expresses her last delight in human contact with "petits sanglots secs" (p. 163). Then she feels her sparse flesh satisfied and contentment steal over her, as it could come only from woman to woman, "odeur . . . rondeur . . . chaleur" (pp. 165-66). Aside from this tenderness, she craves only oil and candy. This summarizes her avidity "de fin du monde" (p. 167). Her *impedimenta* thus stacked up at finger's length for the night, she lies watching the dark hours through.

Before the end, the narrator is not only sad, but inexplicably so, as he watches grandmother send out for violet perfume to please Catherine, but dirty her hands each night. Only Catherine now can be lied to, "le dernier étranger" for whom she can "créer une illusion et en profiter" (p. 174).

The last night of her life, when no doctor can be found, the young man spends alone with his grandmother, holding her warm in his arms, raising her head, having to refuse her summoning of Catherine, and finally having to restrain her wild efforts to swing her cane and call the laundress, who is in any case too distant to hear the summons. Therefore, again at the very end, even at that final moment, the old woman turns her head away from her grandson. Giono's closing passage is superb, for its human pathos and understanding:[9]

---

[9] Maxwell A. Smith also admires this novel, which he finds of a "distressing realism," however, but "ennobled and rendered intensely moving . . . by the devotion of her grandson," etc. (*Giono*, p. 157). On the other hand, Marcel Arland referred to the heroine as "la

"Ah! what remorse! She turned away from me. Her head slid down heavily. Again a velvety vertigo swept through my body. I felt for her wrist. No more pulse. I tried to raise her head. Very heavy. Her mouth opened and closed soundlessly. I said to myself, 'She is dying!' It seemed to me that I should be running somewhere, in some direction or other. But I did not release my hold either on her arm or on her head. And then my vertigo passed. I said to myself: 'She is dying, without pain. Heaven be praised. Stay there. Do not call out.' Once again she opened her mouth.

"I heard a laborer pass by on our street, on his way to work. She still felt warm to my touch. I pressed my ear to her lips. After that, I went to awaken my father, and I said to him, 'Grandma is dead!'" (pp. 182-83).

Although he has struggled against releasing her right up to the last moment, the narrator finally rises and lets her go, for go she will by her own will and weight, and rise he must, and sing again. In her book *Le Mythe d'Orphée dans la littérature française contemporaine* (Paris, 1961), Eva Kushner found that since 1885 French authors, especially, had employed this myth, which apparently responded to what remained on their parts a certain anxiety, or even an anguish that they alone somehow felt obliged to confront. Echoing and apparently making significant, or even comprehensible to them their feeling of solitude, the myth also afforded them escape and a concrete pattern "pour transcender et embellir une reálité décevante" (p. 14). The myth, of course, speaks powerfully to us all of beauty and poetry struggling against a hideous world where doubtless a poet thirsts most for some *Ailleurs*. His notably is that sensitivity privileged to soar un-

---

vieille folle de *Mort d'un personnage*," *La Grâce d'écrire* (Paris, 1955), as cited by Boisdeffre in his *Giono* (p. 240).

der the wings of some "extraordinary love." Most interestingly, Kushner concluded that the authors whom she studied—
and Giono was not included among them[10]—were men apart,
"de grands isolés," without affiliation or tie with any specific
literary group, as was, generally speaking, Giono's habit.
Their works, based upon the myth of Orpheus and Eurydice,
certainly uncover common ground: "They recount an episode, which once revealed turns out to be the symbolic representation of some reality that we feel is much more basic in
the eyes of the author than was the mere episode itself"
(pp. 16-17). As for other modern authors who composed
works based upon this particular myth, it expressed on some
visionary level a reality particularly true for modern man
generally, and for themselves personally and privately. Artists often seem obsessed by one story, which they will repeat
over and again because it illustrates their solution to the
meaning of themselves in the world—as Giono repeated the
Noah legend, for instance. Not only, then, did the myth of
Orpheus suit Jean Cocteau's view of himself, but—although
he found it unnecessary to be explicit—it also suited Giono's
intimate assessment of himself: Julie, the scapegoat modern
artist, the novelist imprisoned.

Explicitly, however, Giono draws closer not to Cocteau in
his treatment of the myth, but rather to Jean Anouilh, because Eurydice also becomes Giono's main thrust. In
Anouilh's *Eurydice* of 1941,[11] a blue-eyed Orpheus also loses
to death a green-eyed beauty, and the scene revolves about
Marseilles. Thus, according to the discoveries of Eva Kushner, Giono would derive in his usage of the myth rather from
the Ovidian / Italian tradition, which understands this legend
as primarily a love story, or which focuses upon its "côté sen-

[10] Segalen, Debussy, Cocteau, Anouilh, Pierre-Jean Jouve, and Pierre
Emmanuel, principally.
[11] *Pièces noires* (1949, 1966).

timentale."[12] Giono neglects what, had he been other, he might have studied, i.e., Orpheus' journey with the Argonauts, his descent into hell, his especial initiation into the secrets of the kingdom of death, his poetic skill, his tragic death.

In the early pages of Chapter II, after the grandmother has designated the narrator by marking his eyes and forehead, she will not allow him to possess her, and she avoids his eyes: "Later, my eyes sought hers, like Orpheus Eurydice's; but the gods had imposed conditions that were too unendurable" (p. 28). In order to reach and join her, he would, in other words, have to descend into hell. During his voyage to Melbourne, the narrator remains absent for ten years. The hope of Orpheus, he says much later (Chapter IV, p. 101), represents the live world's soul, while Eurydice disdains pale earthly joys, preferring "desperately the groves of hell." Grandmother, he says in a refrain repeated during a swift, poetic evocation, "lisse et pointue comme un fuseau, lourde et muette comme un plomb" (p. 104) slipped between loving fingers, each day lower into the lovely depths. Perhaps she found hell more verdurous than earth, its meadows more flowered with asphodels, its perfumed breezes and green peace equivalent. Perhaps down there bloomed pools of *nymphaeae (nénuphars)* beneath noble lindens, nightingales, crystal waterfalls.

"It little mattered that we were all alive, Grandma was very far from us, and even if—jettisoning all the worldly things that one could jettison, and still not die—we tried to join her upon her territory, in order to take her by the hand and draw her back towards the solider ground of earth, she still would not turn her face aside from the valley of shadows

[12] See Kushner's Chapter 1, where she discusses the myth's treatment in its two major sources, Vergil and Ovid.

into which she was sinking, so that we had either to let her perish, or perish" (p. 108).

While Giono may be the first novelist to have associated the son with Orpheus and his mother with Eurydice represented as the object of passionate love, he is not, of course, the first novelist to have depicted the death of a beloved mother. One recalls at once the illness and the death, dispatched in a few lines however, of Eugénie Grandet's abject mother in Balzac's novel of 1833. Far greater emphasis occurs in Leo Tolstoy's most splendid treatment of the narrator's mother, whom he certainly loves as deeply as does Giono's narrator his mother, in the former's autobiographical novels, *Childhood, Boyhood, Youth* (1852-1857), where macabre details of physical deterioration both repel and attract the Jocasta-mothered son. Macabre details add again an especial character to the death of Frau Consul in Thomas Mann's *Buddenbrooks* (1901). All of these novels, and many others as well, may have furnished Giono with ideas.

Not until Maxim Gorky's *Mother*[13] of 1907, perhaps, has a major novelist devoted an entire book, and one that received wide attention, to an aged mother and to her death. Gorky's heroine, Pelagueya Nilovna Vlasova, learns from her son, the revolutionary named Paul, to resent her condition as a mother oppressed, enslaved, persecuted, and unpitied. After having lived in fear all her life, Vlasova finally feels pity for herself so stir in her heart that she becomes, after her son Paul's

---

[13] See *Mother* by Maxim Gorky (New York, 1947), introduction by Howard Fast, trans. Isidor Schneider. The novel, asserts Fast, was written while Gorky was hiding in "a log cabin in the Adirondacks" (p. ix ff.). It takes place in Nizhni-Novgorod, renamed Gorky in 1932. By 1947 the novel had appeared in 106 editions in 28 languages. The author was 39 years old at the time of composition: "This was Gorky, most beloved of Russian writers, as much the reflection of the soul of Russia as Mark Twain was of the soul of America" (p. vii).

imprisonment, a clever and indomitable revolutionary, who goes down fighting. People who listened to her were "impressed by the deep significance of the unadorned story of a human being, who was regarded as cattle are regarded, and who, without a murmur, for a long time felt herself to be that which she was held to be."[14] While there seems no evidence, textual or other, that Giono knew Maxim Gorky's *Mother,* or any other treatment of a mother's death by Gorky or his admirer and adapter Bertolt Brecht, Giono did mention to me in August 1970 that he had read Grazia Deledda's *La Madre* (1920).[15]

The Italian novel, perhaps closely based upon Gorky's *Mother,* recounts the story of a Sardinian peasant woman who has devoted herself entirely to raising and educating her son, also named Paul, for the priesthood. All his life, in school as in seminary, he has been ashamed of her poverty, her origins, and her toil. Like Giono's real mother, this woman performs menial labor for her son, even after he has become a priest and taken a mistress. Supporting her son through his great crisis, she dies alone and in pain rather than disturb

[14] *Mother,* Part II, p. 217. Many traces of this novel and its hero Pavel (Pasha) recur in *Doctor Zhivago,* which is also worth mentioning in this connection because Boris Pasternak of all modern novelists perhaps most resembles Jean Giono, or seems to have derived in many ways, such as in his constant championship of women, from Giono.

The lyrical treatment of old women, so unusual in world letters before Gorky and Giono, has become a commonplace in Soviet fiction, according to Olga G. Sorokin's "The Lyrical Voice in the Contemporary Soviet Russian Short Story," *The Slavic and East European Journal,* Vol. XIII, No. 4 (Winter 1969).

[15] Trans. Mary G. Steegmann as *The Mother* (New York, 1923, 1928), but the London edition (J. Cope) seems to have been entitled *The Woman and the Priest.* Grazia Deledda (1871[?]-1936) seems to be an isolated case in Italian letters, which are remarkable for a total absence of women as characters. Deledda received a Nobel Prize in 1926.

him. Like the Gorky novel, Deledda's book portrays as the central character an admirable old woman and her fatherless son Paul; both mothers were brutalized into conception. Both are uncomprehending slaves, and uneducated, but both die fighting for their sons.

In 1928 D. H. Lawrence wrote a preface for the Steegmann translation of Deledda's *Madre*,[16] in which he admired the "old mystery" as apparent in her novel as in Emily Brontë's, the "female instinctive passion," he called it: "the interest of the book lies, not in plot or characterisation, but in the presentation of sheer instinctive life. . . . The old, wild instinct of a mother's ambition for her son defeats the other wild instinct of sexual mating." In his essay on Deledda, Lawrence says nothing of his own intermediary version of a devoted mother and her son Paul, *Sons and Lovers* of 1913. Here the first four chapters, narrated from the young mother's point of view, amplify the recognition by Mrs. Morel of her son's talent. While Giono confined himself to the recurrent circling of brow and eyes by the grandmother, as experienced without verbalization by the child, and without explanation by the super-narrator, Lawrence had presented her actions, thoughts, realizations, all in detail:

"The baby was looking up at her. It had blue eyes like her own, but its look was heavy, steady, as if it had realized something that had stunned some point of its soul. . . . Its deep blue eyes, always looking up at her unblinking, seemed to draw her innermost thoughts out of her. . . . She felt as if the navel string that had connected its frail little body with hers had not been broken."[17]

---

[16] *Selected Literary Criticism*, ed. Anthony Beal (London, etc., 1955), pp. 292-94.

[17] *Sons and Lovers*, Chapter II (p. 46 in Modern Library Edition, undated).

This recognition by a Jocasta-mother of her child's talent seems very possibly a source of inspiration for Giono, as well as a knowledge shared by him with Lawrence. As we shall see in our discussion of *Jean le bleu,* whatever Lawrence feels about blue eyes and artists, Giono also shared. Furthermore, both men knew about the passionate love some sons feel for their mothers. In fact, the death scene of *Sons and Lovers* suggests in brief Giono's much extended and painstakingly developed treatment. After Mrs. Morel is dead, Paul rushes upstairs to fall across her still warm body, calling " 'My love —my love—oh, my love!' " Then, bending down, he "kissed her passionately" (pp. 466-67). In Giono, the narrator's cry of grief begins, as we have just seen, " 'Ah, quel remords!' "

Before suggesting heirs for Giono, for *Mort d'un personnage,* even if it were confined only to future readers among liberated women throughout the world, may well be artistically Giono's most popular novel, we must not forget what Giono himself labeled his most pervasive inspiration: William Faulkner. *As I Lay Dying* (October 6, 1930)[18] seems to have exerted considerable pressure here, first because only Faulkner and Giono clearly treat in a full-length novel the agony of a mother. But, secondly, both novelists depart radically from the stock, hackneyed, traditional view of motherhood. In the only section where she speaks for herself, Addie (the mother who lies dying) says of her first child Cash: "And when I knew that I had Cash, I knew that living was terrible and that this was the answer to it. . . . When he was born I knew that motherhood was invented by someone who had to have a word for it because the ones that had the children

---

[18] Pierre R. Robert in his *Jean Giono et les techniques du roman* (Berkeley and Los Angeles, 1961) had already noticed a relationship: "Par sa structure *Les Ames fortes* rappelle *As I Lay Dying.*" See note 29, p. 21.

didn't care whether there was a word for it or not."[19] Thus, both Giono's narrator and Addie's children look to the mother for what society has told them they may expect to find but what the mother herself neither is nor can give. Both novelists raise the whole question of the real nature of woman and mother,[20] both far surpassing in artistic integrity Gorky's political novel, another attempt to enslave woman and mother.

Giono's impact may be suggested, at least, by recalling Roger Peyrefitte's hastily written *La Mort d'une mère* (1950), and the much more significant search through hell for his mother and muse of Samuel Beckett, *Molloy* (1951).[21] In Céline's *Mort à credit* (1952) we have the grandmother Caroline as very important in Bardamu's life, and her death occurs in the novel. A more important admirer of Giono's novel seems another southerner, Claude Simon in *L'Herbe* (1958), which, narrated from the niece's point of view, recounts the agony of the octogenarian maiden Marie, already mummified almost to nonexistence, like Pauline confined to her room, blind, deaf, *and* of neither sex, just suffering mankind, stipulates the narrator.[22] As in the Giono passage juxtaposing such dessication to the lush green vegetation of hell, we have Simon's grass and green garden.[23]

[19] *As I Lay Dying* (New York, 1964), p. 163. The few pages (161-68) narrated by Addie are close to Giono's ideas and treatment.

[20] Giono in 1949 is decades ahead of his time. See, for instance, Betty Rollin's "Motherhood. Who Needs It?" *Look*, Vol. 34, No. 19 (September 22, 1970), pp. 15-18: "The notion that the maternal wish and the activity of mothering are instinctive or biologically predestined is baloney" (p. 15).

[21] See my "Molloy's *Musa Mater*," Comparative Literature Symposium, Vol. III, Texas Tech. University (1970), pp. 31-55.

[22] *L'Herbe* (Paris, 1958), p. 81. Marie is described in detail, as in Giono, from p. 76 ff.

[23] Particularly similar, and also very beautiful, is the passage beginning (pp. 142-43 ff.): "Donc: la vieille femme—le vieux, le fragile

249

Simone de Beauvoir's long essay on old age, *La Vieillesse*, where again Giono's book seems unknown, demonstrates most amply his originality. As Beauvoir attests in very learned fashion, literature has always shown a particular disgust for *old* women, from the Greeks, as Peyrefitte and his friend Henry de Montherlant establish,[24] or from early Christianity. French poetry, demonstrates Beauvoir,[25] has always been notorious in its fear and ridicule of old women, from Rutebeuf into Lorris and Meung, Charles of Orleans' *Aage*, the lyric poets from Ronsard to Saint-Amant,[26] and the dramatists, especially Molière. Even French novelists, despite such champions as Brantôme, Marguerite de Navarre, Montesquieu, Diderot, and Sainte-Beuve, generally adopt the contemptuous attitudes reinforced by the weight of Balzac and Flaubert.[27]

Interestingly, one tends to place Giono's narrator of *Mort d'un personnage*, particularly since the title invites us to remain in a world of fictional characters, alongside Perceval, who apparently loved the mother who raised him after his father's death. The Giono narrator would be uncomfortable,

---

amas d'ossements, . . . , d'organes exténués, aspirant au repos, au néant originel, gisant— . . . régnant, . . . étendant sa présence, son royaume . . . dans la nuit silencieuse, la nocturne paix du jardin, des frondaisons . . ."

[24] See *La Mort d'une mère* (Paris, 1950), Flammarion's *Livre de Poche* (p. 33): " 'Non, l'antiquité avait une civilisation par trop masculine.' " The two modern novelists agree to lay the "cult" of motherhood on early Christianity, and on Christ personally, who scorned his mother. See pp. 34-35.

[25] See *La Vieillesse* (Paris, 1970), pp. 147, 160, 183, 224, 426-27, *et passim*.

[26] Including, adds Beauvoir, Marot, Desportes, D'Aubigné, Du Bellay, and Régnier.

[27] Exception must be made, of course, for Félicité in *Trois contes* (1877), heroine of "Un Coeur simple."

to say the least, alongside such fictional company as Aeneas' son Iulus or Camus's character Meursault,[28] neither one of whom wept at the death of his mother.

Jean le bleu (1932)

When in 1961 Pierre R. Robert published a pioneer work[1] celebrating Jean Giono as a master technician of modern fiction, he linked *Jean le bleu* (1932) closely with *Noé* (1947), finding both novels autobiographical, but nevertheless eccentric since neither novel actually granted to the first-person narrator the center of its stage. While the narrator of *Noé* fritters away his time preparing his descent into hell, as we have seen, he meanwhile establishes himself as Scheherazade, another victim before whom the gates of Hades swing ajar: "(Schoolboys) We knew that the oracle speaks only for the victim and that it is only before the victim that swing open the gates of Hades."[2] Therefore, although Noah speaks in the first person, he lives there, as we have seen, interested primarily in describing himself as an aesthetician telling tales. The same was true even to the young Giono nearer the outset of his literary career when in *Jean le bleu* he sketched less himself than his first portrait as an artist: "Whatever one attempts, it is only the self-portrait of the artist, by himself, that one actually writes" (*Noé*, pp. 55-56). Never reticent elsewhere about his poverty, nor embarrassed by his lowly origins and his humble tastes, Giono stressed in *Noé* his matured methods of composition, and in *Jean le bleu* his early education and special orientation, for the poor parents who

[28] *L'Etranger* (Paris, 1942).

---

[1] *Jean Giono et les techniques du roman*, p. 12.
[2] Giono's *Virgile* (1960), pp. 22-23.

bore and reared him were the first to recognize this blond child as very gifted. From babyhood they held him apart. The future artist early knew himself to be "vraiment celui par qui le scandale arrive" (*Noé*, p. 21), a special and a rare person.

After this precocious childhood Giono could never pass certain doorsills of his native Manosque without seeing Oedipus standing somewhere near him, or hear that other prince howling blinded. Down certain streets Lord Romeo's Juliet always passed as in Verona, and the local slaughter-house designated to the artist the underground landscapes of Dostoyevsky.[3] Having become a world-famous novelist, Giono surveyed from the windows of his home on the Mont d'Or one hundred kilometers of Provence, or sprawled, he often said, like Swift's giant over six square leagues of countryside, his feet on the very house where Marie Chazottes was murdered.[4] Comfortably gowned in a woolen robe against cool winds gusting along his native hillside, Giono invited the chestnut tree outside his window to *suggest* not curtains only, but glassware, sets of crystals, then barbarians' drums, wild gallops, long echoes, and hunting horns. In this workroom he daily indulged his everyday need to daydream, "mon goût pour la sieste," for at night, fatigued, he invariably plummeted instantly into nine dream-less hours of sleep.[5] At a time near dawn on the morning of October 9, 1970, the artist died in his bed of heart failure. It was a moment of death that, as Giono often said, he expected instantly, so weary was his heart of bearing what he called a flaming burden of this world's suffering.

Writing novels was for Giono a continuous, continuing process from the publication of *Collines* in 1929: "Finir une,

---

[3] *Noé* (p. 12), but also *Le Moulin de Pologne*, as we have seen.
[4] *Un Roi sans divertissement.*   [5] *Noé*, pp. 12-24, pp. 52-53.

commencer l'autre."[6] Before his receiving eyes, as he daily composed over the decades, ramps on stages lighted up, while words and entire phrases surged unsolicited to mind. It was not so much that he *saw* as that he *saw again* each scene played before his eyes.[7] After writing four pages after supper, the narrator considered that he had earned his evening stroll with his dog. This other activity exchanged one world for another, sometimes more tragic, as the case might be, or in the instance of *Noé*, less so, a mere *opera buffa*.

When during the five hundred days spent writing the 228 pages of *Un Roi sans divertissement*, Giono needed to leave his room to fetch a handkerchief, for example, he often had callously to pass through characters of the novel, all life-sized like himself. None of them Robinson Crusoes, others were similarly traversed by Sylvie Giono going neglectfully out without her sun hat in plain view of her father's window. Giono reflected endlessly about his characters, describing only those gestures useful to each intrigue, but supplying particular *addenda* so that the reader could dredge up details from his own experience ("pour que le lecteur puise de ses propres souvenirs—" *Noé*, p. 32) as he kept up to date an account of each character in his ledger. Sometimes auxiliary narrators like Saucisse lent helping hands (*Noé*, p. 42), as Giono ticked off a tragedy, "Atrides No. 500,000," for instance (*Noé*, p. 47). Each "*curriculum vitae*," added Giono, must above all satisfy the reader's critical faculty.

When of an evening he listened to a concert from abroad on the family radio, Giono found himself descending more and more analytically into each character's individual identity, suddenly recognizing Uncle Eugène's particularities, and this despite a curious phenomenon: that music occurs in an-

[6] *Idem*, p. 42.
[7] "*Voir*" and "*revoir*," *Noé*, p. 55.

other part of a consciousness, he affirmed, from that where fictional creation simmers (*Noé,* pp. 39-43). As he said for Uncle Eugène's personal drama with apocalypse, he found the world of creation occupying various stages that grew dark or bright with brilliant light, where like Saint-Jean the creator also suffered vertigo looking down from atop the ladders in the wings. Fiction differs vastly from both painting and music, because the former depends upon words alone—and readers skip. Fiction can much less express than tangentially convey feeling.

"I am a realist," explained Giono in *Noé* (p. 139 ff.), or, as we have suggested, a New Realist, to whom material objects always existed outside himself and independently of his own sensory experiences. As we shall see was true for him in *Jean le bleu* of 1932, the modern world may be not only green but also blue, not only to Giono, however, but also to Pablo Picasso, or to other foreign contemporaries such as W. C. Handy[8] and George Gershwin.[9] Would one's sensation be blue unless the world were blue in others' eyes also, as in their mirrors, through their windows, in their photographs, and in their eyes and hearts? Giono's experience is therefore not private, but public, because communicable. Thus, although Giono's view of the world as blue may appear to others as mistaken, illusory, or misperceived, it remains illuminative to many because it is supplementary to conceptions currently conveyed in modern music and painting. Persons and objects are never perceived *simpliciter* by Giono but at least double, as by mescaline illusion, before being fixed spatially, tem-

---

[8] The famous Negro composer was born twelve years before Giono, but his autobiography, *Father of the Blues* appeared nine years after *Jean le bleu*, or in 1941.

[9] 1898-1937. *Rhapsody in Blue* appeared as early as 1923.

porally, and verbally. Giono's *esse* means, then, *percipere, sentire, atque fabulare.*

The first sentence of *Jean le bleu*[10] speaks of a world irrecoverably lost to physical actuality, but nonetheless blue—blue—blue in the artist's memory, like the warm blue air that always descended to melt the hoarfrost in the Durance valley, like the blue artisan's apron of father Jean cutting soles out of angel hide in his workshop for a thousand-footed god, the blue cyclone in one's head when an Italian anarchist[11] dedicating his life to liberty fearfully glided into the underground railway station, here the poor Giono flat in Manosque. The child Jean watched him stride blue-faced out again into the night, murmuring liberty, freedom, nakedness. Under the lamp, the child's father Jean fed a blue-winged dragonfly to his caged nightingale, which will die just before the child, this other caged singer, first discovers his own voice. As a child, like a little monkey, he whistled and aped, and from his high apartment window already played the flood, himself Noah in the ark.[12] Very young, the child discovered the awful key to the world in three hushed syllables: *"terrible."* By Chapter IV (pp. 63-65) he hears feeble bird song and poor children singing, so *terrible that one dares not express it* (p. 66), that one can never say it as *terrible* as it is. Thus, *Jean le bleu* es-

---

[10] *Jean le bleu*, along with the Pan trilogy and *Que ma joie demeure* was published by Bernard Grasset in a printing of 1,851 copies, renewed 8 times between 1932 and 1961. The novel is divided into 9 chapters (316 pp.) containing subtitles listed in a final table, but concerning: (I) early memories, (II) school days, (III) the anarchist, (IV) music lessons, (V) the healer and illness, (VI) recuperation at Corbières, (VII) the tutor, (VIII) home again, (IX) the discovery of poetry as a *modus vivendi*, and the arrival at manhood.

[11] Chapter III, pp. 45-59. Page numbers refer to the eighth printing of the original Grasset edition, also entitled *Passage du vent*.

[12] *Singe* (p. 37); Noah, flood, ark (pp. 14, 39-40, 58, 67, *et passim*).

255

tablishes what remains most characteristic of Giono's style: a heartbroken tenderness for men and women, a quivering pity for adults that keeps him always close to tears.

Giono's artistic consciousness moves in 1932 along the wake of the great Gidian works of fiction, particularly here according to Edouard's explicit ideas on the novel.[13] *Jean le bleu* constitutes another *roman de la douleur,* like Giono's *Solitude de la pitié,* which also appeared in 1932. Concurrent with the child's first realizations of the sorrows and griefs suffered by people around him, and with his love for his parents and friends, wells within him the need to share both grief and sorrow, and in his father's footsteps to heal, by songs and persuasions. Thus, also, his feeling of pity stretches out a hand towards others from whom he will not be separated, the ensuing art constituting such a desire grown strong enough to communicate with all who will read books.[14] Too young to understand the reasons for human degradation, *Jean le bleu* himself merely observes the shadowy blue ones floating about him.[15] The day he understands how the years of poverty and toil have weighed upon his own aging father, the son Jean will like the nightingale deliberately leave the cage. At that

[13] Part II, Chapter 3 of *Les Faux monnayeurs* (1926), a work so popular and wide-reaching that by 1947 it had 264 translations. In *Jean le bleu* Giono will descend in depth rather than operate a horizontal slice of life; he will propose his ideal reality juxtaposed to facts; he will furnish a kind of recollected journal; and he will expressly allow his book to become, if not a Bach fugue, at least a Bach Passion. Giono will also dispense with chronology or linear reality to play off thens and nows.

[14] See "Schopenhauer" in Etienne Souriau's *Clefs pour l'esthétique* (Paris, 1970), pp. 41-43.

[15] Giono resembles, in fact, both John Steinbeck and William Saroyan among the authors castigated by Edmund Fuller in his essay "The New Compassion in the American Novel" from *Man in Modern Fiction* (New York, 1949), pp. 32-44.

point, dressed in his blue flunkey's uniform at the bank, *Jean le bleu* quits his brief childhood, like a novice emerging, he says, from the hazy Breton forest of Brocéliande. (A Marseilles street furnished *Noé* the same analogy.)

Most understandably, the very young child Jean became spellbound every time he heard music, as a result of which his father subscribed to classical concerts played by two poor neighbors upon a violin and a flute. In this way and very early, the language of music conveyed Mozart and Bach so thoroughly to this gifted child's attentive ears that notes became words in his mind, and one word chiefly: despair.[16] Thereafter from his apartment window looking down at the dark well "au fond de son malheur" (p. 87), the child whistled a requiem for a dead girl, and listened to the *complaintes* of the animals' skins being tanned, and to the *complaintes* of the solitary Mexican woman weeping ceaselessly for her land of cacti. Up the dark well of the courtyard rose the terrible sobbing of a starving horse as in its agony it ate the wooden door before which it was stabled. The muddy earthen floor of the courtyard served as a pen for terribly crowded sheep, one or two hauled out daily for slaughter. Looking down from a rotting loft above his father's shop—the mother's more prosperous hand laundry occupying a lower floor and engaging two or three girl employees—Jean Giono spent this curious, meditative, dreaming childhood. It was he who learned, and there, that darkness does not fall, that it rises:[17] ". . . sans me faire voir je regardai . . ." (p. 87). Inside his window the narrator cultivated his "beaucoup de mémoire" (p. 91).

When the amateur musicians, *Jean le bleu* attending, played passages from Bach's *Saint John Passion* (1723) to the

[16] Chapter IV, but p. 80 especially.

[17] See the title story *Solitude de la pitié*, where the well of this courtyard has become a well for drawing water within a priest's courtyard.

fat, rich woman and her idiot son, their instruments sobbed for all the inhabitants of the dark courtyard. Even then, the boy narrator understood that somehow elect and elected he stood as intermediary between them and her: "J'étais sur le front de bataille" (p. 94), for which reason he unprotestingly went into the trenches during World War I. Therefore the words of Saint John burned forever into his brain: the chorus No. 28 ("Wir dürfen niemand töten"), the soprano aria No. 63 ("Zerfliesse, mein Herze, in Fluten der Zähren, dem Höchsten zu Ehren"), and the chorale No. 65 ("O hilf, Christe, Gottes Sohn, durch dein bittres Leiden, . . .").[18] Exercising his literary ability, the boy Jean recited to the musicians after each concert what he had comprehended during the playing of the music, and in the Bach aria the singer's voice had streamed from the very center "de la douleur" (p. 93).

In his Kafkaesque Chapter V Jean speaks of his father as a healer, who loved epileptics and wounds, particularly those which were alive, like the festering sores treated by Kafka's country doctor.[19] Graphically and memorably, the man Giono narrates the approach of the boy's diphtheria, the sounds, odors, and colors that heralded his descent into static time

[18] Giono has recalled these three passages in French, all from Part II of this less-well-known *Passion*. See *Jean le bleu*, p. 91. (Giono's *Que ma joie demeure* is a French translation of the Bach Chorale "Iesu, joy of man's desiring.")

[19] Giono seems most affected by "Ein Landarzt" (1919) not only as here in Chapter V (pp. 97-107) of *Jean le bleu* when he describes his father as healer, but also in the closing chapter of *Le Hussard sur le toit* when Pauline and Angélo are lectured by another healing country doctor below his map of Moscow (Marseilles). Contrary to Kafka's pessimism, Giono regards both his healers as successful, but, of course, Angélo had already seen one country doctor succumb to the plague. Thus, we must concur with Claude Mauriac about Kafka: "Son oeuvre préfigure celle de la plupart des écrivains représentatifs de notre époque." See his "Franz Kafka" from *L'Alittérature contemporaine* (Paris, 1958), p. 13.

(p. 112). Recalled years later, this same illness befalls Jason's blond brother in *Deux cavaliers de l'orage*, as we have seen. Become even more the favorite of the family, the convalescent boy grows to understand that his destiny has allowed him to survive this descent of darkness where death, garbed as a great golden bird with blue feathers, hovered over the hills.

FROM Chapter VI (pp. 109-52) to the end of *Jean le bleu*, for which reason we take this novel as our conclusion, Giono sketches the people, incidents, settings, and stories that will over the years furnish his fiction. Mme Massat will become Pauline in *Mort d'un personnage*, plus all the self-denying, self-sacrificing, martyred women in Giono's novels. The various tragedies that occur that summer at the mountain village of Corbières where the child convalesces among the shepherds and their flocks, and the boy's games in the fig trees, supply not only the instantly famous pages of the "Baker's Wife" in *Jean le bleu* but, years later, *Fragments d'un paradis, Noé,* and *Un Roi sans divertissement.*[20] Blanche Lamballe, who hangs herself (pp. 138-60), also prefigures Aurélie and the many other unhappy women whom Giono always pities so deeply. As we have already seen, the stories of the ball, Costes, Costelet, Hortense, and the scapegoat Julie recur twenty years later in *Le Moulin de Pologne.* In the mountain village the children play at hanging themselves, the object of the game being to strangle oneself enough to "see blue."[21] Repelled by both

[20] Mme Massat, pp. 128 and 138, for example; *Fragments*, pp. 129-30; *Un Roi*, p. 131.

[21] Chapters VI and VII of *Jean le bleu* must ultimately be compared, it seems, to Colette's *La Maison de Claudine*, first published ten years earlier. Both are slim but very dense and psychologically profound novels, both are packed with silence and unsaid words; therefore both succeed in eliciting reader collaboration. No one but Giono, it

adults and children with their strange sexual desires, and yet pursuing his playmate Anne with his own appetites aroused, *Jean le bleu* turns in preference to the animals about him, seeing how admirable they are, devoid of "la hantise de la mort," and "l'hypocrisie de l'amour" (pp. 141-42). Aurélie's passion for the shepherd is conveyed to the reader particularly through the ovulation and fertilization of fishes in the swamps.[22] From the eyes of a serpent, the child comprehends the coldness of death, which he had twice seen earlier, in the eyes of Costelet and in those of the young prostitute at Manosque, whom despite protests at home he allowed to kiss him.

Giono's personal indebtedness to a guardian angel, in whom he still believed while writing *Batailles dans la montagne,* derived to some degree at least from the unfrocked young priest whom father Jean engaged to tutor his son that summer at Corbières: "Je lus l'*Iliade* au milieu des blés mûrs" (pp. 164-65). Under a blue sky mirroring the blue reflection of the earth, the blue lucarne of a storm in a fast-approaching distance, the future artist learned a new way to envision the world. There was the delicate, laundered, pampered city

---

would also seem, could equal Colette's poetic gifts of evocation and metaphor. Both understand childhood to be a period of sweet liberty, veiled perversion, and wild savagery, and both understand the importance of the games children play. When one reads such lines, it is difficult to know, by the poetry of such homely words, who is writing, Colette or Giono: "La maison était grande, coiffée d'un grenier haut. La pente raide de la rue obligeait les écuries et les remises, les poulaillers, la buanderie, la laiterie, à se blottir en contrebas tout autour d'une cour fermée" (opening paragraph, *La Maison de Claudine*).

[22] Again, this is a mythical landscape and not a real one in a windswept, bone-dry, cold mountain village. Perhaps here also Giono is indebted to Gide, particularly to the magnificent swamp landscape, *Paludes* (1896).

child imprisoned in schools and the dark well of a tenement, let loose under that turbulence of Provence which Van Gogh represented so well in twisted blues and whites, become, with his "man in black," shepherd to ewes and new lambs. Running wild all day long with children and animals, tucked in warm at night under an eiderdown sprinkled with calico bluebells, the right child matured fast in the right atmosphere. Of all these children, only Giono became a writer, but, then, only Giono had the tutor sent, at great sacrifice on the part of his parents, all the way on foot from Manosque.

With the man in black, the child Jean understood love within himself as he pondered the archetypal friends: Achilles, Patroclus, and Antilochus. What he was learning was textual analysis, "la science du texte" (p. 166) by a method of absorption where "il entrait sensuellement dans le texte," perceiving ultimately "une telle intelligence de la forme, de la couleur, du poids des mots" (p. 167). The whole world of Troy and the Greek camp played itself anew before his eyes, as with "une vie mystérieuse créée devant mes yeux." The study of literature, not an end in itself, leads Jean to self-knowledge: "Je sais que je suis un sensuel" (p. 167). This very sensuality, he adds, hindered him from becoming a musician. Long before he knew this prime characteristic of his being, his father knew it and educated him accordingly, lest as child or as man *Jean le bleu* lose his necessary *purity* and essential *sense of cosmic ecstasy*:

"He shattered nothing, harrowed nothing within me, stifled nothing, erased nothing with a finger moistened with saliva. With an insect-like prescience he prescribed the proper remedies for the young larva I was then: one day this, another day that; he loaded me with plants, with trees, with lands, with men, with hills, with women, with suffering, with goodness, with pride, all of it as remedies, all of it as provisions, all of it in foreknowledge of what could have wounded me. Ahead of time he gave me the right defense for what could have been a wound, for what, thanks to him, became instead, inside me, an enormous sun" (p. 168).

Lying in the tall grass on summer evenings, the young priest further explained to the child (p. 169) the philosophy of New Realism originated by Plato: the real world exists beyond our sensory apprehension.

Giono's pastoral vision of the world's harmony stems also from the young priest's teachings and his concept that one has only to stoop and drink from a common spring to be refreshed. All has its proper weight: the emotion felt by granite or the bark of a tree, all sap flowing under a snake's scales, fenced off by skins, like all blood. "Nous sommes le monde" (p. 172), with our anthills of earth and air, our families and villages of trees, our forests of men.[23]

Rejoining his beloved father who so understandingly shielded him from evil and profanation, the healed youngster with the "regard bleu" returns home to Manosque at the point of manhood. Feeling the need to live, understanding the imperiousnesses of his blood, he experiences at this moment a great sadness (p. 211) against which his father imparts the final sum of his counsel and knowledge: beware of reason, safeguard your sense of hope ("Avec l'espérance on arrive à tout," p. 218), recognize that the ultra-superior strength of men comes from the heart, and that proper justice is nothing

[23] Here Giono celebrates his joyous discovery by telling his wonderful story of how the baker's wife ran off with the shepherd of "Conches" (p. 173 ff.) and knew, exceptionally for a woman, her few days of pastoral bliss. The goddess of the dawn Aurélie spent her brief idyll with a man "as bright as day" (p. 174). Giono's delightful humor punctures their right to the pursuit of happiness as the villagers object: " 'C'est beau, oui, l'amour, mais il faut penser qu'on mange.' " With Aurélie absent, her spouse the baker will not bake bread.

less than hopefulness and confidence in mankind. For the first time, Jean now sees that his father has become an old man, and for the first time he further sees in all its misery the slum courtyard and well where he had spent his childhood. These sights lead him once more to actual *despair*.

With the blues humming their sad refrains in his heart, Jean notices how decrepit and how aged the people and the world of his infancy have become, or really are. The nightingale, he learns, has committed suicide. Above all floats the "terrible" odor of the penned sheep down in their muddy, sunless hole. Telling Jean to keep his sights on the blueness of the distant sea, his musician friend succumbs to cold and hunger. Then the neighborhood optician dies from starvation. Mother Montagnier dies, leaving in this urban blight an orphaned child whom no one claims. In a terrible silence Clara (Julie) weds Gonzales (M. Joseph), who has returned from a pagan Mexico of volcanos, gods of stone, ancient barbarousnesses, and blue finger rings.

In his final Chapter IX Giono develops the one other symbol that has informed this fiction—the verticality of the black, foul courtyard, which represents the depth of consciousness into which he plunges deeper and deeper in self-awareness and self-knowledge. Recounting the stories of the impoverished but once noble Italian lodger Franchesc,[24] Giono implicitly explains how a man can, even in the face of final destitution and starvation, safeguard his cleanliness and like Angélo Pardi nourish his heart on pure water. Singing the blues, Jean celebrates this very courtyard, which usually signifies "defeat and slavery" (p. 272); this slum, which witnesses among its occupants "submission and death": "de temps en temps, le boucher entrait et menait une bête à l'abattoir."

---

[24] These stories and persons bear a strong relationship to Angélo Pardi's home area as portrayed in *Le Bonheur fou*.

With Tolstoyan revulsion before slaughter, Jean chronicles the lives of his fellow-sufferers, their medieval city destroyed by modern civilization, their fields burned, their farms buried under factories, their trades useless, their water and air polluted, their freedom and dignity sold for pennies, their most resolute members often departing to wander *Les Grands chemins*, homeless and destitute.

Through it all, Franchesc is somehow not beaten down, while still being one "des pauvres et des perdus" (p. 275). Even Jesus was powerless before human misery, His hands too small to shelter all the poor, even He, like Jean and Franchesc, with His *blue* eyes! What can the young man do but become a healer of wounds, like his father, so he can in some way apply balm and stanch the flow of blood? Blind chance, then, led young Jean to his blue flunkey's suit at the bank, where, entering rows of figures in ledgers like Melville and like Kafka, opening and closing doors, bowing and scraping to customers, young Giono continued to read and to study "le tragique de la vie" (pp. 295, 297) as he awaited his departure for the front in World War I.[25] His heart broke to see his father descend daily towards death, into definitive loneliness, towards "le terrible" that he as memorialist would all his years strive to avert—the "agonie terrible" of forgetfulness. Art to Giono, or to William Saroyan, would be a long crusade against death.

In the Preface to his edition of *Virgile* (1960), Giono continued his autobiography, castigating the particular middle class of whom he became for a short time a minor employee until André Gide launched him almost overnight into fame and independence. Leaving the forest of Brocéliande, which

---

[25] The final pages of the novel give us the cave-men analogy as developed in *Un Roi sans divertissement* and the opening pages of *Le Grand troupeau*.

was his childhood (v., p. 60),[26] he recalled to mind, he entered the lunar world of the bank, enduring "de grandes nuits de détresse" because of the poor, life's gentle failures, living without the nobility and the joy even of mountain shepherds. Could he sing the golden calf's cult? These years he sought a victorious faith, such as one nourished by miracles (v., p. 67). The poet's function, as Vergil had also understood it, was to add the gods to men, to speak of their admirable pinnacles, and the immense order according to which they regulated the universe. The true poet will meet gods all along the roads.

The poet in Vergil's manner does not enjoy delight himself; he is rather one of those who tell how one takes delight. He is the one who in his works sings of the entire earth. When as a young man he desires to give the world some perfect work, he studies such masters as Vergil and Homer in order simply to inform himself about technique (v., p. 13). With the whole world as subject matter, shall modern poets remain unable to create a poetry of renaissance? Let the first criterion be frank subjectivity (v., p. 41). The youth under the "thousand buttons" of his blue uniform felt hopeful: "Beings and objects were wrapped within that azure zone which foretells the near approach of light" (v., p. 50). The eyes of *Jean le bleu* were, in fact, "yeux bleus puits de tant d'espérance."[27]

On the one hand, then, Giono adopts for *Jean le bleu* a poetic tradition doubtless characteristic of French letters, or one in which the color blue represents the ideal where the soul soars and also the pure realm of the imagination. Thus, the young Giono, speaking of his father's proclivity, and of his own, for healing mankind might be Balzac's La Fosseuse nar-

[26] *Virgile*, p. 60.
[27] Samuel Beckett's "Le Calmant" (1945) from *Nouvelles et textes pour rien* (Paris, 1958), p. 60.

rating her story at the end of *Le Médecin de campagne* (1832-1833):[28]

" 'I had only the blue of the sky as my friend.—I have always become happy whenever I saw the sky entirely blue. . . . Such times I used to dream that I was a great lady. If I gazed at it intently enough, I felt myself immersed in the blue; in imagination I lived up there within it, no longer feeling any sense of weight, soaring up, up, gradually feeling completely happy.' " Around 1859 Victor Hugo had also expressed Giono's feelings many decades later as the latter completed his Pan trilogy:[29]

> Thanks to the great Pan, god of the beasts,
> Son, reality shows its horns
> Under the blue brow of the ideal.[30]

In fact, when Wallace Stevens, another office worker, speaks of blue in Giono's manner, he is placed "plainly in a French tradition": "His (Stevens') recurrent blue and green, north and south, moon and sun are signs for imagination and fact, not symbols."[31] Wallace Stevens himself might often have spoken for *Jean le bleu*, as, for example:

> I am the poorest of all.
> I know that I cannot be mended.[32]

Young Giono's sorrows at the world and its poor and unhappy persons spending their dreary lives around the well of

---

[28] *Scènes de la vie de campagne* from *La Comédie humaine*, Vol. VIII, ed. Marcel Bouteron (Paris, 1949), p. 521.

[29] *Collines* (1929), *Un de Baumugnes* (1929), *Regain* (1930).

[30] *Chansons des rues et des bois*, ed. Zumthor, p. 56.

[31] See William York Tindall's *Wallace Stevens* (Minneapolis, 1961), p. 17.

[32] "Idiom of the Hero" from *Parts of a World* (New York, 1951), p. 21.

the courtyard seems to have been captured thirty years before *Jean le bleu* in the pictures that Pablo Ruiz y Picasso brought to Paris from Barcelona (1904). A watercolor as early as 1902 had portrayed *Les Pauvres,* but the works of the blue period[33] especially belong to Giono's text, and vice versa. Picasso's *Nude, Back View* (1902),[34] which shows a fragile woman with her head resting on her right knee, might well illustrate Giono's forlorn but gallant prostitute. Similarly, Giono's Julie, the dreaming musician from *Le Moulin de Pologne* (1952), finds another visage in Picasso's *Woman in an Armchair: The Dream.*[35] The whole tone and pervasive atmosphere of *Jean le bleu* comes to mind when one considers Picasso's blue *The Two Sisters* (1904). Both women are seated and superbly drawn with their coiffures, round eyes, passive mouths, and watchful postures. Thin, sad, wistful, looking out at the world of unspeakable things, as *Jean le bleu* saw it, they both hold slender fingertips before their lips.[36] Having rejected more practical explanations—that Picasso painted in blue for some years because he was too poor to purchase other colors, or because he was used to working at night, or because he was influenced by the blue tints of photographic plates—art historians Frank Elgar and Robert Maillard conclude in words most applicable to Giono's first portrait of himself as artist: "The exclusive use of blue is better explained by the sensual, if not spiritual, meaning of this colour, the colour of night, ashes, melancholy, and death.

---

[33] See No. 6 (*Mother and Child*, Summer, 1902), No. 7 (*Woman at a Bar*, 1902), and especially the poignant No. 9 (*Les Pauvres au bord de la mer*, 1903) with its forlorn, disconsolate man, woman, and child, three persons in the family as in Giono, from Gertrude Stein's *Picasso* (London, 1939).

[34] Oil on canvas. 18⅛ x 15¾ inches.

[35] Paris (Jan. 24). Oil. 52 x 38¾ inches.

[36] Gouache on paper. 21⅝ x 15 inches. Private collection. Paris.

Bright and vivid shades would be quite inappropriate to the bloodless bodies and dark, frightened faces of human beings wilting beneath a doom they cannot understand. Cold blues and murky greys are more in keeping with that world of suffering and disinherited people."[37]

Not only a portrait of the artist as a young child and adolescent, barely emerging into maturity, then, Giono's *Jean le bleu* may, like the works of Picasso's "Blue Period (1901-1904)" be called "social in theme" and representing an "emaciated, underprivileged world."[38] It seems even very possible that Giono followed Picasso even further, for the paintings of 1943 might well have been reproduced in Giono's portrayal of the stricken Julie, one part of whose face was blue with paralysis, for so in at least two instances has Picasso represented seated women.[39]

Below the actual and social significances of the color blue as emphasized by Giono there may also extend survivals of Celtic lore, which make even more relevant references to the Arthurian forest. Manosque then resembles the blue city or Glastonbury to which the Sun-King, about to create, returns only to be imprisoned by a lunar deity in a penitential maze, encased in blue and thousand-buttoned.[40] Thus the special mark traced on the narrator's forehead by his "grandmother" in *Mort d'un personnage* and the color blue refer similarly to

[37] *Picasso. A Study of His Work*, trans. Francis Scarfe (New York, 1960), p. 24 ff., and here p. 29.

[38] Harriet and Sidney Janis, *Picasso. The Recent Years. 1939-1946* (New York, 1946), pp. 8 and 20.

[39] *Ibid.* Plate 82 (*Seated Woman*. Paris. Sept. 23, 1943. Oil on canvas. 39 x 32 inches). "In this face the right profile and the left profile interlock and overlap. Furthermore, the composite of both makes the full face." In Plate 81 (*Figure Seated in a Wicker Chair*. Paris. Sept. 24, 1943. Oil on canvas. 39 x 32 inches), four planes of the woman's face are blue: forehead, nose, lip, chin.

[40] Robert Graves, *The White Goddess* (New York, 1948), p. 88 ff.

prehistoric Celtic ritual: "This process (wound) is obviously some form of tattooing, and is perhaps the attenuated survival of the ancient British and Pictish custom of tattooing the whole body with blue pigment, a custom which among the witches was not confined to Great Britain, but extended to the Continent as well, particularly to France."[41] To many persons with Celtic educations, in fact, the sacred color blue, whether or not it refers to woad,[42] still attracts a mystical aura, and to French-speaking persons "bleu" may mean "fabulous."

To Giono through the years the blue of eyes remained in several ways significant, towards the end of his life, for instance, indicative of personal heroism: Ennemonde and Camille in *Ennemonde* (1968), M. and Mme Numance in *Les Ames fortes* (1949), Count Pesaro and the major in *Le Bonheur fou* (1957), Ariane du Pavon in *Deux cavaliers de l'orage* (1965), and the widow in *Un Roi sans divertissement* (1947). Both the healer Bobi in *Que ma joie demeure* (1935) and Saint-Jean in *Batailles dans la montagne* (1937) have blue eyes and are associated with heroism and fine blue days. Pauline's father in *Angelo* (1958), on the other hand, more resembles Giono himself in 1953 when he finished *Voyage en Italie*, both "doctors" having blue eyes that made them look vague, distant, never present at the place where they were. Giono's most important allusions outside *Jean le bleu*, however, probably occur in his *Pour saluer Melville* (1943), where he notes that Herman Melville's eyes were gray-blue, lost-looking, but that they were also the fierce blue eyes of a

[41] Margaret Murray, *The God of the Witches* (Garden City, 1960), p. 100.

[42] *Isatis tinctoria*, order of *Cruciferae* is Julius Caesar's *vitrium*, a dye made from leaves by Britons. The Coventry dye from woad carries the mark "true blue." The woaded indigo dyes used in work clothes are fade-resistant.

great and a true poet.[43] D. H. Lawrence had already concurred, and more, that Melville was "magic, . . . abstract, . . .
elemental, . . . and keen," and like all blue-eyed persons, quite
"curious," in fact: "He was a modern Viking. . . . In blue eyes
there is sun and rain and abstract, uncreate element, water,
ice, air, space, but not humanity."[44] It is Melville among all
authors whom Giono most loved and to whom he therefore
turned most often for solace.

Giono's blue is further connected, it would seem, with the
blues, a style of music just receiving its first written study at
about the time of publication of *Jean le bleu*.[45] Surrounded
by the recent miseries of human slavery, Negro jazz musicians, particularly W. C. Handy, with his *Memphis* (1912)
and *St. Louis Blues* (1914), created a style characterized by
rapid alternation of major and minor tonality, the former suggesting happiness, hope, and stability, the latter conveying
dismal, whining, and complaining measures like the several
complaintes that the child heard from his attic window. By
the 1930's it was common to speak of "blue notes" and impossible not to have heard this music of a nature as highly sub-
jective, as tensely emotional, and as socially conscious as the
Giono novel.

Thus, *Jean le bleu* mirrored its century while giving earnest
of works to come, advancing a rationale not only for the early
pastoral novels of Giono but also for his most positive works,
such as *Le Hussard sur le toit*, and his most tragic, such as
Un Roi sans divertissement. Pushing far beyond any ordinary
use of blue or blue eyes in fiction,[46] the young novelist drew

[43] *Pour saluer Melville*, pp. 14, 29, 33.

[44] *Studies in Classic American Literature* (New York, 1923), but
see New York, 1964, edition, p. 131.

[45] Hughes Panassié's *Le Jazz hot* (Paris, 1934).

[46] Most novelists, one observes, attribute blue eyes to characters and
generally without particular significance, although Alan Sillitoe sur-

his self-portrait as a child destined to become an artist. As a youngster he was doubtless, like Gargantua, Chateaubriand, or Apollinaire, dedicated to the cult of the Virgin, for whom he too wore blue. Very soon, as he demonstrated by refusing to recite his piece to her on Easter Monday,[47] he substituted for the green Virgin of his parochial school, a green nymph or Eurydice whom he, like a truly blue Orpheus, conjured up from blotches of mildew on his attic wall.[48] Looking him straight in the eyes, the green muse, lovely earth goddess, not only imposed upon Jean his daydreams and his future poetry, but gave birth in him to all his violets, he confessed, bringing into bloom the jasmine flowers that danced perfumed just over his artist's heart, where, added Giono, in the heart of Jesus flames always flare like exploding suns.

---

prises his readers with the policeman's eyes being called "illiterate blue" (*The Loneliness of the Long Distance Runner* [New York, 1959], p. 27). Blue eyes are either innocent, shrewd, and pure (Dreiser's *American Tragedy*), mild and childlike (Andrić), or blue and innocent (Faulkner's *Sartoris*). Blue-eyed women are often severely castigated, like George Eliot's Rosamund in *Middlemarch* and Balzac's horrible old maid, Sylvie Rogron, with the steel-blue eyes; however, as we have seen, Giono much admired them in heroic, old women— but Giono was always a champion of women, in any case.

[47] End of Chapter II, *Jean le bleu.*
[48] Chapter III, p. 66 ff., and especially p. 69.

Bibliography

Jean Giono. Books.[1]

1924   *Accompagnés de la flûte* (Prose poems)
1928   *Colline*
1929   *Un de Baumugnes*
1930   *Présentation de Pan*
      Regain
      Manosque des plateaux
      Solitude de la pitié
      Naissance de l'Odyssée
1931   *Eglogues*
      Le Grand troupeau
1932   *Jean le bleu*
      Solitude de la pitié

[1] The following list cannot be considered definitive; it aims primarily at placing in context Giono's chief works of fiction, as listed more specifically in our introduction. It may perhaps give, without too much trouble to the reader, some notion of Giono's rhythm of production, and decline beginning perhaps with *Angelo* (1958).

The dates suggested indicate to the best of my present knowledge a first printing, or a printing that contains at least some new material. Giono sometimes reissued works under other titles, and published separately in book form individual works or sections from previous books.

The following list excludes collaborative translations, such as *Moby Dick* (1950), most anthology pieces, such as "Le Grand théâtre" (1964), most of the Prefaces, and the 200 or so contributions (1921-1970) to periodicals. One hundred thirty-eight newspaper articles are listed and studied by Maurice A. Lecuyer in "Les 'Propos et Anecdotes' de Jean Giono, ou un heureux art de vivre," *Rice University Studies*, Vol. 57, No. 2 (Spring 1971), pp. 49-71.

BIBLIOGRAPHY

1933 *Le Serpent d'étoiles*
1934 *Le Chant du monde*
1935 *Que ma joie demeure*
1936 *Les Vraies richesses*
      Rondeur des jours
1937 *Le Bout de la route* (Theater)
      Refus d'obéissance
      Batailles dans la montagne
1938 *Le Poids du ciel*
      Lettre aux paysans sur la pauvreté et la paix
      Entrée du printemps and *Mort du blé*
      Précisions
(1938-1939 *Premières Proses et Premiers Poèmes*)
          (*Cahiers du Contadour*)
1939 *Provence*
1941 *Pour saluer Melville*
      Triomphe de la vie (Addenda: *Les Vraies richesses*)
1943 *L'Eau vive*
      Théâtre (*Le Bout de la route, Lanceurs de graines, La
          Femme du boulanger, L'Esquisse d'une mort
          d'Hélène*)
1947 *Le Voyage en calèche* (Theater)
      Un Roi sans divertissement
      Les Pages immortelles de Virgile
      Noé
1948 *Fragments d'un déluge* (Free verse)
      Fragments d'un paradis
1949 *Mort d'un personnage*
      Les Ames fortes
1950 *Village*
1951 *Les Grands chemins*
      Le Hussard sur le toit
1952 *Le Moulin de Pologne*

274

1953 *Arcadie, Arcadie!* (*Provence,* 1954, 1957)
      Voyage en Italie
1955 *L'Ecossais ou la fin des héros*
      Une Aventure ou la foudre et le sommet
      Notes sur l'affaire Dominici
      La Pierre
1956 *Lucien Jacques*
      Bernard Buffet
1957 *Le Bonheur fou*
      Provence (*Provence, Manosque, Arcadie, Arcadie!,*
         Basses Alpes)
1958 *Angelo*
1959 *Domitien, suivi de Joseph à Dothan* (Adaptations for
         the theater)
      Sur les oliviers morts
1962 *Chroniques romanesques*
1963 *Le Désastre de Pavie*
1964 Preface (Blaise de Monluc)
1965 *Deux cavaliers de l'orage*
1968 *Provence perdue*
      Ennemonde ou autres caractères
1969 *Une Histoire d'amour*
1970 *L'Iris de Suze*
1972 *Les Récits de la demi-brigade*

Critical and Biographical Works[2]

Anonymous. "Giono dans la Pléiade." *Le Monde* (February
   28, 1968), p. v.
——— "Individual traveller: Jean Giono; *Voyage en Italie.*"
   Times Literary Supplement, No. 2,471 (August 13, 1954),
   p. 513.

 [2] I.e., works that in whole or in part directly treat Jean Giono.

Anonymous. "Jean Giono, dernier chantre de la Provence." *Le Méridional—La France* (October 10, 1970), p. 14.

────── "Jean Giono, or Characters in Control of an Author." Special Issue, *TLS* (May 27, 1955), p. 14.

────── "L'Adieu de la Provence à Jean Giono." *Provençal—Dimanche* (October 11, 1970), p. 1.

────── "Les Alpes de Haute-Provence pleurent Jean Giono." *Le Provençal* (October 10, 1970), p. 2.

────── "*Les Ames fortes.*" *Mercure de France,* No. 308 (1950), p. 693.

────── "*Le Hussard sur le toit*": (1) *Nouvelles Littéraires* (December 6, 1951); (2) *Le Monde* (March 26, 1952).

────── "*Le Moulin de Pologne*": (1) *Le Monde* (January 31, 1954); (2) *Mercure de France*, No. 317 (1953), p. 693.

────── "*Les Grands chemins.*" *Mercure de France*, No. 312 (1951), p. 698.

────── "Les Parents d'élèves: le nom de Jean Giono à un etablissement scolaire de la ville." *Le Provençal—Dimanche* (October 11, 1970), p. 5.

────── "Le Théâtre et le cinéma." *Le Provençal* (October 10, 1970), p. 9.

────── "Manosque a rendu un dernier et émouvant hommage à Jean Giono." *Le Provençal* (October 11, 1970), p. 2.

A., Y. "Aujourd'hui: Jean Giono." *Le Canard enchaîné* (October 14, 1970), p. 6.

Antonietto, F. *Le Mythe de la Provence dans les premiers romans de Jean Giono* (Aix-en-Provence, 1961).

Antonini, Giacomo. "Jean Giono e il castigo di Dio." *La Fiera Letteraria*, No. 8 (June 21, 1953), p. 4.

Arland, Marcel. "A la hussarde." *La Nouvelle N.R.F.*, 1re année, No. 10 (October 1953), pp. 687-96. Or see *La Grâce d'écrire* (Paris, 1955), pp. 130-41.

———— "Le Chant du monde." *N.N.R.F.*, No. 9 (1953), pp. 495-505.

———— "Que ma joie demeure." *N.R.F.*, No. 44 (June 1953), pp. 938-39.

Aubarède, Gabriel d'. "Rencontre avec Jean Giono." *Les Nouvelles Littéraires* (March 26, 1953).

Audouard, Yvan. "Giono avait l'art d'imaginer le réel." *Le Provençal—Dimanche* (October 11, 1970), p. 8.

Aury, Dominique. "Un chef-d'oeuvre de Jean Giono—*Le Hussard sur le toit*." *Arts*, No. 341 (January 11, 1952), p. 3.

Bady, René. *Le Problème de la joie: Giono et Claudel* (Fribourg, 1943).

Bailly, René. "Jean Giono." *Larousse mensuel*, No. 13 (1955), pp. 601-02.

Bataillard, A. "Triomphe de la vie." *Formes et Couleurs* (Paris, 1942).

Bauer, Wilhelm. "Die Geburt des Genius." *Neue Rundschau*, No. 47 (1936), pp. 1,116-1,120.

Baussan, F. "Hommage au Roi Jean." *Le Méridional—La France* (October 10, 1970), p. 2.

Béart, Guy. "L'Ame de sa merveilleuse province." *Figaro Littéraire*, No. 1,274 (October 19-25, 1970), p. 19.

Berger, Yves. "*Ennemonde et autres caractères*." *Le Monde* (February 28, 1968), p. v.

Bergeron, Régis. "Le Cas Giono." *Les Lettres Françaises*, No. 450 (January 29 to February 5, 1953), p. 3.

Bersani, J., M. Autrand, J. Lecarme, B. Vercier. *La Littérature française depuis 1945* (Paris, 1970). "Jean Giono," pp. 323-28.

Billy, André. "A Giono le premier prix." *Figaro Littéraire*, "Les Propos du samedi" (February 23 to March 1, 1970), p. 25.

Billy, André. "Jean Giono au pays de ses pères." *Le Figaro* (February 10, 1954).

——— "Naturisme et 'fascisme' de Giono." *L'Oeuvre* (August 29, 1937).

Blanchot, Maurice. "Le Secret de Melville." *Faux-Pas* (Paris, 1943), pp. 282-86.

Blanzat, Jean. "*Le Hussard sur le toit.*" *Figaro Littéraire* (December 22, 1951).

——— "*Le Moulin de Pologne.*" *Figaro Littéraire* (January 31, 1953).

Boisdeffre, Pierre de. *Giono* (Paris, 1965). Illustrated. Bibliography (pp. 251-77) by M. Jean Bottin includes translations, recordings, and films by Giono.

——— *Une Histoire de la littérature aujourd'hui, 1938-1958* (Paris, 1958), Chapter IV, c. p. 249 ff.

——— "Sur les chemins de Giono." *Revue de Paris* (March, 1961).

Bonnier, Henry. "Un Ecrivain farouchement attaché à sa race." *Le Méridional—La France* (October 10, 1970), p. 14.

Borel, J.-A. "Avec Jean Giono disparaît une parcelle du rêve pour un monde meilleur." *Le Méridional—La France* (October 10, 1970), p. 2.

Bosco, Henri. "Le Poète de la terre et des astres." *Le Figaro Littéraire*, No. 1,274 (October 19-25, 1970), p. 16.

Bottachieri, Gabriella. *Le Pittoresque poétique de J. Giono.* Unpublished thesis (Naples, 1954).

Boutang, Pierre. "Ascension classique de Giono." *Aspects de la France* (May 12, 1949).

Brasillach, Robert. "*Batailles dans la montagne.*" *Action Française* (October 7, 1937).

——— *Les Quatre Jeudis, images d'avant guerre* (Paris, 1951), pp. 312-24.

Brayer, Yves. "L'Ami des peintres." *Figaro Littéraire*, No. 1,274 (October 19-25, 1970), p. 18.

Brée, Germaine and Margaret Guiton. *An Age of Fiction and/or The French Novel from Gide to Camus* (Rutgers, 1957, and New York, 1962), pp. 107-13 in either case.

Breyer, José. *Mémoire pour une Faculté de Belgique.* 1954.

Bridault, Yves. "J. Giono: Des fleurs de la solitude et Machiavel." *Arts* (August 22-28, 1952), pp. 1 and 5.

Brisson, Pierre. "*Les Lanceurs de graines.*" *Du Meilleur au pire* (Paris, 1938), pp. 221-27.

Brochon, René. "De Giono à Pétain." *Action Française* (January 5, 1945).

Brodin, Pierre. *Maîtres et témoins de l'entre-deux-guerres* (Montréal, 1943), pp. 203-20.

Chaigne, Louis. *Vies et oeuvres d'écrivains,* II (Lanore, 1957).

Chalon, Jean. "Jean Giono attaque sur tous les fronts, mais garde des réserves." *Figaro Littéraire* (September 9-15, 1965).

Chambert, Nicole. "Jean Giono." *Education* (October 15, 1970), p. 25.

Chamson, André. "De l'épicurisme au stoïcisme." *Figaro Littéraire,* No. 1,274 (October 19-25, 1970), p. 17.

Chapsal, Madeleine. "Un Homme heureux." *L'Express* (March 21, 1960), pp. 33-37.

C., M. "*Noé.*" *Cahiers du Monde Nouveau* (August-September, 1948).

Charpentier, John. "*Que ma joie demeure.*" *Mercure de France,* No. 262 (1935), pp. 576-77.

——— "*Le Chant du monde.*" *Mercure de France,* No. 258 (1935), pp. 355-56.

——— "*Regain.*" *Mercure de France,* No. 225 (1931), pp. 653-54.

Charpentier, John. *"Un de Baumugnes."* *Mercure de France*, No. 216 (1929), pp. 653-54.

Chonez, Claudine. *Giono par lui-même* (Paris, 1956). Illustrated. Bibliography, pp. 190-91.

———— "Une Journée de Giono à Manosque." *Figaro Littéraire* (December 11, 1954), p. 5.

Christoflour, Raymond. "Panthéisme et réalisme de J. Giono." *Mercure de France*, No. 290 (1939), pp. 396-401.

Ciossek, H. H. *Jean Giono: ein Dichter der Provence* (Greifswald, 1934).

Clarke, Katherine Allen. "Interview with Jean Giono." *French Review*, xxxiii, No. 1 (October 1959), pp. 440-45.

———— *Le Lyrisme dans l'oeuvre de Jean Giono.* Unpublished thesis (Grenoble, 1938).

———— *"Pour saluer Melville*—Jean Giono's prison book." *French Review,* xxxv, No. 5 (April, 1962), pp. 478-83.

Clément, R. "Jean Giono et la libération de l'homme." *Grande Revue*, Vol. 155.

———— "Jean Giono vu par un jeune." *Grande Revue* (July 1938).

Clouard, Henri and Robert Leggewie, eds. *French Writers of Today* (New York, 1965). "Jean Giono," pp. 33-34.

Cluny, Claude Michel. "Un Scandaleux bonheur." *N.R.F.* (June 13, 1965), pp. 1,058-62.

Corymbe. "Jean Giono et la Provence." Special Issue (May-June 1937).

Crémieux, Benjamin. "La Littérature et les provinces." *Candide* (February 5, 1931).

Cuny, Alain. "Tout de pudeur et de retenue." *Figaro Littéraire*, No. 1,274 (October 19-25, 1970), p. 19.

Dabit, Eugène. *"Le Chant du monde."* *Europe* (August 15, 1934).

Demazis, Orane. "Un 'vagabond' aux propos captivants." *Figaro Littéraire*, No. 1,274 (October 19-25, 1970), p. 19.

Déon, Michel. "Jean Giono. Le Dernier conteur." *Nouvelles Littéraires* (October 15, 1970), pp. 1 and 6.

Dietzschy, C., *Natur und Mensch in Gionos Sprache*. Festschrift für Tappolet (Basle, 1935).

Dorgelès, Roland. "L'Autodidacte qui nous a tout réappris." *Figaro Littéraire*, No. 1,274 (October 19-25, 1970), p. 17.

Dort, Bernard. "*Les Grands chemins.*" *Les Temps Modernes*, No. 70 (August 1951), pp. 381-83.

Dutourd, Jean. "Pour saluer Jean Giono." *France-Soir* (October 12, 1970).

Epardaud, Edmond. "Une Journée à Manosque avec Jean Giono." *Les Nouvelles Littéraires* (March 13, 1937).

Estang, Luc. "*Ennemonde et autres caractères* de Jean Giono." *Figaro Littéraire*, No. 1,146 (April 18, 1968), pp. 20-21.

Fernandel.[3] "D'*Angèle* à *L'Eau vive.*" *Figaro Littéraire*, No. 1,274 (October 19-25, 1970), p. 19.

Fernandez, R. "De Melville à Giono." *N.R.F.*, No. 55 (August 1941), pp. 206-13.

F., J. A. "Jean Giono, une vision du monde." *Juvénal* (October 14, 1970).

Fluchère, Henri. "Jean Giono." *Cahiers du Contadour* (Summer, 1936).

——— "Hommage à Jean Giono." Rotary-Club de Manosque, December 11, 1970 (Manosque, 1971).

——— "*Le Chant du monde.*" *Cahiers du Sud*, No. 22 (July 1935), pp. 588-91.

——— "Mon Ami Jean." *Le Provençal* (October 10, 1971), p. 9.

[3] Fernandel starred in two Giono films: *Angèle* and *Crésus*.

Fluchère, Henri. "Refléxions sur Jean Giono." *Cahiers du Sud*, No. 19 (1932), pp. 144-49.

Fraud, Michel. "L'Amour de Giono." *Figaro Littéraire* (October 26, 1970).

Frohock, W. M. *Style and Temper. Studies in French Fiction, 1925-1960* (Harvard University, 1967). "First-Person Narration," pp. 91-94.

Ganne, Gilbert. "Giono règle ses comptes." *Nouvelles Littéraires* (April 1, 1965), pp. 1 and 11.

——— *Interviews impubliables* (Bonne, 1952).

Gautier, Jean-Jacques. "*Le Moulin de Pologne*." *Réalités* (April 1953).

Gide, André. *Journal (1923-1931). Oeuvres complètes*, 15 vols., ed. L. Martin Chauffier (Paris, 1932).

Gilman, Wayne C. "The General Neologisms of Jean Giono." *French Review*, XXXIII, No. 5 (April 1960), pp. 469-74.

Godard, Henri. "Deux styles de narration." *Le Monde* (February 28, 1968), p. iv.

Goodrich, Norma L. "Bachelors in Fiction through John Steinbeck and Jean Giono." *Kentucky Romance Quarterly*, Vol. XIV, No. 4 (1969), pp. 367-78.

——— "Further Investigation concerning Jean Giono's *Le Hussard sur le toit*." *The Romanic Review*, Vol. LIX, No. 4 (December 1968), pp. 267-77.

——— "Jean Giono's New Apocalypse Text: 'Le Grand théâtre (1960).'" *The French Review*. Vol. XLIII, Special Issue, No. 1 (Winter 1970), pp. 116-25.

——— "*Le Moulin de Pologne* and Its Narrator." *The French Review*, Vol. XL, No. 1 (October 1966), pp. 65-76.

——— "*Le Moulin de Pologne*. Modern Novel and Elizabethan Tragedy." *Revue de Littérature Comparée* (January-March 1967), pp. 88-97.

Grenier, J. "Réflexions sur la pauvreté et la paix." *N.R.F.*, No. 2 (1939).

Gros, Léon Gabriel. "Pour saluer Jean le bleu." *Le Provençal* (October 10, 1970), pp. 1 and 8.

Guéhenno, Jean. "La Fonction du poète." *Vendredi* (May 5, 1937).

Harvitt, Helen. "Jean Giono. The Abuse of Comparisons with *comme* in *Solitude de la pitié* and *Jean le bleu*." *The French Review*, No. 7 (March 1934), pp. 284-99.

Hoog, Armand. "Le Romantisme et l'existence contemporaine." *Mercure de France*, No. 316 (1952), p. 452.

Jean, Raymond. "Salut à Giono." *Politique Hebdo*, XII (October 15-21, 1970).

Josipovici, Jean. *Lettre à Jean Giono* (Paris, 1939).

Kanters, Robert. " 'Il était une fois' . . . les contes du père Giono." *Le Figaro Littéraire* (March 23-29, 1970), pp. 20-21.

————— "Jean Giono avant et après le déluge." *Figaro Littéraire*, No. 789 (June 3, 1961), p. 2.

————— "L'Homme de la magie des choses." *Figaro Littéraire*, No. 1,274 (October 19-25, 1970), p. 14.

————— "Maturité de Jean Giono." *Figaro Littéraire* (January 10, 1953).

Kemp, Robert. "*Colline*." *Liberté* (May 1, 1929).

————— "*Que ma joie demeure*." *Liberté* (June 10, 1935).

————— "*Machiavel*." *Les Nouvelles Littéraires* (September 15, 1955).

————— "*Regain*." *Liberté* (December 1, 1930).

————— "*Un de Baumugnes*." *Liberté* (November 11, 1929).

Lalou, René. "*Le Bonheur fou*." *Les Nouvelles Littéraires* (May 9, 1957).

————— "*Le Moulin De Pologne*." *Les Annales-Conférences* (April 1953), pp. 15-19.

Lalou, René. "*Les Ames fortes.*" *Les Nouvelles Littéraires* (January 26, 1950).

Larnac, Jean. "Chronique littéraire: la littérature expression de la pensée." *La Pensée,* No. 25 (July-August 1949), pp. 107-16.

Laudenbach, Roland. "L'Homme qui lisait dans les étoiles." *Minute,* No. 444 (October 15-21, 1970).

Le Clézio, J.-M. G. "Les Ecrivains meurent aussi . . ." *Figaro Littéraire,* No. 1,274 (October 19-25, 1970), pp. 15-16.

Lefèvre, Frédéric. "Une heure avec Jean Giono." *Les Nouvelles Littéraires* (December 20, 1930).

Lemarchand, Jacques. "*La Calèche* de Jean Giono." *Figaro Littéraire* (December 23, 1965), p. 14.

Lhoste, Pierre. "Promenade avec Jean Giono." *Paris Midi* (January 21, 1943).

Luccioni, Gennie. "Jean Giono. *Le Bonheur fou.*" *Esprit* (September 1957), pp. 292-97.

Madaule, Jacques. "Jean Giono." *Reconnaissances* II (Paris, 1943), p. 151.

Malherbe, Henri. "*Lanceurs de graines.*" *Revue des Vivants* (December 1932).

Marcel, Gabriel. "*Le Chant du monde* par J. Giono." *L'Europe Nouvelle,* No. 17 (1934), pp. 729-30.

——— "*Le Grand troupeau.*" *L'Europe Nouvelle,* No. 14 (1931), p. 1,654.

——— "*Solitude de la pitié.*" *Quinzaine Critique* (August 10-25, 1930).

——— "*Un de Baumugnes.*" *Quinzaine Critique,* No. 1 (November 25, 1929), p. 80.

Marion, Bernard. *A la rencontre de Jean Giono* (Ghent, 1947).

Maulnier, Thierry. "M. Giono, les paysans et la guerre." *Revue Universelle,* Vol. 1 (1939).

—— "M. Jean Giono, prophète." *Action Française* (January 19, 1939).

Maurin, Mario. *"Le Bonheur fou."* *Les Lettres Nouvelles* (September 1957), pp. 304-05.

Mauron, Marie. "L'Universel de haute Provence." *Figaro Littéraire*, No. 1,274 (October 19-25, 1970), pp. 17-18.

Mazellier, Yves. "Jean Giono et le monde moderne." *Semaine Provence*, No. 511 (October 15-23, 1970), p. 17.

Mendelssohn, Peter de. *Der Geist in der Despotie* (Berlin, 1953).

Michelfelder, Christian. *"Batailles dans la montagne."* *Cahiers du Sud*, No. 25 (1938), pp. 144-47.

—— *Jean Giono et les religions de la terre* (Paris, 1938).

Millau, Christian. "Rencontre avec Jean Giono, Académicien sans uniforme." *Carrefour* (January 12, 1955), p. 12.

Mille, Raoul. "Jean Giono, le dernier des hommes." *L'Action Municipale*, Nice (November 1970), pp. 1, 13-16.

Miller, Henry. *The Books in My Life (January to December, 1950).* (Norfolk, Connecticut, undated), Chapter v.

Missen, François. "Jeudi, il écrivait encore." *Le Provençal* (October 10, 1970), p. 8.

Mondadon, Louis de. *"Le Grand troupeau."* *Etudes* (July 5, 1932).

Moore, Harry T. *Twentieth-Century French Literature to World War II*, 2 vols. (Southern Illinois, 1966), Vol. I, pp. 89-91.

Morand, Paul. "Préface" to *Jean Giono* (1955). See Pugnet, Jacques.

Morelle, Paul. "La Féerie du monde moderne," Propos Recueillis, *Le Monde* (February 28, 1968), p. 4.

—— "Un Homme heureux." *Le Monde*, Supplement au No. 7,193 (February 28, 1968), p. 4.

Morgan, Claude. "Les Partisans de la mort: Céline et Giono." *Les Volontaires*, No. 2 (January 1939), pp. 47-50.

Morrow, Christine. *Le Roman irréaliste dans les littératures contemporaines anglaises et françaises* (Paris, 1941).

Nadeau, Maurice. "Jean Giono sur les toits." *L'Observateur* (January 24, 1952).

―――― "*Le Hussard sur le toit*." *Mercure de France*, No. 314 (1952), pp. 499-503.

―――― *Le Roman français depuis la guerre* (Paris, 1963), pp. 53-55.

―――― "Un Nouveau Giono." *Mercure de France*, cccviii, No. 1,040 (April 1, 1950), pp. 693-97. Or see *Littérature présente* (Paris, 1952), pp. 135-41.

Nizan, Paul. "*Jean le bleu*." *L'Humanité* (December 9, 1932), p. 4.

―――― "*Que ma joie demeure*." *Le Monde* (May 16, 1935), p. 8. (For the reasons behind his attacks on Giono, see Jacqueline Leiner's *Le Destin littéraire de Paul Nizan* [Paris, 1970], pp. 85, 203, 210, and Bibliography.)

Noth, Ernst Eric. "A Manosque chez Jean Giono." *Les Nouvelles Littéraires* (January 1938).

Nourissier, François. "*Deux cavaliers de l'orage*, roman de Jean Giono." *Nouvelles Littéraires*, No. 1,995 (November 25, 1965).

O'Brien, Justin. *The French Literary Horizon* (Rutgers University, 1967), "On *Harvest* (*Regain*) . . . trans. Henri Fluchère and Geoffrey Myers (New York: The Viking Press, Inc., 1939). *The Nation*, June 3, 1939, pp. 257-58.

Onimus, Jean. "L'Expression du temps dans le roman contemporain." *Revue de Littérature Comparée*, No. 28 (1954), pp. 299-317.

Paget, Jacques. "Le Dernier dîner avec Jean de Manosque." *Le Provençal* (October 1970), pp. 1 and 8.

Pagnol, Marcel. "Midi Capitale Marseille. Notre Provence à nous." *Figaro Littéraire* (April 28-May 4, 1969), p. 8. Giono is mentioned only in passing, as a writer of that area.

Perruchot, Henri. "Interview avec Jean Giono." *Réalités*, LXXXI (October 1952), pp. 79-83.

——— "Jean Giono, le barde des paysages dépouillés." *Réalités* (October 1952).

Peyre, Henri, ed. *Six Maîtres contemporains* (New York, 1969). "Jean Giono: Notice," pp. 9-18.

——— *The Contemporary French Novel* (New York, 1955), Chapter V, p. 124 ff. See the revised work, *French Novelists of Today* (New York, 1967), Chapter V, "Jean Giono," pp. 123-53, and Bibliography, pp. 152-53.

——— Review of *Le Hussard sur le toit*: "Flight from Plague." *Saturday Review* (January 23, 1954), pp. 17 and 69.

Picon, Gaëtan. "*Le Bonheur fou.*" *Mercure de France*, No. 1,129 (September 1957), pp. 122-26.

——— *Panorama de la nouvelle littérature française* (Paris, 1960), Part II, p. 80 ff.

Pivot, Bernard. "Guide 66 pour le Paris des lettres." *Figaro Littéraire* (March 24, 1966), p. 9.

Pomerai, Odile de. "An Unknown Giono: *Deux cavaliers de l'orage.*" *The French Review*, v. 39, No. 1 (October 1965), pp. 78-84.

Pons, Maurice. "Leçon de bonheur en voyage." *La Table Ronde* (June 1954), pp. 152-56.

Poulet, Robert. "Giono à l'avant-garde." *Carrefour*, 16e année, No. 751 (February 4, 1959), p. 13.

——— *La Lanterne magique* (Paris, 1956).

——— *Parti pris* (Brussels, 1943).

Pourrat, Henri. "La Pensée magique de Jean Giono." *N.R.F.*, No. 51 (October 1938), pp. 646-58.

Prévost, Jean. *Problèmes du roman* (Lyon, 1943), pp. 150-52.

Prim, Olga. *Le Sentiment de la terre dans l'oeuvre de Giono.* Unpublished thesis (Turin, 1955).

Pugnet, Jacques. *Jean Giono* (Paris, 1955). Preface by Paul Morand, pp. 7-9. Works by Giono listed, pp. 119-21.

Read, Herbert. *Politics of the Unpolitical* (London, 1943, 1946).

Redfern, W. D. *The Private World of Jean Giono* (Duke University, 1967). Bibliography (pp. 197-203) includes: (a) Giono's Books, (b) Giono's contributions to periodicals, (c) prefaces—31 are listed, (d) works in collaboration, (e) translations, (f) correspondence—33 letters to Gide, notably, (g) studies of Giono's works, (h) essays, (i) selected articles, (j) myths and the novel, (k) the provinces and points of comparison.

Remacle, André. "Giono, chantre de la Haute-Provence." *La Marseillaise* (October 10, 1970), pp. 1 and 10.

Richand, Jean. "Jean Giono de Manosque." *Semaine Provence*, No. 511 (October 16, 23, 1970), pp. 6-7.

——— "Un Morceau de Provence disparaît . . ." *Le Provençal* (October 10, 1970), p. 8.

Robert, Pierre R. *Jean Giono et les techniques du roman* (Berkeley and Los Angeles, 1961). *Bibliographie* (pp. 101-07): (a) *Romans de* Giono, (b) *Autres Oeuvres*, (c) *Ouvrages critiques*, (d) *Revues*, (e) *Ouvrages sur le roman en général.*

Robichon, Jacques. "Dialogue avec Jean Giono." *La Table Ronde*, No. 86 (February 1955), pp. 50-60.

——— "Jean Giono." *Arts*, No. 345 (February 8, 1952).

Roche, Alphonse. "Les Provençalismes et la question du régionalisme dans l'oeuvre de Jean Giono." *PMLA*, Vol.
LXIII, No. 4, Part 1 (December 1948), p. 1,322 ff.

Rougon. *Mémoire* présenté à la Faculté des Lettres d'Aix.
1952.

Rousseaux, André. *Ames et visages du XXme siècle* (Paris,
1932), pp. 184-96.

——— "Jean Giono, seconde manière." *Figaro Littéraire*
(May 7, 1953), p. 2.

——— *Littérature du XXme siècle* (Paris, 1938), pp. 194-203.

Roy, J. "*Un Roi sans divertissement* et *Noé.*" *Les Temps Modernes,* No. 31 (1948).

Roz, Firmin. "La Manière de M. Jean Giono." *Revue Politique et Littéraire* (October 16, 1937).

Rudin, J.-P. "Jean Giono ou le goût du bonheur" (Paris, 1970).

Sadoul, Georges. "Où en est Giono?" *Commune* (March
1939).

Seize, Pierre. *Au Grand jour des Assises* (Paris, 1954).

——— "Quand Jean Giono réclame à la Justice justice pour
ses personnages." *Figaro Littéraire* (July 16, 1955).

Séligmann, J.-P. "A Manosque et dans son temps." *Le Méridional—La France* (October 10, 1970), p. 14.

Simon, Pierre-Henri. "*Noé* de Jean Giono." *Le Monde*
(June 14, 1961), pp. 8-9.

——— *Témoins de l'homme* (Paris, 1951).

Smith, Maxwell A. "A Visit to Giono." *Books Abroad,* XXXIII
(Winter 1959), pp. 23-26.

——— "Giono's Cycle of the Hussard Novels." *The French
Review,* XXXV, No. 3 (January 1962), pp. 287-94.

——— *Giono. Selections* (Boston, 1965), pp. vii-viii, ix-xii,
1-2, 55, 71, 95, 113, 135, 147-48.

Smith, Maxwell A. "Giono's Trilogy of Pan." *Tennessee Studies in Literature*, No. 2 (1957), pp. 73-80.

———— "Giono's Use of the Ulysses Concept." *The French Review*, Vol. 31, No. 1 (October 1957).

———— *Jean Giono* (New York, 1966). Notes and References, pp. 179-82. Selected Bibliography, pp. 183-87. Index.

Spaziani, Marcello. "Jean Giono in Italia." *Fiera Letteraria* (April 4, 1954), pp. 1-2.

Starr, William T. "Jean Giono and Walt Whitman." *The French Review* (December 1940), pp. 118-29.

Susini, Jean. "A Manosque avec Giono." *Le Pays Cévenol et Cévennes* (October 17, 1970).

Taos, Marguerite. "A Manosque avec Jean Giono." *Les Nouvelles Littéraires* (January 13, 1955).

Tavernier, R. "*Manosque des plateaux* et *Pour saluer Melville*." *Confluences*, No. 3 (1941).

Testanière, Jean. " 'La Mort pour moi est une bénédiction,' déclarait récemment Jean Giono." *Le Méridional—La France* (October 10, 1970), p. 14.

Thévenet, Jacques. "Cavalcade dans les collines." *Figaro Littéraire*, No. 1,274 (October 19-25, 1970), p. 18.

Thiébaut, Maurice. "Les Deux Giono." *Revue de Paris* (June 1957), pp. 143-51.

———— "Stendhalisme de Jean Giono." *Revue de Paris*, No. 2 (February 1952).

Tzara, Tristan. "Un Romancier de la lâcheté." *Les Lettres Françaises*, No. 24 (October 7, 1944).

Ullmann, Stephen. *Style in the French Novel* (Cambridge, 1957), pp. 217-31.

Valmont, Jacques. "Jean Giono." *Aspects de la France* (October 15, 1970).

Varillon, François. "Jean Giono, de Paris au Contadour." *Etudes*, Vol. 230 (February 5, 1937), pp. 337-51.

——— *"Les Vraies richesses." Etudes*, Vol. 230 (December 20, 1937), pp. 469-83.

Vial, Fernand. "Jean Giono at the Académie Goncourt." *The American Society Legion of Honor Magazine* (Spring 1955), pp. 9-25.

Vigneaux, Jean. "Jean Giono, le dernier seigneur des lettres." *Pourquoi pas?* (October 22, 1970), pp. 164-68.

Villeneuve, Romée de. *Jean Giono, ce solitaire* (Avignon, 1955). *Bibliographie*, pp. 298-302.

Villiers, François. "Pendant nos prises de vues, sa simplicité." *Figaro Littéraire*, No. 1,274 (October 19-25, 1970), p. 19.

Vox, Maximilien. "Croissance de Giono." *Livres de France*, No. 2 (1951), p. 3.

Voyenne, Bernard. "Avant-propos" to *Regain* (Paris, 1948). Limited Edition.

Walker, Hallam. "Myth in Giono's *Le Chant du monde.*" *Symposium* xv (Summer 1961), pp. 139-46.

English Translations[4]

Brown, Alan. *Two Riders of the Storm* (London, 1967), trans. *Deux cavaliers de l'orage.*

Clarke, Katherine Allen. *Joy of Man's Desiring* (New York and London, 1949), trans. *Que ma joie demeure.*

——— *Blue Boy* (New York, 1946; London, 1949), trans. *Jean le bleu.*

Fluchère, Henri and Geoffrey Meyers. *Harvest* (London and Toronto, 1939), trans. *Regain.*

——— *The Song of the World* (New York, London and Toronto, 1938), trans. *Le Chant du monde.*

Glass, Norman. *To the Slaughterhouse* (London, 1969), trans. *Le Grand troupeau.*

---

[4] This list is limited to those translations which I have examined. Boisdeffre, for example, alludes to two others that I have not located.

Griffin, Jonathan. *The Hussar on the Roof* (London, 1954), trans. *Le Hussard sur le toit*; or *The Horseman on the Roof* (New York, 1953, 1954).

Johnson, Phyllis. *The Straw Man* (New York, 1959), trans. *Le Bonheur fou*.

Le Clerq, Jacques. *Hill of Destiny* (New York, 1929), trans. *Colline*.

—— *Lovers Are Never Losers* (London, 1932), trans. *Un de Baumugnes*.

Mendelssohn, Peter de. *The Malediction* (London and New York, 1955), trans. *Le Moulin de Pologne*.

Murch, A. (Alma) E. *Angelo* (London, 1960), trans. *Angelo*.

—— *The Battle of Pavia* (London, 1965), trans. *La Bataille de Pavie*.

Vay, David le. *Ennemonde* (London, 1970), trans. *Ennemonde*.

Index

INDEX

302